Understanding and Designing Your Active Directory Infrastructure

Neall Alcott, et al

SAMS

201 West 103rd St., Indianapolis, Indiana, 46290 USA

Understanding and Designing Your Active Directory Infrastructure

Copyright © 2002 by Sams Publishing

International Standard Book Number: 0-672-32185-8

Library of Congress Catalog Card Number: 2001089502

Printed in the United States of America

First Printing: December, 2001

04   03   02   01   4   3   2   1

Trademarks

Warning and Disclaimer

ASSOCIATE PUBLISHER
Jeff Koch

EXECUTIVE EDITOR
Terry Neal

DEVELOPMENT EDITORS
John Gosney
Steve Rowe

MANAGING EDITOR
Matt Purcell

PROJECT EDITOR
Andy Beaster

COPY EDITOR
Kezia Endsley

INDEXER
Erika Millen

PROOFREADER
Kay Hoskin

TECHNICAL EDITOR
Brian Lich

TEAM COORDINATOR
Denni Bannister

INTERIOR DESIGNER
Anne Jones

COVER DESIGNER
Aren Howell

PAGE LAYOUT
Gloria Schurick

Contents at a Glance

Contents

About the Authors

Neall Alcott is a consultant, trainer, and writer. He has been designing and managing networks for over 10 years. He has also been providing Microsoft-based training for the past four years. He resides in Deptford, NJ, with his wife Ginny, and children, Lauren, Lindsey, and Jake. Neall can be reached via e-mail at nalcott@yahoo.com.

Shannon Kalvar is a professional consultant with 10 years of infrastructure architecture and project-management experience. He has worked with federal and state governments, financial corporations, the health care industry, primary and secondary education, utility companies, non-profit organizations, and the occasional dot.com. Shannon currently lives in Longmont, CO, working as a project manager and occasional IT consultant. Questions for him can be directed to kalvars@msn.com.

Daniel Wilt has over eight years of network infrastructure and project management experience. Dan currently resides in Moorestown, NJ, with his wife, Susan, and son, Ethan.

Bob Bello currently works as a supervisor\LAN Admin III of ADP's EBS LAN division. His current environment consists of a mixture of Windows 2000, Windows NT 4, Windows 9x, AS/400 RISC, and Warp boxes. In addition, he has worked as a consultant and instructor for the past four years. During this time he has been involved in architecting various networks and presenting Novell CNA, Microsoft MCSE, SMS, Cisco CCNA, and Citrix CCA courses. Bob resides in Bellmawr, NJ.

Dedication

*This book is dedicated to Ginny, my lovely wife, who puts up with more than she really needs to...
but don't tell her I said that!*

Neall Alcott

*I would like to dedicate this work to my wife, who puts up with my manic bouts of writing. I would also
like to thank Neall, who gave me the chance to rant in public again.*

Shannon Kalvar

Acknowledgments

Thanks go to my wife, Ginny; my daughters, Lauren and Lindsey; and my son, Jake. Thank
you for always being there.

Many thanks also go the contributing authors of this book: Daniel Wilt, Bob Bello, and especially Shannon Kalvar. All of your contributions really provided great insight into the various
portions of Active Directory. Thanks guys!

I'd also like to thank my own personal NetWare guru, Mark Marshall, for his assistance in
doing the research and screenshots for Chapter 2. He still thinks that NDS is better though...

John Gosney deserves many thanks for his development of this book. John was a great help in
developing the overall content and, with his large mallet, hammering the ton of Active
Directory information out there into useful morsels.

Brian Lich did a great job as technical editor. He added some great technical bits and pieces
that we may not have thought of originally, and generally kept all of us in check.

Neil Salkind, my agent, deserves credit for helping me get the contract in the first place and
taking care of all the details that most authors don't really think about. I always appreciate his
help. It's good to know that someone wants to help.

Finally, I'd like to thank Terry Neal, Steve Rowe, Andrew Beaster, Kezia Endsley, and the rest
of the Sams staff for their assistance in bringing this book to print. Sams really has a great
editorial staff and you deserve many kudos!

Tell Us What You Think!

As the reader of this book, *you* are our most important critic and commentator. We value your opinion and want to know what we're doing right, what we could do better, what areas you'd like to see us publish in, and any other words of wisdom you're willing to pass our way.

As an Associate Publisher for Sams, I welcome your comments. You can fax, e-mail, or write me directly to let me know what you did or didn't like about this book—as well as what we can do to make our books stronger.

Please note that I cannot help you with technical problems related to the topic of this book, and that due to the high volume of mail I receive, I might not be able to reply to every message.

When you write, please be sure to include this book's title and author as well as your name and phone or fax number. I will carefully review your comments and share them with the author and editors who worked on the book.

Fax: 317-581-4770

E-mail: feedback@samspublishing.com

Mail: Jeff Koch, Associate Publisher
Sams Publishing
201 West 103rd Street
Indianapolis, IN 46290 USA

Introduction

Active Directory was one of the most anticipated operating system features released by Microsoft since the release of the GUI interface in Windows 95. But to simply call Active Directory a feature of Windows 2000 is a huge understatement. Active Directory is a full-fledged directory service that is meant to act as the switchboard for an organization's network infrastructure.

Active Directory provides a place to centrally store information about network devices or objects, such as users, files, printers, and applications. Other devices, such as routers, switches, and network appliances can also interact with Active Directory. Active Directory provides a consistent way to implement and manage network resources.

For most organizations, implementing Active Directory provides a path to simplified management, strengthened security, and network interoperability.

Unfortunately, the path is lined with many traps and pitfalls that can ensnare all but the most careful and diligent network planners. *Understanding and Designing Your Active Directory Infrastructure* is meant to provide insight into the origins of Active Directory and its competitors, teach you how to plan for Active Directory, help you implement and integrate Active Directory into your environment, and finally help you troubleshoot Active Directory when and if problems occur.

Who This Book Is For

This book was written for an intermediate to advanced level reader. It assumes that you have experience with network operating systems, such as Windows NT and Windows 2000. It's targeted towards someone who wants to perform tasks quickly without spending a lot of time reading theories. (Of course, some theory does appear in the book for explanation purposes.) The reader can be anyone from a network architect/planner to a person studying for a certification exam. If you're in the target audience, you'll find the learning materials fast paced and packed with lots of tips and helpful information.

Understanding and Designing Your Active Directory Infrastructure focuses on the main considerations when planning an Active Directory infrastructure and the kinds of tasks that you commonly perform. Chapters such as Chapter 4, "Planning AD", will appeal to network architects and planners who are responsible for the design and implementation of Active Directory. Likewise, Chapter 6, "Creating the Components Within the Active Directory," will appeal to network administrators responsible for creating and managing objects in Active Directory. Although most of this book is task oriented, it offers a broad range of Active Directory information that will make everyone who uses Active Directory want this book.

Conventions Used in This Book

There are several conventions used within this book that help you get more out of it. The first is the use of special fonts or font styles to emphasize a special kind of text; the second is the use of icons to emphasize special information.

- There are some situations when I'll ask you to type something. This information always appears in bold type like this: Type **Hello World**.

- Code normally appears on separate lines from the rest of the text. However, there are some special situations when small amounts of code appear within the paragraph for explanation purposes. This code appears in a special font like this: `Some Special Code`.

- Definitions are always handy to have. I'll use italic text to differentiate definitions from the rest of the text like this: A *CPU* is a required part of your machine.

- URLs for Web sites are presented like this: `http://www.microsoft.com`.

- This book also includes a real-world example/case study that is expanded and discussed at the end of each chapter.

NOTE

Notes help you understand some principle or provide explanatory information. In many cases, a note emphasizes some piece of critical information that you need.

TIP

All of us like to know special bits of information that will make our job easier, more fun, or faster to perform. Tips help you get the job done faster and more safely. In many cases, the information found in a tip is drawn from experience, rather than from the documentation.

Sidebar Element

In several areas throughout the book, there are sections presented as sidebars. These sidebars serve as a sort of FYI relating to that chapter section. Sidebars help bring real-world context to the section's topic.

CAUTION

Any time you see a caution, make sure that you take special care to read it. This information is vital. I'll always uses the caution to designate information that will help you avoid damage to your application, data, machine, or self. Never skip the cautions in a chapter and always follow their advice.

An Introduction to
Windows 2000 and
Active Directory

IN THIS CHAPTER

This chapter provides an introduction to Windows 2000 and Active Directory. It begins with an overview of the entire Windows 2000 family. This includes each version of Windows 2000 and its respective features. It also discusses how those features are typically deployed.

Following is an introduction to Active Directory. This section includes a brief overview of many of the chief components found in Active Directory. The section also discusses some of the benefits derived from the implementation of Active Directory in an organization.

Windows 2000 Overview

In mid-2000, Microsoft officially released the much-heralded upgrade to the Windows NT operating system. Windows 2000 included many new features, as well as greatly improved stability and reliability.

Microsoft released four flavors of Windows 2000: Professional, Server, Advanced Server, and Datacenter Server.

As a whole, the Windows 2000 operating system is much more reliable and stable than previous versions of Microsoft operating systems such as Windows 95/98 and Windows NT 4.0. Windows 2000 includes modifications to the operating system core that prevent crashes and enable the operating system to repair itself.

Each version of Windows 2000 operating system is geared toward a particular market segment. Although the core of the operating systems is the same, each version contains particular features and capabilities ideal for the market it is intended to serve.

The following sections provide a brief overview of these particular features and capabilities.

Windows 2000 Professional

Windows 2000 Professional is meant to be used on home PCs and corporate desktops. Based on its predecessor, Windows NT Workstation 4.0, Windows 2000 Professional includes a number of new features geared toward the desktop and mobile computing market, such as the Encrypting File System (EFS), offline folders and files, Universal Serial Bus (USB), and plug-and-play support. It also provides support for up to two processors and 4GB of RAM.

Windows 2000 Server

Windows 2000 Server is the member of the Windows 2000 family that's used in workgroup and departmental environments requiring more than a workstation-based peer-to-peer network.

Windows 2000 Server enables you to create more advanced client/server-based networked environments. Windows 2000 Server can be used for file and print sharing. It can also be used for more advanced purposes, including a messaging and database server.

Windows 2000 Server can also provide advanced network services such as Domain Name System (DNS), Dynamic Host Configuration Protocol (DHCP), Remote Installation Services (RIS), Windows Internet Naming Service (WINS), and Active Directory.

Windows 2000 Server provides support for up to four processors and 4GB of RAM.

Windows 2000 Advanced Server

Windows 2000 Advanced Server includes capabilities that provide high availability and fault-tolerance. As such, Windows 2000 Advanced Server is targeted towards Internet-based applications and e-commerce.

All of the features found in Windows 2000 Server can also be found in Windows 2000 Advanced Server. Advanced Server includes clustering capabilities that provide two-node failover. It also includes a 32-node network load-balancing feature that allows you to create sophisticated Web server farms.

Windows 2000 Advanced Server provides support for up to eight processors and 8GB of RAM.

Windows 2000 Datacenter Server

High-end market segments, such as online transaction processing (OLTP) and data warehousing, have long been the domain of mainframes and variants of the Unix operating system. Windows 2000 Datacenter Server marks Microsoft's entry into this high-end market.

The demands of this market segment, such as applications that require more processing power and larger memory needs, have excluded previous versions of Microsoft's operating systems including Windows NT 4.0 from penetrating the market.

Datacenter Server builds on all of the features found in Windows 2000 Advanced Server but now includes increased clustering capabilities that provides up to four-node failover.

It's important to note that Windows 2000 Datacenter Server has very stringent hardware requirements, and as such, organizations looking to implement Datacenter Server will need to consult with a major hardware vendor.

Windows 2000 Datacenter Server provides support for up to 32 processors and 64GB of RAM.

Table 1.1 lists the hardware requirements for the different versions of Windows 2000.

TABLE 1.1   Hardware Requirements for the Windows 2000 Operating System Family

Windows 2000 Professional	Windows 2000 Server	Windows 2000 Advanced Server	Windows 2000 Datacenter Server
133MHz Pentium compatible CPU	133MHz Pentium-compatible CPU	133MHz Pentium-compatible CPU	Pentium III Xeon or higher CPU
64MB RAM	256MB RAM	256MB RAM	256MB RAM
2GB disk space	2GB disk space	2GB disk space	2GB disk space
			Minimum 8-way capable server platform

What Is Windows 2000 Active Directory?

The most exciting new feature found in Windows 2000 is, of course, Active Directory.

For many years, Microsoft operating systems have been plagued by their limited directory services capabilities.

So, what exactly is a directory service? A directory service is a database that contains information about every object on the network. This information can help network administrators and network engineers manage large enterprise-wide networks. For example, information about a particular user is stored in a standard defined user object. This object includes information pertinent to user such as the username, password, group membership, contact information, as well as any system information unique to the user.

Other types of objects in the directory service include groups, applications, computers, printers, and files, and folders. The directory service makes these objects accessible throughout the entire enterprise-wide network.

Other networking companies have previously released their own directory services. A com-pany named Banyan Systems released one of the first directory services, called StreetTalk. StreetTalk was one component in Banyan's overall networking service named VINES. Banyan VINES was a distributed network environment for inexpensive PCs. Although the Banyan products have long since been discontinued, they are still widely regarded as the first directory service.

Novell, one of Microsoft's main competitors in this area, also released NetWare Directory Services (NDS). Chapter 2, "Novell NDS and Windows NT 4.0 Directory Service," explores NDS in more detail.

Definition of an Active Directory

Now, don't let this discussion mislead you. Windows NT 4.0 includes what Microsoft considered a directory service. In the strictest sense, Windows NT 4.0 provides information about objects throughout the network, so it does include a directory service. However, in all practicality, NT 4.0's directory service is very limited. Its database has a flat structure that provides no form of delegation or inheritance of user and group rights. A database is also limited to approximately 40,000 objects. As a result, the directory service is not feasible for very large enterprise-wide networks. Many of these large networks have to use StreetTalk or, more likely, NDS.

Microsoft's first real foray into the exciting world of directory services was marked by the release of Windows 2000 and Active Directory.

Active Directory extends Windows NT 4.0's directory service to overcome many of the earlier limitations. It also includes many new features that are important for organizations in the new Internet age.

Some of these new features are briefly described in the following sections.

The New Domain Model

As I stated earlier, the directory service in Windows NT 4.0 has a very limited database size. A domain in Windows NT is limited to 40,000 objects. In Active Directory, a domain can contain a virtually unlimited number of user objects.

The new domain model in Active Directory also provides for hierarchical organization of domains. Domains can now be organized into trees and forests. As a result, administrators can subdivide Active Directory into multiple domains that follow the organization's structure. These subdivisions allow more efficient delegation and inheritance of rights.

Trust Relationships

One of the most difficult aspects of implementing and administering Windows NT 4.0 directory services is the management of trust relationships. A *trust relationship* provides a way for two or more separate domains to authenticate user accounts from outside their domain. If an organization needs to overcome the 40,000 objects limitation in Windows NT 4.0, they have to create multiple domains and configure trust relationships between them. These trust relationships need to be created manually and, to add insult to injury, are *unidirectional*. In other words, for two domains to trust one other, to trust relationships needs to be manually created. If three domains need to trust one another, six trust relationships need to be created. As more domains are added, the number of trust relationships grows exponentially.

In Active Directory, trust relationships are created automatically by the directory service. These trust relationships are bi-directional and transitive. As a result, the management of trust relationships is greatly simplified. For organizations that require special needs, Active Directory still provides the capability to create manual, unidirectional trust relationships.

Multimaster Replication

In Windows NT 4.0 directory services, the directory database is replicated between the Primary Domain Controller (PDC) and Backup Domain Controllers (BDCs). There was only one PDC per domain. The PDC contains a read-write copy of the directory database. As a result, the PDC must always be available for changes to be written to the directory database. If the PDC is down, a user can still model to the domain via a BDC. A BDC contains a read-always copy of database.

Active Directory supports a form of replication known as *multimaster replication*. Simply stated, every domain controller in Active Directory contains a read-write copy of the directory database. Changes made to each copy are then replicated to all other domain controllers. With multimaster replication, it is very unlikely that the directory service will ever be unavailable.

Open Standards

Although Windows NT 4.0 includes support for some open standards such as TCP/IP, it is mostly based on proprietary standards. In the interoperable world of the Internet, this is a serious limitation.

Active Directory is based upon and supports many of the open standards that make up the Internet today. Standards such as DNS, Kerberos, and Lightweight Directory Access Protocol (LDAP) allow third-party vendors to integrate their applications and directory services into Active Directory.

Group Policy

Windows NT 4.0 uses system policies. A system policy enables the administrator to control the computing environment. This can be as simple as limiting the background color of the user's desktop or as extensive as limiting the user's actions within the operating system. System policies are contained in a file stored in the NetLogon share of a domain controller.

In Active Directory, group policies are stored in the directory database. They can be assigned to practically any object in the directory and contain myriad features such as the installation of new software as well as the configuration of security parameters.

Global Catalog

In any directory service, the capability to search for a particular object or object attribute can be severely impeded depending on the size of the directory database. Because of this, Active Directory includes a feature known as the *global catalog*. The global catalog contains a subset of each object's attributes. The attributes included are ones that are most likely to be used in searches. You can think of the global catalog as a partial copy of the Active Directory database. As a result, searches are much more efficient and take less time.

Windows NT 4.0 does not have any method for searching directory objects.

Complementary Components of Active Directory

As mentioned earlier, Active Directory in Windows 2000 includes a number of complementary components that are based on open standards. Three of these components—LDAP, DNS, and Kerberos—are critical and required for the proper operation of Active Directory.

The following sections provide a brief overview of each of these components.

LDAP

LDAP, or *Lightweight Directory Access Protocol*, is a smaller subset over the Directory Access protocol. It is a key component of the directory service standard X.500.

LDAP enables you to locate resources, whether the resource is a user, an organization, or simply files or folders on a public Internet or corporate network. You use the LDAP directory to perform the search. The LDAP directory, much like DNS, resembles an upside-down tree. The beginning of the LDAP directory is called the root. Below the root lie the country branches. Each country branch designates an actual country throughout the world. For example, the United States could be represented by a US branch, whereas the United Kingdom could be represented by a UK branch. Within each country branch lie the organization branches. These represent individual businesses and organizations within that particular country. Within the organization branches are the organizational units that represent a hierarchy of the organization. These organizational units reflect structures such as departments and working groups. Individual resources—such as people, applications, files, and folders—are located within each organizational unit (see Figure 1.1).

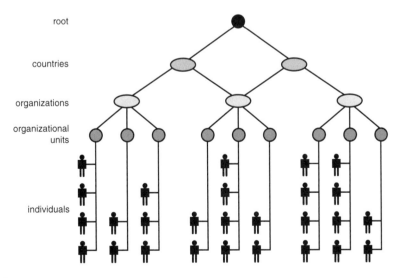

FIGURE 1.1
The structure of an LDAP directory.

Many companies and organizations support LDAP, including Cisco, Novell, and, of course, Microsoft.

DNS

The *Domain Name System*, or more commonly known as DNS, is a standard that defines how host names are mapped to IP addresses. A domain name is a more easily remembered as well as more meaningful alias for an Internet address.

Back in the dark, early days of the Internet and TCP/IP, the same resolution was accomplished via a simple text file known as the HOSTS file. An administrator simply typed the host name into the file along with its IP address. When the operating system needed to resolve the host name, it looked into the HOSTS file for the corresponding IP address.

As you can imagine, the HOSTS file became more unwieldy as a network grew. To make matters worse, the HOSTS file needed to be copied and updated on every computer on the network. Because of the inefficiency of this system, Internet engineers decided to define a new system for host-name resolution.

DNS is a distributed database that enables administrators to control their portion of the DNS database. Although control of the database can be limited, the entire database as a whole can be accessed across the entire network. Therefore, administrators can add or remove the host names under their jurisdiction while the rest of the network can query and access host names in the database. The solution overcomes many of the limitations found in the hosts file, such as its static nature.

The DNS database structure looks like an inverted tree. At the top of the tree is the root domain. It showed simply as a period (.).

Below the root domain are the top-level domains. Anyone who has used the Internet or e-mail will recognize the top-level domains, which include *com*, *edu*, *net*, *org*, and *mil,* as well as specific country domains such as *uk* for the United Kingdom and *au* for Australia. The Internet Corporation for Assigned Names and Numbers (ICANN) is currently developing an expanded top-level domain-naming standard. This standard will include easier-to-recognize top-level domain names, such as *biz* for businesses.

Below the top-level domains are the actual subdomains for businesses and organizations. Administrators for these organizations are responsible for managing the subdomains (see Figure 1.2).

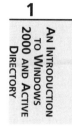

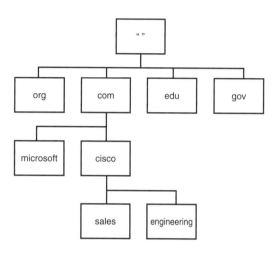

FIGURE 1.2

The structure of DNS.

DNS contains three primary components. The first is the host name's database, which includes a listing of all host names and domain names and their corresponding IP addresses. A second component is the DNS client. Most operating systems include a DNS client built into the operating system's TCP/IP stack. The DNS client takes host names entered into an application, such as Internet Explorer, and queries a DNS server for the corresponding IP address. The last component in DNS is the DNS server. The DNS server responds to queries from DNS clients. The DNS server locates the requested host names in the DNS database and returns the corresponding IP addresses (see Figure 1.3).

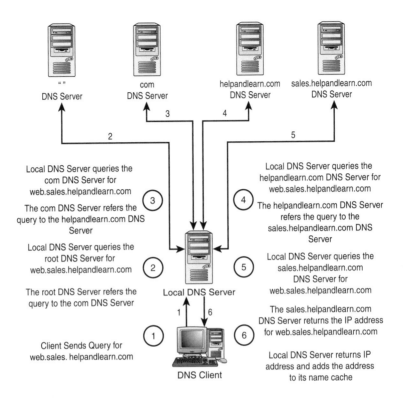

FIGURE 1.3

Querying the DNS database.

So what does all this have to do with Active Directory? Active Directory uses DNS to store critical information.

Just as DNS can be considered the heart of the Internet, DNS is also the heart of Active Directory.

Kerberos

In a search to provide a method for single sign-on access to network resources, Microsoft decided to use the Kerberos authentication protocol. The concept of single sign-on is to allow access to services within a domain or residing in trust domains with a single set of credentials.

Kerberos is an authentication method designed by the Massachusetts Institute of Technology (MIT). Kerberos allows the request for a network service and the user to be mutually authenticated.

So how does Kerberos authentication work?

Initially, the users enter their domain credentials at a Windows 2000 logon prompt. At this point, Windows 2000 uses DNS to locate an Active Directory server and the Kerberos authentication service. Once located, the Kerberos service will issue a ticket to the users. The ticket is a temporary certificate that identifies the users to network resources, such as servers and applications. This ticket can then be used to request other Kerberos tickets to provide access to network services. The entire process runs transparently to the users.

As a result, the Kerberos authentication process reduces the number of usernames and passwords that users have to remember.

Kerberos is the default authentication protocol in Windows 2000. Prior to Windows 2000, the default authentication protocol was NT LAN Manager (NTLM). Windows 2000 includes backwards compatibility with the NTLM authentication protocol to support previous versions of the Microsoft operating systems such as Windows 95/98 and Windows NT 4.0.

Benefits of Active Directory

If you take a look at most networks in the corporate world today, you'll see a number of directories used for many purposes. There may be a directory for e-mail, one for the phone system and voicemail, one for security access to buildings and facilities, and a directory for human resources and payroll. Having many separate directories creates a cumbersome burden and results in inefficiency.

As a result, many organizations can benefit from a single centralized directory service, such as the Active Directory.

With Active Directory, employees of an organization can quickly locate information about resources in the network or systems and applications connected to the network.

The following sections provide a brief overview of a handful of Active Directory's benefits.

Fault Tolerance

One of the main benefits of Windows 2000 and Active Directory is its capability to improve the fault tolerance of a network. Fault-tolerance means that if a failure occurs, the service being provided is still functional. As stated earlier, prior Microsoft operating systems provided little if any fault tolerance. Windows NT 4.0 provided limited fault tolerance with the use of the PDC/BDC relationship.

In Windows 2000, domain controllers use multimaster replication to replicate Active Directory data. As a result, the directory database maintains a loosely consistent state. All domain controllers contain a read/write copy of the directory database for their domain. If the domain controller or even multiple domain controllers fail, Active Directory is still fully available.

Extensible

All objects in Active Directory are defined in the Active Directory schema. When an object is being created, Active Directory uses the schema definition to determine how to create the object, including which attributes to include.

There might be situations in which the default schema is insufficient and do not meet the needs of the organization. For example, if an organization were implementing a new e-mail system such as Exchange Server 2000, the new e-mail system would require new schema changes.

Active Directory allows the schema to be extended by adding or modifying schema objects dynamically. Therefore, after the Active Directory schema is extended, the new objects and attributes are immediately available.

Because of this extensible capability, Windows 2000 and Active Directory can grow and change as your organization changes.

It is important to note that any modification of the schema is considered a major change and, if planned or implemented poorly, can have disastrous implications throughout the entire directory. Because of this, only members of the Schema Administrators group are permitted to make changes to the schema.

Scalable

Active Directory is inherently capable of scaling to a very large size which, let's face it, is a critical requirement of any directory service.

Recall that the directory service in Windows NT 4.0 is limited to 40,000 objects and its database.

Active Directory stores directory information within domains. Domains are used as a partition that enables you to distribute the directory across the network. This allows the directory to be available, as well as grow without limitations such as network speed or reliability.

Active Directory can virtually hold an unlimited number of objects per domain. Because of this, Microsoft recommends that most organizations use a single domain as much as possible.

However, there are situations in which you should use multiple domains. Some of these situations include deferring security requirements, and decentralized or autonomous administration.

Active Directory also uses DNS to locate objects within the directory. DNS is highly scalable and, as you might know, is used throughout the Internet.

Summary

This chapter provided an overview of Active Directory and the likely benefits it will bring to an organization. It also discussed the Windows 2000 operating system family and its various components.

CASE STUDY

Learning by Example: The "Molly Pitcher Pharmaceuticals, Inc." Company

Background: Molly Pitcher Pharmaceuticals, Inc. is a multibillion-dollar pharmaceutical firm headquartered in the United States. The headquarters houses approximately 5,000 employees. These employees are members of various departments, such as:

- Sales and marketing: 500 employees

- IT: 150 employees

- Research and development: 1,000 employees

- Executive staff: 850 employees

- Shipping and receiving: 500 employees

- Manufacturing: 2,000 employees

Molly Pitcher also has many remote office locations in North America that are utilized by sales personnel. The sales personnel spend most of their week visiting doctors and hospitals in their territories. They introduce Molly Pitcher Pharmaceuticals, Inc.'s new pharmaceutical products as well as field any concerns the physicians have with other Molly Pitcher products. At various times during the week, these sales personnel visit the remote office locations to attend meetings, update their offline address books, and retrieve any files needed from the corporate network. There are 12 remote offices and each office houses 50 employees, including sales personnel.

Geography: The Molly Pitcher Pharmaceuticals, Inc. headquarters is located in Valley Forge, PA. The headquarters campus is composed of five buildings that house various departments. Remote offices are located in New York, Washington, D.C., Philadelphia, Atlanta, Dallas, Detroit, Chicago, Denver, Las Vegas, Los Angeles, San Francisco, and Seattle.

Network infrastructure: All remote offices connect back to headquarters via T1 leased lines. Headquarters connects to the Internet via a T3. Most servers, running Windows NT Server 4, are located in the Valley Forge datacenter. They are used for a variety of functions, such as file and print services, messaging, intranet, and several other applications. All desktop computers at headquarters are connected to a 100Mbps switched backbones. Desktops at remote offices are connected via a 10Mbps nonswitched backbone. Client computers, both desktops and portables, have already been upgraded to Windows 2000 Professional during the past year. The company currently has an Internet presence, `mollypitcher.com`, and the Web infrastructure is currently housed at the Valley Forge datacenter.

Existing IT environment: Molly Pitcher currently utilizes Windows NT 4.0 in a master domain model. There is a master domain at headquarters that houses all user accounts for headquarters employees. There are several resource domains, one for each department at headquarters. Also, each remote office contains a resource domain. Domain controllers for all resource domains and the headquarters master domain are located in Valley Forge. Backup Domain Controllers (BDCs) for the master domain have been placed at each remote office to speed up user authentication. The company also has an existing dial-up infrastructure, which utilizes Novell NetWare 3.12 servers for authentication. The sales personnel use this dial-up infrastructure to check e-mail and place orders for physicians.

Current business situation: Molly Pitcher has decided to move the corporate network to Active Directory. The existing master domain model has been difficult to administer. The company has also had to spend a lot of time training IT employees in the proper way to securely administer the resources within the various domains. Because the dial-up architecture is housed on a Novell NetWare 3.12 platform, each user who requires dial-up access must be assigned a separate Novell NetWare user account. This results in cumbersome situations where the user must remember two user accounts and passwords, whereas administrators need to provide NetWare clients on remote user's portable computers.

Novell NDS and Windows NT 4.0 Directory Services

IN THIS CHAPTER

To fully understand Active Directory, you must come to understand the operating systems and directory services that came before.

Novell's NDS is one of the most common directory services. It has been around for almost 10 years and is very stable. Despite this, thanks to a superior marketing effort as well as an ever-improving product line from Microsoft, many organizations have decided to move to a network operating system that is overall easier to use. As a result, the number of new NetWare installations has steadily declined, whereas installations of Windows NT and Windows 2000 continue to rise. In the near future, as Novell's market share continues to decline, more and more NDS-based networks will be migrated to Active Directory. For the NDS-based networks that are not migrated, Active Directory will need to interoperate with it.

Windows NT Directory Services is the other most common directory service. The most recent release, Windows NT 4, took significant market share from NDS. With the upgrade to Windows 2000, Microsoft is expecting all Windows NT Directory Services-based networks to be migrated to Active Directory if they expect to be supported in the future.

In a world where interoperability between operating systems and directory services is very important, understanding how NDS and NT Directory Services work together will make you a more well-rounded systems engineer. You can then design Active Directory systems that can interoperate with and successfully migrate these earlier directory services.

Novell NetWare and NDS

In the early to mid-1980s, a little known software company named Novell released a product that revolutionized the networking world and made networking affordable for many small and medium-sized businesses.

This product was named NetWare.

Novell NetWare used standard IBM-compatible PCs to create a distributed networking environment. This new networking environment allowed groups of PCs to share files and resources attached to a central file server. Prior to this, networking was accomplished using expensive mainframe computers and terminals. Many small and medium-sized businesses could not implement networking technology because of the restrictive cost of such equipment. NetWare was fast and reliable compared to other networking products available. NetWare allowed an organization to create a network using inexpensive PCs, thus bringing networking to the masses.

There have been many versions of Novell NetWare over almost 20 years. The following section provides brief descriptions of some of the more widely used versions.

Historical Overview of NetWare

NetWare has a very interesting history. You can correlate the development of Microsoft operating systems and their capabilities by understanding the different versions of NetWare. As a new version of NetWare was released, Microsoft responded competitively and added similar or better features to Windows.

NetWare 3.x

NetWare 3.x was released in 1989. NetWare 3.x could handle up to 250 concurrent users per server. It could also mount very large disk volumes to provide more than ample disk space for file sharing.

NetWare 3.x also added multiprotocol capabilities. Prior to NetWare 3.x, NetWare relied on IPX/SPX for its network protocol. NetWare 3.x added support for TCP/IP and AppleTalk, allowing communication between DOS, OS/2, Unix, and Macintosh-based networks.

NetWare 3.x had a directory service called the Bindery. Bindery directory services were on a per-server basis. In other words, if you needed access to three NetWare 3.x servers, you would need a user account on each of the servers.

Many organizations continued to use NetWare 3.x despite the release of the superior NetWare 4.x. These organizations had networks that were rather small and did not require all of the firepower (and overhead) that NetWare 4.x brought. For this reason, Novell continued to support and release updates for NetWare 3.x.

The last release of this NetWare version was NetWare 3.2. Novell discontinued the NetWare 3.x line at the end of 2000.

A decade of use—not a bad run for a network operating system.

Microsoft released Windows NT 3.51 during this timeframe. Windows NT 3.51 was the first version of NT to be seriously considered by most organizations. This version of NT saw the introduction of the domain-structured directory service. It suffered from its old and quaint Windows for Workgroups-style user interface. Most users by now had grown accustomed to the Windows 95 user interface.

NetWare 4.x

Released in 1993, NetWare 4.x included all the features in NetWare 3.x, but added even more capabilities, the most important of which was Novell Directory Services, or NDS.

NDS introduced the concept of a single sign-on (SSO). As in the previous example, if you needed access to three NetWare 4.x servers, you would need only one NDS user account. NDS is described in more detail later in this chapter.

NetWare 4.x boosted the number of concurrent user connections up to 1,000 per server. It also added sub-block allocation and file compression for more efficient disk space usage.

NetWare 5.x

NetWare 5.x was unveiled in 1999. With NetWare 5.x, Novell fully embraced the Internet by providing native TCP/IP support. Earlier versions of NetWare relied on IPX/SPX for their networking protocol. Although TCP/IP could be utilized to connect TCP/IP-based workstations, IPX/SPX was required to operate a NetWare server. Because of the native TCP/IP support, NetWare 5.x servers could now be used on the Internet for Web sites, FTP, e-mail, and so on.

NetWare 5.x added support for Java and a more robust selection of administration tools.

NDS was also improved. NetWare 5.x's NDS (also known as NDS 8.x) could support more than a billion objects in its database!

With the release of NetWare 5, Novell announced that it was dropping support of both NetWare 4.x and NetWare 3.x.

Understanding NDS

Novell Directory Services, or NDS, is a distributed database that accesses and manages resources on a network. All servers on the network share this database, and it allows users to access the database from any point within the network.

NDS is known for the following characteristics:

- A distributed database
- A logical, not physical, directory structure
- Not platform specific
- Flexible replication topology

NDS is based on a logical structure and, because of this, does not need to reside on a particular server or group of servers. Other operating systems, such as Windows NT and even Windows 2000, require the use of domain controllers to house the directory database. In NDS however, there is no special server for housing the directory database. All servers are treated as equals and can hold or not hold a copy of the database. The network designer can designate which portions of NDS (known as replicas) are placed on which servers. The capability to place replicas throughout the network increases the availability and fault tolerance of NDS.

NDS is not platform specific. Novell has released versions of NDS that will run on Windows NT, Windows 2000, Linux, Solaris, IBM AIX, Tru64 Unix, and, of course, NetWare. For a heterogeneous environment, NDS might be the answer an organization needs.

NDS Structure and Replication Topology

NDS stores information in a hierarchical manner. This allows NDS to reflect the organizational needs, whether they be regions, departments, or user groups, rather than the physical topology of the network. This allows the user community to better understand and find network resources because the structure of NDS reflects the structure of their organization.

NDS Objects: [Root]

The [Root] object represents the beginning of the NDS tree.

An NDS tree can have only one [Root] object. This object cannot be renamed or deleted, although it is still considered a security principal (which means it can be assigned rights to other objects).

It's important to remember that networks with separate [Root] objects cannot communicate or share data with each other. Users that require access to both NDS trees would require a valid user account in each tree, thus the primary reason for using NDS, SSO, is not possible.

The [Root] object can only contain Country, Organization, and Alias objects.

Country

The Country object is a container object that is utilized directly below the [Root] object. It is limited to two characters.

If an organization is organized along country boundaries (such as regional offices in the US, England, Japan, and so on), the Country object can represent these offices. In reality though, most organizations do not use the Country object and prefer to use the Organization object to represent different regions.

Organization

The Organization object is a container object.

There must be at least one Organization object in an NDS tree, either immediately below the [Root] object or below a Country object. It can contain leaf objects or Organizational Units (OUs), but it cannot contain other Organization objects.

Typically it represents the name of the organization. For example, instead of using the more limited Country object, the NDS tree could have Organization objects representing different regional offices or countries.

Organizational Unit (OU)

The Organizational Unit (OU) object is a container object. OUs can only be used under an Organization object or under another OU. It cannot be used directly under the [Root] or Country object.

The OU object is the most common container object in NDS and often subdivides the NDS tree according to the organization's needs. OUs typically designate special functions, such as location, department, responsibility, access needs, and the like (see Figure 2.1).

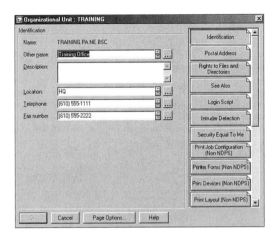

FIGURE 2.1

Viewing the attributes of an NDS Organization Unit (OU) object.

OUs can also contain their own login scripts. An OU login script can automatically prepare and configure a standard OU user environment. All users who are members of the OU would process the login script (see Figure 2.2). This allows an organization to configure the user's environment depending on the department to which he belongs. The user's computer will automatically have mapped network drives pointing to areas on the file servers where his department's data is stored.

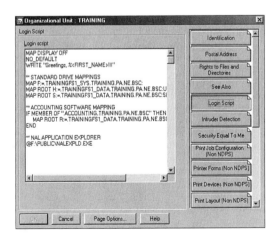

FIGURE 2.2

Viewing the login script attribute of an NDS Organization Unit (OU) object.

OUs are used as security principles as well and in turn can be used much like groups are typically utilized. For example, if all members of an OU needed access to a directory, the OU itself could be given a trustee assignment (access control list in Windows 2000) to the directory. As a result, all members of the OU would inherit the permissions to the directory.

Alias

The Alias object is a leaf object that points to an existing leaf or container object.

Aliases are typically used to make life a little easier for users. Take for example a university that has printers on every floor of every building throughout its campus. To ease network administration, all printers, print queues, and print server objects would be created in a single OU aptly named, PRINTERS. Users, however, prefer to only see the printer objects that are relevant to them (such as the printers in their building on their floor). Aliases work great in this situation. In the users OU, an Alias object can be created to point back to the appropriate print queue in the PRINTERS OU. As a result, the users can view only the printers that are relevant to them.

Group

The Group object is one of the two most used leaf objects in an NDS tree. This object creates a collection of User objects that have the same security requirements. In turn, the object is assigned permissions to the objects (OUs, Servers, Directories, and so on) (see Figure 2.3).

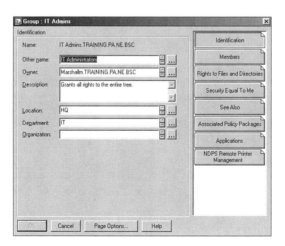

FIGURE 2.3
Viewing the attributes of an NDS Group object.

OUs and Groups have similar functions, however Groups can contain User objects from other container objects (see Figure 2.4).

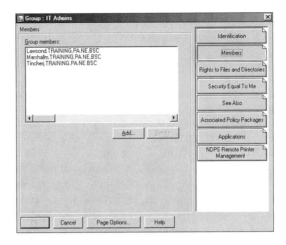

FIGURE 2.4
Viewing the membership of an NDS Group object.

Printer

The Printer object represents a physical network printer. If a user sends a print job to a printer object, the print job is automatically placed in the printer's print queue (see Figure 2.5).

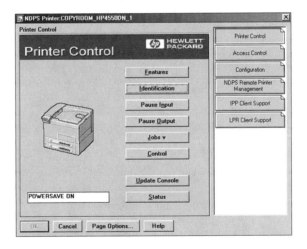

FIGURE 2.5
Viewing the properties of an NDS Printer object.

Server

The Server object represents a NetWare server in the NDS tree. The data volumes of the server are represented as Volume objects below the Server object in the NDS tree (see Figure 2.6).

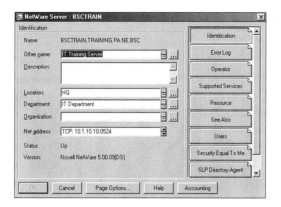

FIGURE 2.6

Viewing the properties of an NDS Server object.

User

The User object is the most used leaf object in an NDS tree. The User object represents an individual user account that a person uses to log on to the network.

A user object contains a number of attributes, such as home directory, login restrictions, intruder lockout, as well as many others (see Figure 2.7).

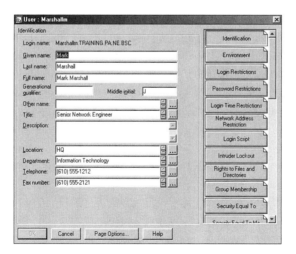

FIGURE 2.7

Viewing the attributes of an NDS User object.

One of the attributes of a user object is the group membership list (see Figure 2.8)

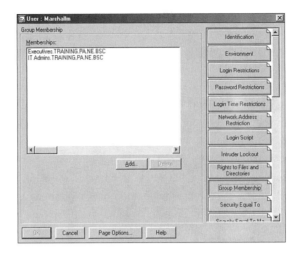

FIGURE 2.8

Viewing the group membership attribute of an NDS User object.

User objects also contain a login script attribute. This attribute allows an individual user's environment to be automatically configured when they log on.

Special user objects can be created as user templates with certain attributes already defined. These templates can then in turn be utilized to create new user objects.

Volume

The Volume object represents the actual physical volume located in a NetWare server. You can manage the file system on the volume using this object.

By default, the name of the Volume object consists of the name of the NetWare server followed by an underscore and finally the name of the volume. For example, for a NetWare server named NW5 with a volume named DATA, the Volume Object's name will be NW5_Data.

NDS Replication Topology

NDS is a loosely consistent partitioned database. The database can be divided into logical portions, which are then known as *partitions*. Copies of these partitions can then be placed on other NetWare servers. The copies are known as *replicas*. NDS keeps the replicas loosely synchronized. In other words, two replicas of a partition are not exact copies of one another. NDS continually synchronizes the replicas and makes decisions about which replica contains the most up to date data (see Figure 2.9).

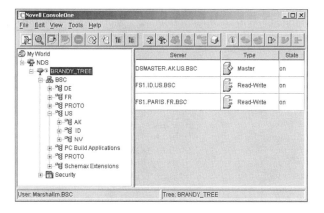

FIGURE 2.9
Viewing a partition along with which NetWare servers are holding replicas of the partition.

There are four replica types in NDS (see Figure 2.10).

Master

The Master replica is the initial copy of a new partition. When a new NDS tree is created, a Master replica of the [Root] partition is created on the first NetWare server installed.

Read/Write

The Read/Write replica can be created if another copy of a partition is needed on a NetWare server. A Read/Write replica is created because the Master replica already exists for the partition.

Read/Write replicas can administer the NDS database as well as authenticate users to the NDS tree.

Read-Only

The Read-Only replica contains, obviously, a read-only copy of the partition. Any changes attempted to the NDS tree via this replica are redirected to either the master replica or a Read/Write replica for the partition. The change is then replicated back to the Read-Only replica.

The Read-Only replica is rarely used in NDS. Novell recommends not using this replica type because it can create unwanted synchronization traffic throughout the tree. This replica type was included in NDS to make NDS X.500 compliant (X.500 requires a Read-Only replica type).

Subordinate Reference

The Subordinate Reference replica type is created automatically by NDS wherever a server holds a parent partition but not the master. In other words, if there are child partitions below a parent partition but the server does not contain the master replica for the child partitions, the server will have subordinate references to the child partitions.

FIGURE 2.10
Viewing a NetWare Server along with the various replicas it is holding.

NDS Versus Active Directory

Although NDS and Active Directory are similar in many ways and attempt to accomplish the same tasks, there are some significant differences in the architectures of the two directory services.

Security Principles

One of the most obvious differences is in how security principles are handled. In NDS, any Container or Leaf object can be a security principle. For example, an OU object can be given read/write permissions to a particular folder in the file system. In Active Directory, only User, Group objects, and Computer Objects can be security principles. As a result, even if you had created an OU for a department and moved all of the department members' user accounts into the OU, you will still need to create a group. This group's membership list would contain the department users as well, who can then, via the group, be assigned the appropriate rights to resources. In NDS, you can use the OU to assign permissions. In AD, you cannot.

Replication Partitioning

Another significant difference between NDS and Active Directory is Replication Partitioning.

The heart of any directory service is the way that directory data is replicated and distributed within the directory. Directory data must be replicated in a timely and validated method. If it isn't, the data would become corrupted and useless. As a result, some portions, if not all, of the network would become inaccessible.

The NDS database is considered loosely consistent. The database can be divided into partitions and replicas that can then be placed on *any* NetWare server. As a result, a simple file and print server at a remote office could contain a replica of the partition the remote office users utilize the most.

Active Directory uses multimaster replication and is also loosely consistent. Multimaster replication allows directory updates to occur at any domain controller, but domain controllers only. By deploying multiple domain controllers in one domain, fault tolerance and load balancing can be obtained. If one domain controller within a domain fails, other domain controllers within the same domain can provide necessary directory access because they contain the same directory data.

Active Directory also manages directory replication through the use of Site objects. The Site object manages replication schedules over WAN connections.

Windows NT 4.0 Directory Services

Previous Microsoft operating systems (DOS, Windows for Workgroups, and Windows 95) relied on a very loose network administration and security model called Workgroups. Workgroups provided an easy way for users to locate network resources, however, network security was still supplied on an as-needed basis. In other words, each computer contained user accounts, passwords, and access control functions to maintain network security. If a user needed access to data on three separate computers, the user would need three separate user accounts. Because of this loose model, network administration and security would become more burdensome as the network grew. Workgroups are sometimes referred to as peer-to-peer networks. Novell NetWare 3.x's bindery is comparable to a workgroup.

With Windows NT, Microsoft introduced a new model of network administration and security called *domains*.

Domains

A domain is a client/server model that allows users to have a single user account for the network. The user logs on to the domain and in turn can access any resources on any computer that is a member of the same domain (provided of course that the user has been assigned the appropriate security privileges).

Although not as robust, domains are roughly comparable to NetWare 4.x and 5.x's NDS.

Windows NT Server Roles

Being a client/server model, domain security and administration is handled by certain Windows NT servers in the domain. Each server in a Windows NT domain must fall into a particular role, roles which are described in the following sections.

Primary Domain Controller (PDC)

The Primary Domain Controller, more commonly referred to as the PDC, is responsible for maintaining the domain security database. This database is called the Security Account Manager (SAM). The SAM contains all user accounts and their associated information, such as username, the user's Full Name, a Description, password, and so on as well as any account restrictions (such as account disabled, logon times, and so on).

There is one server per domain that acts as the PDC. The first Windows NT Server in a domain must be the PDC and its role is determined during installation. The name of the domain must also be determined during this installation.

The PDC holds a read/write copy of the SAM. The PDC then replicates the SAM to all Backup Domain Controllers or BDCs.

When a user logs on to the domain, the PDC validates the user's username and password against the security information contained in the SAM. If the username and password are valid, the PDC creates a security token and returns this token to the requesting client. This security token represents the users and their group membership lists. Windows NT uses this token to provide seamless and single logon access to all resources throughout the domain.

Backup Domain Controller (BDC)

The BDC contains a read-only copy of the SAM and assists the PDC in authenticating users, whether the PDC is simply busy or not available.

The BDC can also be used for disaster recovery in the event that the PDC is unavailable. A BDC can be promoted to be the PDC for the domain. Once promotion is complete, the new PDC (that is, the former BDC) holds the read/write copy of the SAM for the domain.

So, what happens to the former PDC? Well, it depends on the operational state of the old PDC. If the PDC was fully operational (up and running on the network), the PDC is automatically demoted to a BDC when the new PDC is promoted. If the PDC was not operational, it will still think it is the PDC when it is brought back up. In this case, the Netlogon service will be automatically disabled once it detects the new PDC. After the Netlogon service is disabled, the server cannot authenticate user logons or participate in domain security. The administrator would then have the option to go into the Server Manager Utility to demote the PDC to a BDC.

Member Servers

Member servers are simply Windows NT servers that are members of the domain but do not participate in domain security or administration. Member servers are also sometimes referred to as standalone servers. Member servers contain their own SAM that is used for administering the server's resources. The member server's SAM, along with the domain SAM found on the domain controllers, work together to provide security to all domain resources. The connection between SAMs (between domain controllers and member server or workstations, as well as domain controllers in different domains) is referred to as a "trust relationship."

Trust Relationships

Remember that domains are more effective than workgroups because the user needs only a single logon to access multiple resources within a domain.

But, what happens when the network environment consists of multiple domains?

Well, Microsoft included a piece of functionality in Windows NT called a trust relationship. A trust relationship is basically a conduit that allows two or more security entities to exchange authentication tasks regarding a user account or access.

An important piece in the authentication puzzle is the way Windows uses *pass-through authentication*. Pass-through authentication occurs when a user cannot be authenticated to the local computer the Netlogon service on this computer will pass the credentials to the domain controller. The domain controller will find the user account and return all of the appropriate SIDs to the local computer. The local computer then completes the logon process.

When a trust relationship is established between two domains, their users (depending on the type of trust relationship) can access the resources in each domain.

For example, Adara is a member of the Engineering domain. The Engineering domain is trusted by the Marketing domain. Adara can log on to the Marketing domain without needing a separate user account in that domain. This is possible through trust relationships.

Notice the key word "trusted." With a trust relationship, there are two sides to the trust. The "trusted" side represents the domain that contains the user accounts that will be permitted access. The "trusting" side represents the domain that contains the resources to be accessed. This domain is "trusting" user accounts from the "trusted" domain. An easy way to remember which side is which is this simple phrase: "Trust Ed," as in "Please trust Edward the user." The trusted domain always contains the user accounts.

Two types of trust relationships can be established. The one-way trust was described previously, where one domain trusts another domain. The two-way trust is essentially two one-way trusts, where one domain trusts another domain and vice-versa.

Trust relationships are not transitive. This was an important point to remember when designing Windows NT networks. Figure 2.11 illustrates this point. Domain A has a trust relationship with Domain B. Domain A trusts Domain B. Domain B also has a trust relationship with Domain C. Domain B trusts Domain C. Therefore, authentication requests cannot occur between Domains A and C. Because the trusts are not transitive, a separate trust relationship between Domain A and Domain C would need to be established or user from Domain C would need to have valid user accounts in Domain A.

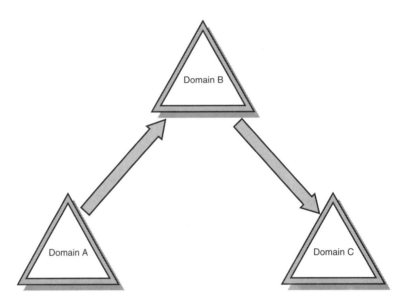

FIGURE 2.11
Example of non-transitive trusts.

Luckily for all of us, Active Directory simplifies a lot of the management of trust relationships. But make no mistake. Beneath the user friendly veil of Active Directory lays the old, tried and true trust relationship. As a matter of fact, Active Directory creates transitive two-way trusts between domains by default. Active Directory even allows you to create trusts the old fashion way if the situation arises.

Directory Database Size

One of the critical limitations found in Windows NT directory services is the directory database size.

The Microsoft recommended limitation for the size of the SAM is 60MB. This recommendation is because of the limitation of the size of the NT Registry (wherein the SAM resides).

To understand the limitation of the database size, one must realize the size of objects in the database itself, such as user, group, and computer objects. Each of these objects takes up 4KB of space. As a result, the practical number of objects in a domain is 40,000 objects.

Because of this limitation of 40,000 objects, Windows NT domains were not the greatest solution for large complex network environments.

Domain Models

To overcome the limitations in the directory database size, Microsoft recommended that Windows NT-based networks be designed to fit into one of the following domain models. These domain models can be implemented according to geographic scope or security requirements.

Single Domain Model

The Single Domain model is simply a default Windows NT domain configuration. It contains no trust relationships and is centrally administered, which makes it the most easily managed domain model.

The main disadvantage to the Single Domain Model is the directory database size limitation.

Single Master Domain Model

The Single Master Domain model contains one domain that contains all user accounts for the organization. This domain is sometimes called the Master Accounts Domain. This model allows all user administration to be centralized to this single domain.

Resources are decentralized in other domains. These domains are called Resource Domains. This allows the resource domain administrators to manage and control their own resources.

The trust relationships in this domain model are all one-way with the resource domains trusting the master accounts domain.

This domain model is still limited to 40,000 user accounts however (see Figure 2.12).

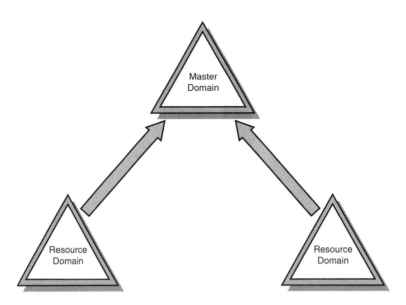

FIGURE 2.12
The Single Master Domain model.

Multiple Master Domain Model

The Multiple Master Domain model contains two or more Master Accounts Domains that contain all of the users for the organization. All user administration is centralized between the Master Account Domains.

Again, resources are decentralized in other domains and managed by the respective domain administrators.

Trusts in this domain model consist of two-way trusts between all Master Accounts Domains and one-way trusts between each Resource Domain and all Master Accounts Domains.

This domain model overcomes the directory database size limitation (see Figure 2.13).

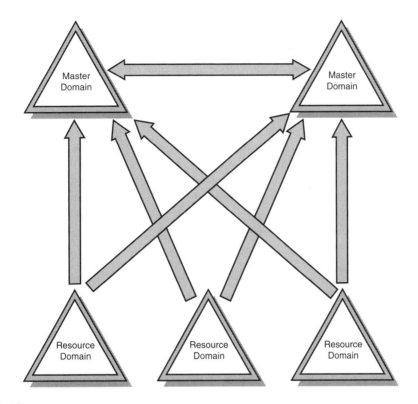

FIGURE 2.13
The Multiple Master Domain model.

Complete Trust Domain Model

The Complete Trust Domain model takes into account that user accounts and resources are mixed throughout the domains. This model allows decentralized account and resource management.

Trusts in this domain model consist of two-way trusts between all domains.

This domain model is the most difficult to manage in Windows NT because of the large number of trusts required and its decentralized nature (see Figure 2.14).

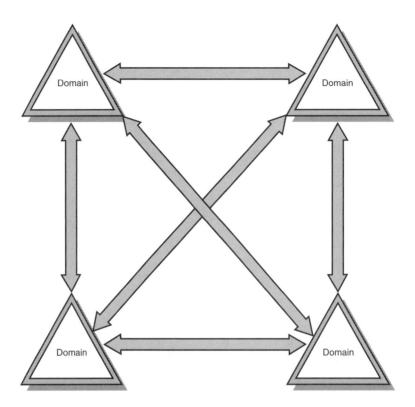

FIGURE 2.14
The Complete Trust Domain model.

Summary

This chapter looked at the two directory services that provided the foundation to Active Directory. It covered NDS in detail, describing the history of the NetWare operating systems as well as the objects and replication scheme NDS uses. It also discussed Windows NT domain-based directory service and the various methods that Microsoft employed to provide scalability.

The remainder of this book is dedicated to the discussion of Active Directory and how you can implement it into your network environment, whether large or small.

CASE STUDY

Learning by Example: The "Molly Pitcher Pharmaceuticals, Inc." Company

After reviewing the case study for Molly Pitcher Pharmaceuticals, Inc., there are a couple of issues that need to be analyzed.

First, Molly Pitcher is utilizing Novell NetWare 3.12 for their dial-up architecture. NetWare 3.12 utilized a directory service called the bindery, which stored user and group accounts on a per-server basis. There were also no means of synchronizing accounts from Novell NetWare 3.12 to Windows NT 4 or Active Directory. Because the company is looking to eliminate this dial-up architecture, these Novell NetWare 3.12 servers must be migrated or, more likely, simply eliminated. Windows 2000 Routing and Remote Access Servers (RRAS) can be deployed to provide a new dial-up architecture that is compatible with Active Directory.

Second, the company is currently using a single master domain model. This model contains one domain that houses all user accounts for the Molly Pitcher. This model allows all user administration to be centralized to this single domain. There are one-way trust relationships between the resource domains and the master domain. The resource domains are administered by the individual departments and remote offices. Due to the complex nature of the Windows NT 4 domain models, as well as the issue of training administrators, Molly Pitcher wants to eliminate this model with a streamlined Active Directory design.

Describing Active Directory Components

IN THIS CHAPTER

There are many components that make up Active Directory, and it is critical that you understand these components and the concepts surrounding them. In later chapters, you will learn how and why to create these components.

This chapter describes some of the most critical components in Active Directory, as well as Microsoft's recommendations for their use. These components need to be thought out beforehand, as they can have a serious impact on the function and performance of your Active Directory. Some of these components include

- DNS and the domain namespace
- Domains
- Forests
- Trees
- Sites

Domain Namespace

Active Directory in Windows 2000 utilizes the Domain Naming Service (DNS) standard for naming objects.

All hosts on a TCP/IP-based network must have a valid and unique IP address. An IP address is a 32-bit binary number. It is represented using dotted decimal notation, such as 192.168.0.1. As you can imagine, most humans cannot remember many IP addresses.

DNS was implemented to make the TCP/IP networking world more user friendly. DNS allows user-friendly names to be mapped to IP addresses. For example, instead of trying to remember 192.168.0.1, a DNS mapping (known as a resource record) could be created stating that COMPUTER1 maps to 192.168.0.1. The user only needs to know about COMPUTER1, not 192.168.0.1.

Another benefit of DNS is that IP addresses can and do change. The IP address of COMPUTER1 could change to 192.168.0.37. In this case, the DNS record for COMPUTER1 would be updated from 192.168.0.1 to 192.168.0.37. The users and applications would still be looking for the host name COMPUTER1 and thus would not need to be notified of the change.

DNS is a hierarchical naming system and a distributed database. As you can see in Figure 3.1, DNS looks much like an inverted tree. The root of the tree (aptly named "root") is represented by a period. The root signifies the beginning of the domain namespace. A domain namespace, in either Active Directory or DNS, defines an area with boundaries in which any object contained within must adhere to the domain-naming standard. Objects or hosts that do not adhere to the domain-naming standard will not be considered to be part of the domain namespace. As a result, they might not be able to properly access information provided by DNS. For example, when clients attempt to access Active Directory to perform logons or look up directory information, they use their domain name to determine their location within Active Directory. If they are misconfigured, the operation will fail.

Domains are branches off of the root. Figure 3.1 represents the Internet Domain Namespace, where directories below the root are the main Internet categories, such as COM, NET, and ORG. Domains can contain hosts, such as computers and servers, and also subdomains. On the Internet, these subdomains are companies and organizations, such as `microsoft.com`, `compaq.com`, `npr.org`, and `pbs.org`.

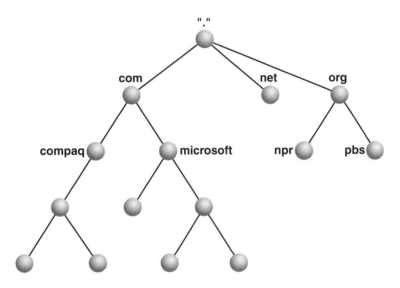

FIGURE 3.1
The Internet domain namespace.

The Active Directory domain hierarchy uses the same rules and procedures as DNS to resolve domain and computer names.

For example, an organization named Help and Learn, Inc. is beginning to plan its implementation of Active Directory. They have two regional divisions in their organization, called East (representing the East Coast of the United States) and West (representing the West Coast). Their plan calls for the use of `helpandlearn.com` as their domain namespace. All objects within Help and Learn, Inc.'s Active Directory structure would be within this namespace. The East and West regions could be implemented as subdomains in Active Directory. They would be named `east.helpandlearn.com` and `west.helpandlearn.com`. A computer object named LAPTOP1 located in the east subdomain would have the Active Directory name `laptop1.east.helpandlearn.com`.

Possible DNS Names

There are two very important rules when it comes to naming objects in DNS:

- A child domain can have only one parent domain. For example: If the domain `public` is a child of microsoft.com, it cannot be a child of `msn.com`. Looking at the FQDN of the domain, it becomes apparent: `public.microsoft.com` is not the same domain as `public.msn.com`.

- Two children of the same parent must have different names. For example: If two domains are created under the same parent domain, their names must be different due to the hierarchical DNS structure. Look at the following FQDNs: public.microsoft.com and `private.microsoft.com`. You cannot rename the `private` domain to `public` because `public` already exists.

A DNS name consists of different portions separated by periods (.). Each portion represents a domain or subdomain in the namespace. This is known as an FQDN (fully qualified domain name).

As in the previous example, a computer named LAPTOP1 in the East subdomain of Help and Learn, Inc. would have a fully qualified domain name (FQDN) of `laptop1.east.helpandlearn.com`.

Reading an FQDN from right to left, one can understand the DNS hierarchy. `com` is the root domain; `helpandlearn` is a subdomain of `com`; `east` is a subdomain of `helpandlearn`, and so on. Each domain and subdomain in the hierarchy contains its own portion of the DNS namespace.

A host's name can also be resolved by using its relative name. The relative name is simply the host name without the DNS hierarchy. To resolve a relative host name, the requester must be located in the same domain.

Back to the example, LAPTOP1 is the relative name of `laptop1.east.helpandlearn.com`. To query DNS for LAPTOP1 using its relative name only, the requester would need to be a member of the east domain.

Internal Versus External Namespace

If an organization that is implementing Active Directory requires Internet connectivity, the organization would need to register their root domain name with one of the Internet naming registrars. Once a unique domain name is registered (and thus a DNS namespace created), the

Active Directory namespace is implemented as one or more subdomains of the Internet root domain (see Figure 3.2).

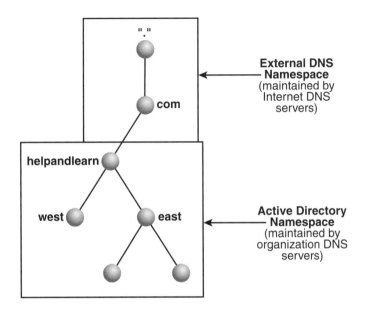

FIGURE 3.2

Utilizing an external namespace.

If an organization does not require Internet connectivity, the organization can opt to utilize an internal DNS namespace. But it must be noted that Active Directory does require DNS. Active Directory uses DNS to locate servers and services within the directory. If the organization opts for an internal DNS namespace, they must still design and install the internal DNS infrastructure, including servers, domains, and so on (see Figure 3.3). It is also strongly recommended that the organization still registers its internal and external domain namespace in case of future changes.

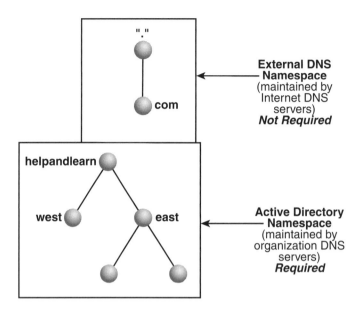

FIGURE 3.3
Utilizing an internal namespace.

Overcoming Name Limitations

One of the most difficult tasks faced by an organization looking to register an Internet domain name is name availability. Many names have been registered and it may really take some creativity to find the name you want or a name that even makes sense.

An organization can register their domain name themselves or through their Internet Service Provider (ISP). If they are registering the domain name themselves, they can use one of several Internet registrars, such as Network Solutions (www. networksolutions.com). Network Solutions provides a simple Web-based form where you can enter the desired domain name. It will search the database to determine whether the domain name is available. If it is, you can proceed to register the name. If it is not, you will be presented with a number of optional domain names (see Figure 3.4).

Of course an organization should also consult its legal department to verify that the domain name is not infringing on any other copyrights or trademarks.

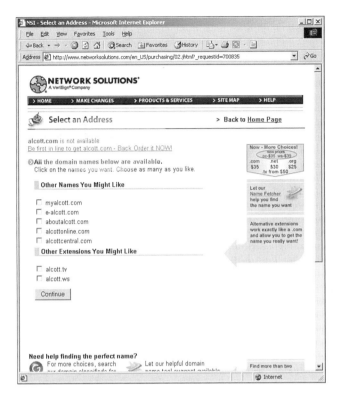

FIGURE 3.4

Registering a domain name using Network Solutions.

Domains

The most basic component in Active Directory, domains are used to implement directory security and manage resources. User accounts are administered in a domain, whereas member servers and other resources use domain security to determine who is granted access to their resources. An Active Directory domain controller can host only one domain. The domain controller holds a read/write copy of the domain security database.

When creating a Windows 2000 domain, there are a number of items that will need to be considered, all of which are described next.

TIP

It is important to realize that a domain is simply a partition of the Active Directory forest. These partitions can also be referred to as boundaries. This is described in more detail in the next section, "Administrative Boundaries."

The Active Directory database can be distributed across domain controllers, resulting in fault tolerance and more efficient access for the database. Although not as flexible, AD domains are comparable to NDS replications in that they are used to partition the directory database.

Administrative Boundaries

Any administrative rights granted to groups and users within a domain are only valid within that domain. For example, the Domain Administrators group by default is granted Full Control access to the domain. Members of that group cannot administer other domains where they are not in the Domain Administrators group.

The same principle applies to Group Policy Objects (GPO). GPOs do not take effect in domains they were not created in. Active Directory does allow GPOs from differing domains to be explicitly linked, however.

Domain Security Policies

Security policies are determined on a per-domain basis. These policies include the Password Policy, the Account Lockout Policy, and the Kerberos Ticket Policy.

- The Password Policy determines important security parameters related to user passwords. Some of these parameters include password length, password history, and password expiration.

- The Account Lockout Policy determines how intruder lockout is implemented in the domain.

- The Kerberos Ticket Policy defines the lifetime of a Kerberos ticket. A Kerberos ticket, like the access token previously found in Windows NT, is used for authentication and object access.

Creating Domains

When creating a domain, there are a number of things you must consider and determine before creation:

1. Select a forest root domain. One of the first decisions to be made when creating an Active Directory Domain is to select the forest root domain. The forest root domain is the first domain created in a forest.

   - If the domain to be created is the first Active Directory domain, by default it will create a new forest and become the forest root domain.
   - If the domain to be created will join an existing Active Directory forest, you need to specify the forest root domain. It is important to note that the Domain Administrators group for the forest root domain will be able to modify the membership of both the Enterprise Administrators and Schema Administrators groups.

2. Select a DNS domain name for the domain to be created.

   - If the domain will be the tree root domain of a new forest, simply specifying the DNS domain name will suffice.
   - If the domain will be joining an existing tree, the domain name must be part of the DNS namespace described earlier in this chapter. In other words, it must be contiguous with the tree root domain's hierarchy (see Figure 3.5).

helpandlearn.com

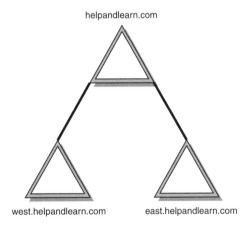

west.helpandlearn.com   east.helpandlearn.com

FIGURE 3.5

Creating a new Active Directory domain in an existing tree.

3. Implement the DNS infrastructure. Recall that DNS is a required component in Active Directory. When creating an Active Directory domain, the Active Directory setup program (DCPROMO) will verify that there is a DNS infrastructure available. If the infrastructure is not in place, you can tell DCPROMO to install and configure a DNS server automatically. Also note that once you create the DNS namespace, it cannot be changed. If you need to change your DNS namespace, you will need to run DCPROMO and

remove Active Directory. You would then need to recreate the DNS namespace and reinstall Active Directory.

Creating Multiple Domains

The limitations found in Windows NT 4 domains, such as limited database size, are not issues in Windows 2000. As a result, Microsoft recommends that one domain be used for Active Directory.

However, there are situations in which you need to create more than one domain.

- **Security requirements**—The most common reason for implementing multiple domains is the existence of differing security requirements. It is important to remember that security policies are determined on a per-domain basis. For example, the Password Policy determines the password length for the entire domain. If your organization requires that some users have a longer password length than others, you need to create a separate domain for these users.

- **Autonomous situations**—Multiple domains also need to be created for autonomous situations. Members of the Domain Administrators group are granted full control access to all objects in a domain. If a portion of your organization does not want its data to be comprised by members of the Domain Administrators group, you can create another domain and give administrative control to those members of the organization.

- **Replication requirements**—Remember that Microsoft recommends the use of a single domain in a forest? Although it is a great idea when it comes to administering the directory, domain controllers in a single large domain can become burdened by replication traffic. In a single domain in a forest, every object in the forest is replicated to every domain controller in the forest. This results in inefficient use of network bandwidth and domain controller processing resources. By breaking the large single domain into smaller, more manageable pieces, you can better control replication traffic. Only objects in that domain are replicated to that domain's domain controllers.

TIP

Networks incorporating headquarters with branch offices and WAN links can benefit from the use of multiple domains.

- **Existing Windows NT Domain Structure**—Another reason that you might choose to have multiple domains is to retain an already existing Windows NT domain structure. However, unless one of the two previous situations (security requirements and replication requirements) are still valid after an upgrade to Windows 2000 and Active Directory, most organizations benefit more from the consolidation of domains than the preservation of the prior Windows NT domain structure.

Trees

A tree in Windows 2000 simply signifies a DNS namespace. More simply, an Active Directory tree is a collection of domains. It consists of a single-tree root domain with subdomains completing the Active Directory hierarchy (see Figure 3.6).

There are two types of namespaces that you need to consider when implementing Active Directory.

- **Contiguous**—A namespace in which each level of the domain hierarchy is directly related to the levels above and below it. For example, the tree root for Help and Learn, Inc. is `helpandlearn.com`. The subdomains are named `east.helpandlearn.com` and `west.helpandlearn.com`. As you can see, all domains share the root `helpandlearn.com` domain name.
- **Discontiguous**—A namespace that is based on different root DNS domain names. For example, `microsoft.com` and `helpandlearn.com` are two separate (that is, discontiguous) namespaces. A discontiguous namespace is used with multiple trees in a forest.

The namespace for an Active Directory tree is contiguous, because each domain in the hierarchy is directly related to the domains above and below it in the tree.

3

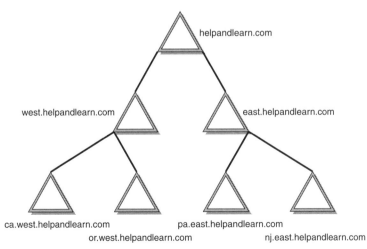

helpandlearn.com Active Directory Tree Structure

FIGURE 3.6

The hierarchy of an Active Directory tree.

Creating Trees

Like DNS, Active Directory trees are represented as inverted trees. Trust relationships between the domains in the tree are created automatically in Windows 2000, unlike Windows NT, which requires all trust relationships to be created manually.

An Active Directory tree is created automatically when a new root domain is installed.

Forests

Whereas the namespace for an Active Directory tree is contiguous, the namespace for an Active Directory forest is discontiguous.

A discontiguous namespace is based on different root DNS domain names. A discontiguous namespace is used with multiple trees in a forest. For example, the tree root for Help and Learn, Inc. is `helpandlearn.com`. Help and Learn, Inc. acquires another company named Marshallsoft. Marshallsoft uses Active Directory with a root DNS domain name of `marshallsoft.com`. Because the two organizations have different root DNS domain names, their combined Active Directory environment consists of two trees in a forest.

A forest can consist of a forest root domain (described next) and multiple trees below (see Figure 3.7).

NOTE

The first domain created in Active Directory is a forest root domain.

It is important to decide how the forest root domain will be used:

- If the forest root domain is used as a *regular domain* (that is, there are user and groups accounts, as well as resources in the domain), you must consider that members of the Domain Administrators group for this domain are by default members of the Enterprise Administrators and Schema Administrators groups for the forest. This might pose a security issue because they are the most powerful groups within the forest.

- Using a *dedicated forest root domain* provides a number of benefits. First, the security threat posed by the Enterprise Administrators and Schema Administrators group is minimized. Because the scope of the forest root domain is limited (the only user accounts in the domain will be created for forest administration only), better control of these groups is provided. Lastly, replication traffic for the domain is minimal.

CAUTION	

It is important to implement a fault-tolerance policy for the forest root domain. This can involve the use of multiple domain controllers (which should be included in any domain) as well as implementing RAID (Redundant Array of Inexpensive Disks) and tape backup on domain controllers. Implementing RAID will minimize the risk of failure in the event of a hard drive failure. Tape backup allows you to restore a domain controller in the event of a failure.

If a forest root domain is lost and cannot be recovered by tape backup, the Enterprise Administrators and Schema Administrators groups will be permanently lost. A forest root domain cannot be reinstalled or delegated to another domain. As a result, the Active Directory forest will be, for all purposes, inoperable.

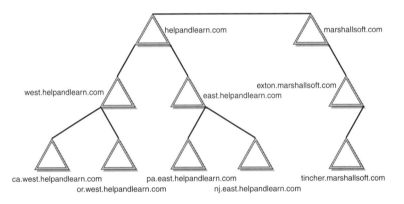

FIGURE 3.7
The hierarchy of an Active Directory forest.

Creating Forests

A forest is a group of Active Directory domains. A forest provides for simpler management of multiple domains, while also simplifying the user's experience within the directory. Users and administrators interact with Active Directory through a common forest.

An Active Directory forest must have the following characteristics:

- **Single Schema**—The *schema* in Active Directory defines how objects are constructed and which attributes are used in all domains in the forest. The schema is replicated to every domain controller within the forest. Only members of the Schema Administrators group can modify the schema.

> **CAUTION**
>
> It is very important to strictly limit the membership of the Schema Administrators group.

- **A Single Global Catalog**—The global catalog is used for searching or logging on to the directory. A limited set of attributes from every object in the directory is copied to the global catalog. This allows for more efficient use of directory information, because all attributes are not used in the search, only select attributes that are most commonly used. Users log on to the directory using their User Principal Name. The User Principal Name resembles an Internet e-mail address. It consists of two parts, `username@domainname`. The username portion is simply the user's logon name, whereas the domain name portion is the DNS name of the Active Directory domain where the user's account is located. As a result, the User Principal Name uniquely identifies the user in the directory.

- **A Single Configuration Container**—The Configuration Container stores Active Directory configuration objects for the entire forest. These objects contain information such as directory partitions, sites, services, and any directory-enabled applications. The naming context for the Configuration Container is `cn=configuration, dc=forestRootDomain`. Any changes to the Configuration Container are replicated to all domain controllers in the forest. The Enterprise Administrators group has full control of the Configuration Container.

- **Complete Trust Domain Model**—Active Directory by default creates two-way transitive trust relationships between all domains in the forest. As a result, users and groups from any domain can be incorporated in access control lists. Unlike earlier versions of Windows NT, Active Directory's default behavior eliminates the need to manually create trusts between domains.

Active Directory Sites

Active Directory uses the concept of *sites* to logically represent the physical network topology. Active Directory uses the site topology to route replication traffic efficiently. Site topology is also used to route queries and authentication requests.

Site topology is not related to the domain hierarchy! A single domain can appear in many sites, and a site can contain many domains as well (see Figure 3.8).

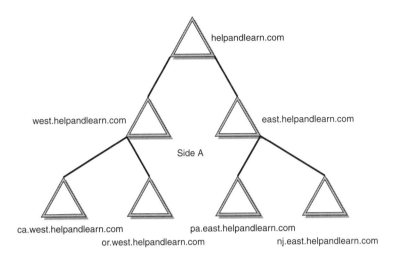

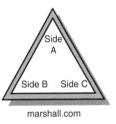

FIGURE 3.8
Sites versus domains in Active Directory.

Creating Sites

Microsoft considers a site a group of TCP/IP-based subnets connected by fast and reliable connections. So, in layman's terms, what does that mean? The best rule of thumb is to consider any networks with 10MBps or faster (that is, LAN speeds) a site. Sites that are separated by WAN links must be separate sites.

A *site link* is the connection between two or more sites (as its name implies). Site links are used by Active Directory to determine the amount of available bandwidth between two sites.

Site links consists of four factors:

- **Cost Active Directory**—Uses the cost value of a site link to ascertain when a site link should be used for replication traffic. The cost values of various site links determine the route that replication traffic follows throughout the network. For example, sites that are connected via low-speed modems and dial-up lines have a higher cost than sites connected with high-speed network backbones. Costs are a good way of creating fault-tolerant site links. For example, if you have two site links between two sites and assign a higher cost to one of the links, replication will only occur across the link with the lower value. If that link fails, the link with the higher cost will be utilized.

• **Replication Schedule**—The replication schedule of a site link indicates when the site link is available to replication traffic. This can be used to force replication traffic to only occur during off-peak hours (such as late at night).

• **Replication Interval**—The replication interval value determines how often replication changes are requested from the other side of the site link. By default, the replication interval is three hours or 180 minutes. The minimum period is 15 minutes.

• **Transport**—The transport determines the transport protocol used for replication traffic. Replication between sites can occur synchronously by RPC (Remote Procedure Calls) over the IP transport or asynchronously via SMTP (Simple Mail Transport Protocol) over IP transport.

TIP

RPC over IP should be used most of the time, unless, due to firewall or router configurations, RPC traffic is denied. In this case, SMTP over IP should be used.

It is important to note that site links using SMTP over IP will ignore any replication scheduling parameters. SMTP mail is transmitted according to the configuration of the e-mail infrastructure.

Clients and Servers Are Associated with Sites

When booting up, Windows 2000 clients query a domain controller for their respective domain. The domain controller analyzes the client's IP address and determines which site the client belongs to. The domain controller returns the site name to the client and the client caches the information. The client will use the site name to determine resources at the site.

KCC Uses the Site Topology to Create Replication Connections

The Knowledge Consistency Checker (KCC) uses the site topology to determine and create replication connections between domain controllers. Site link information and site boundaries are used to make these determinations.

Intrasite Versus Intersite Replication

There are two types of replication traffic in Active Directory, intrasite and intersite. Intrasite replication traffic is between domain controllers within the same site. Intersite replication traffic is between domain controllers in different sites. The KCC tunes intrasite replication to minimize replication latency, whereas it tunes intersite replication to minimize bandwidth usage.

Table 3.1 describes some of the differences in the two forms of replication traffic.

TABLE 3.1   Intrasite Versus Intersite Replication

Intrasite	Intersite
Traffic is uncompressed.	Traffic is compressed (to save bandwidth).
Replication partners notify each other when changes must be replicated (to reduce latency).	Replication partners do not notify each other (to save bandwidth).
Replication partners poll one another periodically.	Replication partners poll one another during scheduled intervals only.
RCP over IP transport only.	RCP over IP or SMTP over IP transports.
Replication connections can be created between any two domain controllers in the same site.	Replication connections can only be created between bridgehead servers. A bridgehead server is designated by the KCC. A bridgehead server is a domain controller that has been designated to perform all intersite replication for a particular site.

Site Topology Information Is Stored Within the Configuration Container

All information related to site topology (sites, site links, subnets, and so on) is stored in the configuration container. The configuration container is replicated to every domain controller in the entire forest. As a result, any change to the site topology is replicated to every domain controller in the forest, thus creating replication traffic.

Summary

This chapter described many of the critical objects found in Active Directory and its structure. Active Directories are created using forests (to define a common schema), trees (to define the domain namespace), and finally domains (to define security and replication boundaries).

This chapter also provided descriptions of Active Directory replication and the components that are involved. Sites are used to define areas of high bandwidth, where intrasite replication can take place between domain controllers. Site links are used to link sites together to perform intersite replication.

CASE STUDY

Learning by Example: The "Molly Pitcher Pharmaceuticals, Inc." Company

After reviewing the case study for Molly Pitcher Pharmaceuticals, Inc., there are some issues that need to be analyzed.

Domain namespace: Currently, Molly Pitcher Pharmaceuticals has an Internet presence at `mollypitcher.com`. As a result, they already have an external namespace. You have two choices to consider here: to keep the existing external namespace (`mollypitcher.com`) and use it for Active Directory, or create a subdomain off of `mollypitcher.com`, such as `ad.mollypitcher.com`. This domain would become the forest root for Active Directory. I would recommend using `ad.mollypitcher.com`, because the company is already utilizing `mollypitcher.com` for its Web infrastructure. Using a subdomain gives you more flexibility.

Forest/tree structure: From the case study, there are no obvious reasons to utilize multiple forests (that is, differing schema) or multiple trees (this is, discontiguous namespaces). Because of this, Molly Pitcher's Active Directory infrastructure will be implemented in a single forest/tree structure, where `ad.mollypitcher.com` is the forest root domain.

Using existing Windows NT domain structure: You could retain the existing Windows NT domain structure, which in this case is a single master domain model. However, the company has stated that the reason they are implementing Active Directory is to avoid the complexity that is inherent in their existing domain structure.

Site structure and replication: Molly Pitcher is a geographically dispersed company, with 13 locations throughout the United States. There are 12 remote offices and headquarters located in Valley Forge, PA. These remote offices are connected to headquarters via T1 lines. Because of this WAN topology, you need to implement Active Directory sites to route replication traffic efficiently. It will also help make directory queries and authentication requests more efficient for users in the remote offices. In this design, you need to create 13 sites and their associated site links. In this case, a single site link is created between the headquarters and each remote office. There are no site links between remote offices. The transport for the site links should be RPC over IP, because the network infrastructure is considered stable.

Planning Active Directory

IN THIS CHAPTER

The previous chapters discussed what Active Directory (AD) is, how it differs from similar products, and how it is organized. This chapter examines a variety of issues that you should consider when planning for and implementing AD in your organization.

The most important thing to realize about these considerations is that the majority of them are only marginally "technical." They are sourced in political, logistical, and communications issues that, if not properly understood and managed, can result in a drastic mismatch between the AD design and the actual work environment.

You can divide the issues that you need to consider in a variety of ways. For these purposes, though, the easiest way to approach them is as follows:

- **Migration considerations**—Implementation issues that affect the WINS, DDNS, DHCP, OU, User, and Group strategies.

- **Administrative considerations**—Operational issues that can affect your OU, GPO, User, and Group structures.

- **Security considerations**—Access and data protection issues that can affect your OU, Group, and GPO structures.

- **Installation considerations**—Logistical and technical issues that can affect your migration plan and server/workstation build procedures.

- **Organizational considerations**—Communications and legal policies that might affect your roll-out plans, security design, access design, and administrative policies.

All the advice in this chapter can be summarized in the following statement: Understand the environment before you begin our design. Don't just try to understand how the computers are arranged; look at how the network is administered, how the users do their jobs, and how the network needs to improve to better serve the users. Then, and only then, should you begin to consider a design.

Migration Considerations

One of the things that you should do to begin your AD planning is to stop and take a good, hard look at your current environment. Do you really understand what is going on? Do you know what kinds of computers you have? How many calls do you normally receive about account lockouts? How often does WINS fail to correctly resolve names? How many groups do you have, and how are they used? Do you need to keep all of your domains, or should you collapse some in order to simplify administration? How is group membership determined?

The list of questions you can ask is almost endless. Each answer is a data point that will help you to decide how to go about migrating your current environment to Active Directory. In essence, this decision involves the following issues:

- How much of your current administrative overhead do you want to bring into the new environment?

- How well does your current architecture match the business needs?

- How much will you have to change to use the new features in Windows 2000?

- Would it be easier to reorganize the current environment or to build a completely new one?

In order to answer these questions, you need to understand your options. So, this discussion focuses on the ramifications of each of these options. The options are as follows:

- Upgrade or parallel migration—Choose between upgrading your current environment or building a new one and moving into it.

- Mixed moved or native mode—Choose between moving quickly to an all Windows 2000 authentication environment and moving very slowly towards one.

- Server upgrade, rebuild, or domain shift—Choose between upgrading a server to Windows 2000, rebuilding it from scratch, or just bringing it as it stands into the new Windows 2000 domain.

- Client upgrade, rebuild, or domain shift—Choose between upgrading your clients to Windows 2000, rebuilding them from scratch, or just bringing them as they stand into the new Windows 2000 domain.

- Creating or migrating users and groups—Choose between creating all new users and groups or migrating the existing users and groups with a migration tool.

After you understand the ramifications of each option, you can make intelligent decisions about how, what, and when to migrate your resources.

Upgrading the Domain to Windows 2000

One of the first decisions that you should make is whether you are going to upgrade your current Domain structure or build a parallel AD and migrate users and resources into it. This section discusses the pros and cons of upgrades; the next section addresses what happens in a parallel migration.

During an upgrade migration, you will:

1. Take a BDC from each Master domain and put it off-line. This is your "recovery" server, and will protect the account database if something goes horribly wrong.

2. Upgrade the PDC(s) of the Master domain(s).

3. Update the infrastructure servers (DHCP, WINS, and DNS) in the Master domain(s).

4. Upgrade the BDC(s) of the Master domain(s).

5. Upgrade the PDCs of any Resource domains.

6. Upgrade the BDCs of any Resource domains.

7. Upgrade the member servers of the domains.

> **NOTE**
>
> More information about the detailed migration procedure is in Chapter 8, "Migration Planning and Migration Tools."

By doing this, you preserve your account databases, groups, security settings, file system settings, and domain structure. It reduces the chance that you will accidentally miss user settings, thereby rendering them unable to do their jobs. It also preserves your old naming and IP addressing standards; servers continue to function with their original names and addresses, removing the need to reconfigure client workstations, applications, and services. All in all, this dramatically cuts down the work that you have to do in setting up the new AD.

Or does it? Yes, you've preserved all of your old accounts. More importantly, you've preserved all of your old SIDs, which means that you still have your old access rights. But, you've also inherited all of the mistakes made in the old domain. Now, rather than being able to build the new environment the "right" way, you have to audit and potentially change your old work.

More importantly, you can almost guarantee that your old environment does not take advantage of the new organization and security features of Windows 2000. Now you have to plan how to change what you currently have into something that leverages new capabilities. In some cases, this is almost impossible.

Furthermore, an upgrade migration makes it very difficult to rationalize your infrastructure services. In order to reap the logistical benefits of the upgrade, you should leave the majority of your services (WINS, DHCP, and possibly even DNS) in the same basic configuration that you currently use. This means that you will have to plan additional steps, and manage additional risk, in order to refine your configurations. Contrast this with the parallel upgrade, where managing these tasks and risks is inherit in the project itself.

There are also logistical issues to consider. After you begin an upgrade of your current NT infrastructure, it can be very difficult to turn back. Administrators need to be brought up to speed very quickly on how to perform basic user maintenance tasks. Servers need to be upgraded to meet new hardware requirements. When the IT department is centralized and the network is not, someone will have to travel to each site to upgrade the local servers.

In any in-place upgrade, you will run a mixed Windows 2000/Windows NT environment for some period of time. This can result in some very complex interactions, especially when you have multiple master account domains. It also forces the first and second level support staff to understand and track an environment that can shift on a daily basis. The support staff needs constant updates on the status of account moves, security changes, and any other changes to the environment that affect the user community.

You also need to consider what tools you'll use to support your network. If you are going to change tool sets (such as use a new backup or asset management package), how do you roll that out? Do you leave the old package alone and put the new one on migrated servers? Do you install the new package into the environment first (assuming that it even works in our old environment) and then do the Windows 2000 upgrades?

When you are weighting all of these issues, you need to consider the following advantages that upgrading gives you:

- Preserves the account database, including the SIDS. This means that you do not have to recreate the user, group, and machine accounts for the domain.

- Preserves the file system of each server. This means that you do not have to reapply security settings to your NTFS partitions or your shares.

- Maintains existing IP and naming conventions. This means that the users will not have to remap their printers or shares. Furthermore, the administrator does not need to reset the IP addresses of basic infrastructure services like DDNS and WINS.

- Reduces the window of cross-platform security interactions. This means that it is less likely that a user will encounter a significant security error during the migration, because most or all of the security information is stored in the Windows 2000 environment.

You also need to consider the following disadvantages that come from choosing the upgrade option:

- Preserves the mistakes made in the original environment. This means that if you want to clean up the environment, you have to do so with the existing errors, rather than starting with a pristine state.

- Creates a variance in server security settings. Settings on an upgraded server or workstation are different from those of a freshly built one. In particular, an upgraded machine has few restrictions in the security of its system files and Registry settings, creating the potential for a mismatch between what you think you are installing and what you actually get. This problem can be resolved by using the Security Configuration Manager utility.

- Poses logistical, technical, and procedural difficulties when several authoritative security directories (such as NT, Novell, and a Unix Kerberos domain) must be centralized into one system. In an upgrade migration in which you intend to collapse security, you must first rationalize and document the upgraded environment, and then define all of the proper conversion relationships. This can be much more time consuming than simply defining an ideal state and using the data from your sources to get there.

- Creates a "two-tool" production situation. This means that you must migrate your current environment to your new tools first. Otherwise, you increase the risk of administrative error during the migration state.

You also need to answer the following questions when you accept the upgrade option:

- Which of the domains (if you have more than one) is going to be the upgrade domain?
- How, when, and by whom are your off-site domain controllers and servers going to be upgraded?
- How, when, and by whom are your domains going to be collapsed and rationalized?
- How, when, and by whom are your printer queues, intranet servers, application servers, file security, and groups going to be upgraded?
- What criteria will you use to get though the existing security identities (user accounts, local groups, global groups, and so on) to determine which ones you'll keep and which you'll change?
- How will you communicate with your support organization to ensure that they can support the user community during the migration?

Your environment is a good candidate for an upgrade migration if:

- You have few (typically less than 15) geographically dispersed authentication and server sites.
- Your current environment is well organized, documented, and contains a small number of other directories.
- You have just come though a comprehensive hardware refresh cycle.
- You have an adequate understanding of your disaster-recovery tools and can verify that they work in a mixed environment.

If the work involved with the issues is greater than the amount of benefit that you'll receive from the in-place migration, consider other migration options. The next section deals with the other main option—the parallel migration.

Parallel Migration

Some organizations analyze the upgrade migration path and find that it is fraught with problems. Perhaps the logistics are simply too much to handle. Perhaps they have several directory systems that need to be collapsed. Perhaps they simply want to avoid all of the clean up associated with upgrading the old environment and prefer to start fresh.

For the purposes here, a parallel migration is one in which you:

1. Create a new Windows 2000 domain/tree/forest.
2. Decide what the new environment should look like.
3. Decide what information migrates from the old environment to the new one.
4. Create a mapping between the new environment and the old.
5. Migrate users, groups, files, and servers as indicated by the map.

> **NOTE**
>
> More information about the detailed migration procedure is in Chapter 8.

In other words, you create a pristine environment, into which you migrate your data as you see fit. This gives you a number of advantages: control of the data, control of the migration pace, the capability to set appropriate standards, and the capability to ensure compliance with those standards. These advantages address, almost point by point, the problems of the upgrade migration.

For example, your support staff still needs accurate information about which users and resources are scheduled for migration. However, in a parallel migration there is a much clearer demarcation—some things exist only in the new environment, others are not intended to be moved to the new environment, and the remaining are scheduled to move on a particular date. The interactions can be much less complex. They certainly have clearer boundaries.

A similar analysis holds for each of the previous points. In a parallel migration, because you have two separate environments, you have much clearer boundaries between support processes, tool versions, and infrastructure services. Anything you can think of that might get muddled in the upgrade migration is clearer in the parallel migration.

At the same time, you do have to be more careful about how, when, and why you change login scripts, printer mappings, and similar activities. A parallel upgrade is a classic "infrastructure installation," with users migrating from an older environment into a new, sometimes radically different one. This increases your need for user communications and feedback, which can increase the time that you spend on the project-management side of the deployment work.

You also need to realize that the "pristine" parallel migration is nearly ideal for collapsing several security directories into a single directory. Consider the example of a mixed Novell and NT environment for analysis. If you upgraded the Windows NT to Windows 2000 directly, you would have to:

1. Determine the "perfect" state for Windows 2000.

2. Determine your existing state.

3. Determine the mapping of the Novell to the current state.

4. Determine the mapping of the Novell to the existing state.

5. Alter the Windows NT to more closely match the perfect state.

6. Upgrade Windows NT to Windows 2000.

7. Migrate security information from Novell to Windows 2000.

If you have a pristine, parallel migration you instead follow these steps:

1. Determine the "perfect" state.

2. Determine the mapping of Windows NT to the perfect state.

3. Determine the mapping of Novell to the perfect state.

4. Migrate the appropriate security data from either Novell or Windows NT, as appropriate, into the Windows 2000 environment.

The other issue to consider is that one of the primary advantages of the upgrade migration, preserving the SIDS, is accomplished by almost all of the existing migration tools. Any native mode domain has a SID history attribute for every object, allowing newly created objects to have the same SID as the object they were migrated from.

When you are considering the parallel migration option, you need to consider the following advantages that it provides:

- Creates a clear demarcation between the old and the new environment. This results in few interactions within the migration environment, generally leading to a cleaner, more controllable upgrade.

- Preserves (with the proper tools) the SID of the migrated object. This means that you can migrate data and security settings with relative impunity, and clean them up later.

- Enables very granular control over when resources and users migrate into the new environment. This is especially important in large organizations or organizations that have legal or auditing requirements.

- Provides a pristine environment into which you can map several existing security providers, picking and choosing which source best fits particular needs.

You also need to consider its primary disadvantage, which is that it requires considerable amounts of new server hardware. If the Windows 2000 upgrade coincides with the standard hardware refresh, this is less of an issue. However, if the intention is to purchase new servers out of the refresh cycle in order to support AD and other Windows 2000 services, you'll have to establish a serious cost-benefit justification.

Also realize that you must answer the following questions when you accept the upgrade option:

- How will you monitor and manage the interactions between the existing environment(s) and the Windows 2000 domain during the migration? The enterprise will be running in a dual mode for some time, and without proper planning could be exposed to unacceptable risks.

- How are you going to map security information from each of your existing environments?

- How will you manage and maintain your login scripts, printers, file shares, and shared resources that might change during the migration, and could potentially (as in the case of login scripts) require several versions?

Your environment is a good candidate for the parallel migration if:

- You are coming up on or in the middle of a hardware refresh cycle.

- You have multiple security providers that you want to collapse into one domain.

- For technical reasons, you cannot upgrade your domain directly.

- You have a large number of physical sites, and need the additional control over the migration provided by the pristine environment.

If you can afford it, the parallel migration provides a number of advantages. However, be aware that transitioning from an upgrade migration to a parallel migration can be difficult and extremely costly. Avoid this pitfall by carefully considering your options *before* the project begins, and sticking with your decision throughout the duration of the effort.

Mixed Mode or Native Mode Domains

One of the biggest questions that comes up during AD design, and therefore is the cause of the biggest misconceptions, is the difference between mixed mode and native mode domains. People ask: "Should we go to a native mode domain?" They treat it like some kind of mystical journey, which once engaged upon will lead to a promised land.

The real question you need to ask about the mixed to native mode conversion is not "if," but "when." Everyone eventually goes over to native mode; it's more a question of when the event occurs in your project plan than whether or not you will do it at all.

First, lets clear up the misconceptions. Going to native mode does not:

- Enable group policy objects

- Ensure better replication

- Compact the AD database

- Prevent down-stream clients from logging in
- Prevent legacy applications from working
- Alter the way that AD interacts with other Kerberos systems

It does:

- Enable some attributes in the directory
- Enable universal groups
- Permit the AD to begin ignoring the SAM, thereby bypassing its limitations

If you intend to perform an upgrade migration, you should carefully plan your switch to native mode. You can switch to native mode only after all of the domain's DCs (the PDC and all BDCs) are upgraded to Windows 2000. Otherwise, you could end up with clients who cannot log onto the domain at all, because the domain controller trying to authenticate them can no longer receive updates from the active security databases.

If you intend to perform a parallel migration, you should switch to native mode as quickly as possible. Leaving your directory in mixed mode ensures that most (if not all) of the existing migration tools will not be able to migrate your users into your lovely new AD structure.

Server Migration

When you consider your server migration strategy, you can divide servers into four categories: those that you will replace, those that you will consolidate, those that you will upgrade, and those that you will move without changing.

Each category is handled slightly differently in terms of design and planning.

You should generally replace servers that cannot be upgraded to Windows 2000. Perhaps they are too old and you cannot bring them up to your minimum hardware specification. Or perhaps they are out of warranty, so you no longer want to run the system without coverage. Whatever the criteria, when you replace a server you must:

1. Be absolutely sure that you know which services the server provided.
2. Make provisions for those services to be available during the migration.
3. Make sure that the services work on their new locations.
4. Replace the server, test it, and then put the new server into production.
5. Decommission the old server.

You should generally consolidate servers that are under used or that cost more in maintenance than they provide in business value. These servers are typically legacy servers that you would either upgrade or replace anyway, but their utilization is such that you cannot cost-justify the purchase. When you prepare to consolidate several servers, you must:

1. Identify the utilization on each server.

2. Ensure that the server you are consolidating to can handle all of the utilization.

3. Verify that the data-access patterns of the various services being consolidated do not conflict. For example, it is often difficult to stabily consolidate mail and database services onto a single Wintel platform.

4. Schedule the consolidation during non-business critical periods.

5. Test the consolidation thoroughly. Consolidations of different services onto the same box can introduce unusual utilization patterns that create instability.

6. After performing the consolidation, monitor the server for at least one business quarter.

7. Decommission the old server.

You should generally upgrade servers that are under warranty, are easily boosted to hardware specification, display reasonable utilization levels, and do not run services that require a legacy environment. When you prepare to upgrade a server, you must:

1. Verify that all of the services offered by the server (applications, databases, and so on) are compatible with Windows 2000.

2. Prepare and test the upgrades for those services that are not compatible with Windows 2000.

3. Schedule the upgrade during normal maintenance hours.

4. Upgrade the server hardware, OS, and services to Windows 2000 and compatible software versions.

Realize that the complexity of an upgrade migration comes not from the OS, but from the services that the server provides. In particular, database and ERP software can take months to plan for a move, and you might spends months afterwards monitoring the server to ensure that nothing has gone wrong.

You generally move servers that run business-critical applications that do not have Windows 2000 compatible versions and that do not participate in domain security (either as a PDC or BDC). The effort of retiring business critical legacy software can be greater than that of the entire Windows 2000 project. When you prepare to move a server, you must:

1. Verify that the legacy application does not have any dependencies on other servers you are upgrading, consolidating, or replacing.

2. Schedule the move during normal maintenance hours.

3. Remove the server from its old domain.

4. Put the server into its new domain.

5. Verify that the security settings on the server are appropriate for the server's function.

4

PLANNING ACTIVE
DIRECTORY

6. Monitor the server and its legacy application for at least one quarter after the migration.

7. Transition monitoring and operational tasks to regular support personnel once the migration is deemed successful.

The actual schedule and order of precedence of the migration of servers will depend on the size of your organization, the members and skill set of your project team, and your ability to quickly and accurately assess the environment. The greatest risk you run to overshooting the schedule is in the conversion of business-critical or legacy applications; this risk can only be addressed by the creation and implementation of a comprehensive and relatively time-consuming testing plan.

Client Migration

Migrating servers is easy because you generally have a good idea of where they are, what is on them, and how the business uses them. Migrating client computers is an entirely different matter.

The logistics of finding, identifying, assessing, recording, sorting, scheduling, and finally actually working on the client computers can easily take up the majority of the time you spend on the Windows 2000 project. Figuring out all of these pieces is outside of the scope of the current discussion.

What does lie within this scope is determining what to do with all of those clients once you determine where they are, what they are, who is using them, and what they are used for. Generally, you can lump them into three categories:

- Clients you'll replace
- Clients you'll upgrade
- Clients you'll leave as they are

Clients you'll replace are typically those that are either so old that you cannot upgrade them to meet specification or about to be retired due to accounting policy (lease refresh or capital budgeting). With these machines, you need to consider the logistics of identifying, moving, and decommissioning the old hardware, as well as the impact of receiving a new workstation on the user. You can control your installation risk by pre-staging the new hardware, and then testing and configuring it before it is given to the user.

Clients you'll upgrade meet the minimum hardware specifications (sometimes with additional hardware) or are not going to be considered for replacement for accounting reasons within the next year. With these clients, you need to be especially careful to consider the upgrade time, installation method, and restoration method for the client. One of your greatest challenges is accurately moving all of the users' individual settings and data from the old state to the new.

Clients you'll leave as they are tend to be machines that run legacy applications that the user simply cannot function without. If no other solution can be found, the user needs to be given a new PC. Sometimes (if a group of users needs an application sporadically and asynchronously), you can leave a single legacy workstation for a group of users, freeing you from the responsibly of maintaining several out-of-specification machines.

User and Group Migration

From a planning and design standpoint, one of the most complex tasks that you have to consider is how, when, and why you will migrate your user and group accounts. It's easy to get into "analysis paralysis" with this issue. There are literally hundreds of factors you could consider, and probably thousands of variations on the basic themes.

Rather than spend hours discussing every variation, take a moment to step back and consider what it is that you have to plan here:

- If you upgraded your domain, you have to determine how you are going to alter your groups to fit in with the current design.
- If you are using a parallel migration, you have to determine the mapping between the old and the new group structure.

In both cases, you need to create a change map. This document tells you what to delete, what to collapse into what, what to create, and what to simply move. The actual work of migrating the information though the change map occurs either before the migration begins or after the migration is finished. Doing this work during the migration can cause unpredictable changes in people's access to resources, and so isn't recommended.

When creating the change map, pay special attention to:

- Service accounts or administrator accounts that are used as service accounts. These might require different permissions than you are used to under Windows 2000.
- Accounts that are only allowed to log on to specific machines, or during specific times of the day. If you are changing the client machine or the working parameters of the account, you will have inadvertently changed the security policy.
- Groups that have access to more than one resource (either though file or share permissions). These groups might have more scope of control than you think; due diligence here will save you a lot of help-desk phone calls later on.

As discussed, migration considerations affect your logistics and your change plans. Don't discount the difficulties and opportunities they pose when considering your Active Directory design.

Administration Considerations

Looming beyond the horizon of your migration is that fabled state called production. Your servers will hum quietly away, users blissfully content within the protective web of your IT operations. Security will properly shield data from unauthorized access. Users will never lock themselves out, or forget their passwords.

After the delusion has passed, you face the hard reality that someone is going to have to manage the Active Directory you design. Most likely, that someone will be you. So, you need to understand exactly what it means to manage the network and then account for those issues in your design.

In order to facilitate this discussion, consider the following issues:

- Differences between NT and Windows 2000—Changes to the operating system that affect how you think about administration
- The Role of OUs—How to use Organizational Units to make your administrative tasks easier
- How and when to delegate control—How to use the ability to delegate control of particular directory objects to simplify administration
- Security (who and when)—Measuring the need for access against the risk associated with granting that access
- Group policies—How many, and what to use them for

By trying to understand these issues, you can produce a directory that not only looks good on paper, but that you can actually support over time. The two conditions are not necessarily mutually exclusive.

Understanding the Administrative Differences Between NT and 2000

Just taken on the face of it, this section might seem useless. After all, you already know that Windows 2000 is different from Windows NT. Heck, that's half of the reason that you've decided to go ahead with the project.

Be that as it may, it's helpful to take a minute to clearly articulate the differences between Windows 2000 and Windows NT from an administrative standpoint. By clearly understanding the differences, you can make intelligent decisions about how you are going to leverage the changes for the future.

The first, and most important, difference that you need to consider is the least obvious. In Windows NT, you couldn't force a machine to use a local domain controller in an IP environment. In Windows 2000, machines use their site information to find the closest available controller to log into.

Why is this important?

- In a multimaster account database (like Windows 2000) changes are not propagated automatically. This means that you either need to change the database nearest the user or tell the users to wait for their account changes.
- If database corruption is causing login problems, you have to log onto the system that is experiencing the difficulty to diagnose it.
- You need to keep a very careful eye on the File Replication Service, because it registers errors when it cannot synch properly with a domain controller. This can help you diagnose Group Policy problems and login script errors that you thought you fixed.

Note that replication between sites is a scheduled process. For most procedures (like changing group membership), the schedule dictates when changes are propagated from the site in which they are made to the other linked sites. If you have a network with multiple jumps, the time that it can take for a change to replicate across your environment is equal to total replication time of the entire chain of links.

Also, be aware that group membership is propagated as a single block of information. That means that if an administrator changes the membership of group foo in Britain, and you change the membership of group foo in the US, one of the groups will be overwritten.

Consider the implications of the multimaster model when it comes to restoring your domain controllers.If the directory has not been damaged it is usually easier in small organizations (say, under 10,000 objects) to simply let the domain controller replicate the AD database rather than trying to restore it. In a large organization, you need to be more careful about the directory backup and restoration procedures, because getting a full replication could take more time than you can afford.

Consider also the impact that tools like the Taskpad have on your administrative model. With a little careful planning, you can give specifically built tools to your first level support that both give them the abilities that they need and restrict them from functions they shouldn't have. For example, you can build a Taskpad that just gives administrators access to changing user passwords, thereby letting them do their jobs without having to learn the Users and Computers MMC snap-in.

Furthermore, you should plan for changes in the way that you think about login scripts. You now have the ability to set up scripts that run when computers come on-line and when they shut down, as well as scripts that run when the user logs on or off. Combine this with the possibilities of Visual Basic and ASDI, and you have almost limitless configuration options.

With all of these changes, it is easy to get lost. The options are nearly limitless when it comes to making changes. If you actually want to be able to deploy Windows 2000 in anything resembling the product's lifecycle, you need to limit your scope for the initial migration.

Experience suggests that the best limit to place on the scope of administrative change is to first attempt to duplicate the current functionality. Migrate scripts, study your administration tools, and be careful not to exceed your initial capacity. Only after you can duplicate your original functionality should you consider addressing problems in your current environment. For example, if you have a serious problem with your Help Desk's inability to change passwords without having Domain Administrator access, this will become a listed problem that you consider correcting. After you've duplicated functionality and corrected problems, you can move on to actually implementing administrative enhancements.

How OUs Play a Role

One of the newest tools in the Microsoft administrator's tool kit is the Organizational Unit. OUs are logical containers of directory objects; they can nest infinitely deeply, and represent nearly anything that you can imagine.

The question is what do you do with these things? You can group users and computers in almost as many ways as there are companies and network designers. It seems that there might, in fact, be no one right answer.

And, in truth, there is no single answer to "what is the best OU structure?". There are guidelines you can use, though, that help you to get the most out of them.

The first and most important rule to remember when designing OUs is to avoid overly complicating your scheme. There is no theoretical limit to how deeply you can nest OUs. You could pile them 10, 20, or even 30 deep before ever seeing another object. Practically, however, you should be careful not to get too much more than three deep. Any deeper than that, and the rules for sorting directory objects into the various OUs become very complex.

Also, you should be very careful about what OUs you actually include. Because an OU is a logical grouping of computers, groups, and users, you should be willing to ask yourself "What role does this OU serve?". If you cannot come up with a good answer, most likely the OU should be removed from the design.

> **TIP**
>
> It is generally considered good design to avoid so-called "container" OUs. These are empty OUs that have no function other than to hold other OUs. Take the example of an OU called Countries, with sub-OUs of United States, France, and Japan. The Countries OU is a container OU. What function does it serve? Do you really need it?
>
> This is not to say that such OUs are categorically bad. Each container should go through the same functional justification process as every other OU. If you have a valid need to organize a goodly number of OUs, it will be reasonably clear early on.

OUs are excellent for representing specific boundaries of configuration settings, security policies, or special groupings. For example, some companies have OUs for Web servers, file servers, and application servers. Others have OUs for machines that require access to network resources, but have radically different functional requirements than other workstations (such as a PC that gathers real-time data from a set of laboratory equipment and posts that data to the network).

OUs are also good for designating zones of control within the company. The more decentralized a company is (by choice, legal restrictions, or political necessity), the more group-specific OUs required to exist to facilitate the delegation of control. In a completely decentralized IT organization, it might even be necessary to have multiple geographically specific OUs.

The factors that you need to consider when designing your OU structure are as follows:

- Are you a centralized or decentralized IT organization? What are the various organizations' boundaries of control?
- How many functional roles do your servers play? Examples include Web, file and print, and application servers.
- How many categories of functional roles can you create for your workstations? Examples include desktops, laptops, remote workstations, and data-gathering equipment.
- Do you have workstations, servers, or users that require special exclusion from the general domain/GPO/Organizational security? Examples include Executive Users, Help Desk Personnel, and Network Administrators.
- Do you have an administrative, financial, or legal need to separate users or computers? Examples include contractors (for contract workers), disabled users (a place to put accounts you disable), and restricted workstations (a place to put workstations with exceptionally stringent security requirements).

4

PLANNING ACTIVE DIRECTORY

- How will your OU structure impact any future applications that intend to use the Active Directory? For example, are there any special dependencies within your ERP package upgrade that you should be aware of?

These considerations force you to question very carefully what you intend to do with each OU. The more detail you can provide to answer that question, the more likely it is that your design will match well with your environment and your future administrative needs.

Delegate Control

One of the most highly touted features of Windows 2000 Active Directory is its capability to granularly assign administrative rights, even down to a specific attribute on an object. This is a tremendous departure from the days of Windows NT, when the assignment of restricted administrative rights was a challenge.

With a little planning, you can assign to each user the right to change his or her personal information. You can assign secretaries the right to change the address information of any user in their department. You can give help desks the rights to change users' passwords without giving them the right to add workstations to the domain. Anyone can be assigned the right to do anything, anything at all!

Exciting, isn't it? But first, consider what exactly it is that you need to delegate and how you are going to go about doing it. This is one of those features that require very careful analysis before you just jump in and start handing out permissions to everyone who might possibly need them.

The first question is the most challenging: What do you need to delegate? It's good to rephrase the question to put it into perspective:

What sensitive, personal, confidential, or security-related data do you want to grant access to?

This is really the question that you are asking. When you delegate control of an attribute, you are giving whoever you grant control to the right to go in and change that attribute. You are also implicitly giving them both the administrative and the legal right to access and control that information.

You also need to be concerned with change control in your IT organization. How are you going to best facilitate data integrity and auditable change within your environment? What impacts do these changes have on the integrity of data in enterprise use? What do you have to be concerned about?

That said, take a look at the various roles in a typical IT organization that need security permissions to specific functions:

- **Level 1 (Help Desk)**—Interfaces directly with users. They reset passwords and accounts, verify group membership, resolve usage issues, clear print queues, and use basic tools to troubleshoot hardware and software malfunctions, and assist users in finding resources.

- **Level 2 (Immediate Desktop and Server Support)**—Interfaces with Level 1 and the user community. They work with users to resolve problems that are either outside of the security scope of the Level 1 support group or that simply require more time than L1 can give to any single problem. They need administrative access to specific hardware as well as the capabilities of Level 1. Most will also need the capability to add workstations to the domain, and potentially the capability to create mailboxes.

- **Level 3 (Advanced Technical Support)**—Works on complex user or system-wide challenges. They need the capability to perform complex tests, analyze specific data, and read any part of the security/information directory to identify potential unintentional errors. Most Level 3 technicians are granted the capability to alter group memberships, change passwords, and add and remove servers from the domain.

- **Operations**—Works with the back end processes that keep IT shops running. They manage and monitor servers, printers, file systems, enterprise software, software distribution, and similar functions. They are typically responsible for backups, account maintenance, server maintenance, software maintenance, and sometimes telco and building security as well. Depending on how fragmented these functions are, you might need several levels of "operational" security, granting specific rights only to those who need them.

- **Architecture**—This group is concerned with the creation of business value though the integration of people, process, and technology. They typically need to be able to access utilization data, error logs, and view the entire directory structure. Architects might not need access to sensitive personal data (like a personal address), depending on the exact architectural function being performed.

- **Software Testers**—Work with the architecture group to ensure that software that needs business requirements is safe and supported in the environment. They need fairly broad access to the directory, servers, and workstations, but this access can easily be confined either to a separate test environment or to a single OU.

- **Developers**—Tend to have special needs based on whatever application environment they are using. As they build and test applications, they typically find that they need broad security access to deal with code issues. Because a well-run software development project provides considerably more visible business value than an infrastructure project, they will typically get this access in the production environment unless reasonable provisions are made before they request the access.

4

PLANNING ACTIVE
DIRECTORY

Note that most organizations mix these roles to create job descriptions. For example, it is not unusual to see a Help Desk that combines both level 1 and operational functions. This meshing can create role conflicts for the individual team members if not carefully managed, but that is a topic for another book.

When you have a decentralized organization, you multiply and magnify the number of individuals filling specific roles and the complexities of their interaction. You must be very careful to designate the zones of control of each part of the organization, and rigidly enforce those zones. Otherwise, the difficulties of administrating your directory and ensuring its data consistency will become overwhelming.

Fortunately, Microsoft provides a good tool for helping to separate the zones of control possessed by these roles (even in a decentralized organization). Although it is theoretically possible to go in and discretely give security permissions to each attribute, most people use the Delegate Security Wizard, which is tied directly to OUs.

What? If that's true, why did you just go through this tedious exercise of talking about roles and job functions? You can just hand out permissions using the Wizard and be done with it. Well, how you carve up your security permissions has a great deal to do with how you build your actual OU structure.

For example, lets say that your Help Desk has broad administrative access to file and print servers, but none to Web, Exchange, or application servers. They can add users to groups, modify passwords, and unlock accounts. However, they cannot add users, computers, or groups to the domain, and do not have the right to change user directory data.

In this a scenario, you might need to have OUs for users, groups, file and print servers, Web servers, Exchange servers, and application servers. That way, you can use the wizard to granularly control the access that members of the Help Desk group have to each OU and the objects that the OUs contain.

So, when you begin to consider the implications of delegating control, you need to be concerned with the following issues:

- What is the sensitivity level of the data that you can give access to?
- How are you going to control the change of directory data?
- What access is appropriate for which roles within your organization?
- How do these considerations affect your Organizational Unit design?

> **TIP**
>
> Always remember that the delegation of security is only partially an IT function. It is mostly a business exercise—who has legitimate need to specific information, and who should be excluded from that information on business grounds.

Security

It is entirely justifiable to make an argument that IT departments exist to defend an organization's data integrity. Indeed, in many organizations this is the IT departments' primary function. When a company's data is lost, destroyed, or corrupted it can cost millions of dollars and thousands of hours of lost work. As companies become more interconnected, incorrect data passed from one supply chain member to another can derail an entire multi-company process, leading to catastrophic failures in many enterprises.

With that in mind, you should approach data security and directory security with the utmost caution. It is one of the most important functions you can undertake, and deserves to be treated with respect.

The good news in all of this solemnity is that there are a number of clearly defined rules that you can follow to protect your users from undue harm:

- Use the principle of least access
- Create an audit trail
- Balance the need for restriction with the business needs of the users
- Always obtain proper authorization
- Include restoration and business continuance plans in the security scheme

The principle of least access states that a user should only be given access to the data and services that she or he justifiably needs to perform a job function. All other data is restricted, no matter what the user's political or organizational importance.

In Windows 2000, you can apply the principle of least access by carefully separating your OUs into functional lines, ensuring that only those resources available for corporate-wide use have the Domain Users group in their security profiles, and by carefully auditing which groups have access to which resources. Perfect control allows for perfect protection.

Unfortunately, no security scheme is perfect. IT organizations are designed, built, and run by humans for humans. This means that mistakes will happen. The only way to identify and correct security mistakes is to establish clear audit trails for security principle creation (the creation of user accounts), access to secured resources (a log of successful and unsuccessful access attempts), and security principle alteration (adding a person to a group).

The density and frequency of the audit information must be carefully balanced with your IT organization's ability to process the data in meaningful ways. It does no good to gather hundreds of megabytes of detailed data that no one ever reads. You need to apply some common-sense principles to cut down on the flood of data that you could encounter:

- Monitor the most sensitive data access points first
- Monitor the groups with access to those data access points
- Manage the creation of users and groups
- Allow only trusted administrators to grant membership to designated secured shares

In addition to auditing, there is one more piece of the data access puzzle you need to consider: how intrusive are you going to be? In the best of all possible worlds, you would lock secured data into a safe, drop the safe into a vat of concrete, and then dump the whole thing into the nearest river. Although your data would then be safe, no one could use it to produce value.

As IT professionals, you have to balance the need to protect the data with the need of users to get access to it. There are countless methods suggested for doing this: rational analysis, six-sigma analysis, and locking everything in a room.

The most effective measure by far is simply to institute *and follow* a process by which proper authorization by designated data owners is required before granting access to any data. For example, if there is a share that contains all company financial data, you probably want the CFO to be the designated data owner. No one is placed into a group with access to the share without the CFO's expressed permission. The process you use for this authorization could be automated (an e-mail is sent to the data owner), paper based (a form is sent to the data owner), or explicit (the data owner requests the access for the user who requires it).

You should also be prepared to respond to data corruption, deletion, or destruction in an organized fashion. This means that you have to plan not only for the restoration of services, but for that mythical state called "business continuance," in which your organizations continue to function at some level without their business-critical computer systems.

You need to be careful not to understate the importance of security considerations. It's easy to gloss over security when doing an Active Directory design; doing so exposes your organization to unacceptable risks that, at the end of the day, are your responsibility to mitigate.

Group Policies

Group Policy Objects (GPOs) are one of those features that can easily get out of hand without proper planning and execution. With some 600 settings out of the box, and the infinite capability to add and modify what they do, you can easily build an administrative structure so complex that you can never determine exactly what is going on.

GPOs are, at their heart, a way of altering the Registry in a predictable and controllable fashion. They allow the network administrator to enforce specific configuration settings, ensuring predictable behavior from disparate systems. A GPO can be linked to several OUs or sites, and can be filtered based on security group membership.

When building GPOs, you should keep a few basic rules in mind. These rules make your design much easier to implement and troubleshoot:

- Decide early on whether you are going to link single GPOs to single OUs or whether you are going to use GPO filtering.
- Use as few GPOs as possible.
- Apply as few GPOs as possible.
- Only configure settings that will be enforced.
- Set the settings you want to enforce as close to the target in the GPO chain as possible.

There are two basic ways to apply GPOs to users or computers: link a single GPO to a single OU or link multiple GPOs to a single OU and filter them based on group membership. Both options have their advantages and disadvantages; what is important is that you make a choice and apply it consistently. If you decide to link a single GPO to a single OU, you might need more OUs to ensure that users or computers get the settings they require. If you decide to link multiple GPOs to a single OU you require fewer OUs but more security groups to segregate user and computer roles.

The chapter has not discussed the idea of linking a single GPO to multiple OUs. Although this is certainly possible, this is not a design decision that provides a great deal of value. Because it is difficult to audit which OUs a GPO is linked to, linking a GPO to multiple OUs can easily lead to unintentional interactions and inappropriately configured settings.

Another way to avoid unintentional interactions is to avoid creating a large number of GPOs. When building a GPO structure, you should apply Occam's Razor: when choosing between answers, the simplest is usually the best. This not only protects you from attempting to trace back through a large number of GPOs, but also saves you processing time during the log-on and log-off processes.

4

PLANNING ACTIVE
DIRECTORY

If, after selecting the simplest path though your various concerns, you have a large number of GPOs you should try to create a GPO path that is as shallow as possible. This means that you should try to apply as few GPOs to a user or computer as you possibly can and still meet your design and security needs. A shallow path also reduces the amount of time spent processing GPOs during log in and log out, impacting the user experience quite drastically in some cases.

The reasoning for specifying only those values that you intend to change follows much the same lines as the previous argument. Because GPO processing takes place every 45 minutes by default as well as at log in and log out, the fewer settings you change in each GPO, the fewer values need to be processed. If there are no settings in the user part of a GPO, for example, simply deactivate processing of that part of the GPO.

Because GPO settings are a cumulative set of all of the settings in all of the GPOs you apply, and the GPO closest to the user or computer in the OU structure is applied last, you should be careful to place settings that are particular to account in the GPO closest to the account.

The other way to ensure enforcement of a particular function is to enforce the application of a GPO. Be careful with this functionality—the entire GPO will be forced down, denying you the ability to customize settings further down the line. You should use this feature only with settings that are particular either to a specific site (a special security notice at a secured facility) or with settings that apply to a very large subset of your users (such as your domain-wide settings).

GPOs are a tremendous tool for administrators, but without careful consideration and planning, they can become an administrative nightmare. By judiciously applying Occam's Razor, you can protect yourself from the dangers of a complex system, and reduce the likelihood that you will unintentionally disrupt your users ability to perform their jobs.

Security Considerations

As the chapter has already discussed briefly, data security is one of the primary responsibilities of an information technology organization. A large part of your jobs is made up of making sure that your user community has access to the data they need, when they need it, with a reasonable expectation that it has not been changed or corrupted since finding its way onto the network.

This section discusses in detail some of the data-access concerns that might affect your Windows 2000 Active Directory design. The ones highlighted in this discussion are:

- Access to Active Directory information—Who should have access and under what context?

- Administration of Active Directory—Who should have the ability to administer and control AD objects?

- Publishing shares and printers in AD—What are the ramifications for data visibility and security?
- Searching the Active Directory—What needs to be available and what does not?

As in any security situation, the principle of least access always applies. When applied rigorously in conjunction with a reasonable audit and change control scheme, this principle creates a solid security foundation upon which your organization can grow.

Access to AD

The Active Directory is a repository for the organization's security and identity information. You can think of it as a giant searchable address book, filled with data that many people might need to access. The more data you store in the Active Directory, the more likely it is that multiple (and perhaps conflicting) groups within the business will need access to the data stored in it.

There are three basic methods for accessing Active Directory information:

- The administrative tools provided by Microsoft
- ASDI scripts that search for particular information on available objects
- LDAP queries using LDAP-enabled query clients

There are dozens of books and hundreds of white papers about how to use these tools to access the information in your Active Directory. Unfortunately, most of these miss the point.

The point is simple, yet fairly profound:

Who actually needs access to this data and why?

Until you answer these two questions, you cannot even begin to consider how you are going to provide security for your data.

Let's pause for a moment and take a look at the information that is really contained in AD for most objects:

- **Identification information**—address, phone number, full name, and direct report
- **Location information**—physical location, network location, and business position
- **Group information**—groups that the user participates in
- **System information**—passwords, login scripts, home directories, and similar information
- **Custom information**—whatever attributes you have added to your objects

What services need access to this information? Who needs it in your organization? Why do they need it? Where is it sourced from, and who is responsible for changing it?

Generally, you'll find the following answers to these questions:

- **Identification information**—Controlled by HR and changed by operations. It can be used by ERP-type systems to create consistent identity for the users.
- **Location information**—Controlled by HR and changed by operations. It is used by network equipment and servers to correctly route data.
- **Group information**—Controlled by data owners and changed by operations. It can be used by ERP software, databases, and other applications to grant appropriate access.
- **System information**—Controlled by the individual user and the architecture/operations roles equally. The information is used by applications to grant appropriate access, and can also be used by other security providers to grant access to their resources.
- **Custom information**—Controlled by designated data owners and can be either proprietary or confidential. This data is usually accessed by an ERP or other custom application, and might be legally sensitive.

Carefully examine exactly who needs access to what and why. In a typical network, you grant read permissions to those who need to reference the data, change permissions to those who have the right to alter the data, and full control *only* to the data owner.

Administration of AD

Administering Active Directory is in reality no different from administering any other network system. The tools are different, but the rules and restrictions are the same.

However, Active Directory does provide the opportunity to very closely match good policy with network design. Unlike Windows NT, in which most of the policy was dictated by limitations in the system, AD is extremely flexible about how it is organized, who has access to which features, and what jobs you can parse out.

This is another topic where Occam's Razor is your most useful tool. Keep things as simple as possible while still meeting the security goals. Avoid needless steps, layers, or complexity. Cut down the number of steps between the data owner (whoever that is) and the individuals who control the access without sacrificing needed auditing ability.

Shares and Printers in AD

It is possible to publish information about shares and printers into the Active Directory. Hypothetically, this makes it easier for users to find and access the resources that they need when they need them.

In practice, publishing shares into the Active Directory is not always a wise idea. It's not so much that you can protect data by hiding it from those who shouldn't have access to it, but simply that there are dozens of better ways to handle the users search for this information. Many companies use intranets, document management systems, the Distributed File System, or shared departmental drives. The list of solutions is endless, and much more flexible than AD publishing.

Publishing printers, on the other hand, can be highly useful to the user community. Rather than presenting your users with a seemingly endless list of cryptic printer names, you can sort your printers by location for easier access. They can then search printers local to them, or search for printers in a different location if they need to print for a colleague somewhere else in the company.

Generally, the data-access concerns related to printers in the Active Directory are reasonably low. The risk associated with printers is simply not great enough to warrant detailed security settings on the network. Most printers do require some level of physical security, however, as users may print documents containing sensitive information that does need to be protected from inappropriate access.

Searching AD

Users can search Active Directory to find users, computers, and printers. Generally this is a function that you would like to encourage—the more information that your users can find, the more likely they are to be able to execute their job functions.

However, in a multi-domain environment, you need to be careful to include all of the attributes that you want users to be able to search on in your Global Catalogue servers. Refer to Chapter 3, "Describing Active Directory Components," for more information.

Installation Considerations

The logistics of an installation can complicate the most carefully designed directory. How quickly you can implement specific features, preserve and migrate functionality, and mitigate the risk of data loss are key to how you consider phasing in your designs.

This section discusses two basic tools:

- Using the Remote Installation Service—RIS allows you to boot a workstation to the LAN and rebuild it using a specified image.
- Using GPOs to distribute software—You can use GPOs to distribute software packages to users or computers based on their location in the OU structure.

This chapter does not discuss the use of automated build scripts, automated build CDs, or third-party tools. These tools are discussed in full in Chapter 8.

Using the Remote Installation Service

The Remote Installation Service (RIS) is a native Windows 2000 method for multicasting a workstation image to several clients in need of a build. It is bandwidth intensive, hard drive intensive, and occasionally difficult to manage.

Generally RIS is used in small environments (under 100 workstations) where the DHCP and the RIS services are located on two or more separate servers. It allows for the quick imaging of several machines at once.

RIS can also be used in a central staging area, where multiple workstations are imaged simultaneously in preparation for deployment. This can greatly speed workstation migrations, but only when the logistics of moving the workstations to the central build facility do not take more time and coordination than simply building the machine closer to the user.

Software Installation through Group Policy

Each nding on how you structure your GPOs, this could be extremely useful or simply an odd feature that you ignore for now.

It is useful when you have patches that need to go to the entire organization, programs that are specific to a particular site or security profile, or application packages that change on a regular basis and that affect a large portion of the organization.

It is less useful when your organization manages application availability by user, rather than by security profile or group. Because GPOs are enforced on an OU and group level, they are not well suited for deploying applications to individual users.

In terms of ideal management, it would be good for an organization to achieve application management by security profile or group membership. Unfortunately, it is not always politically possible for an organization to take this approach. It is also sometimes not wise to do so; in some environments each user's security profile and business needs are different enough to warrant individual management.

Political Considerations

In one of those unkind twists of fate that sometimes happen in life, IT people cannot simply ignore the rest of the world and play with our computers. Our work takes place within a larger context, a context that includes business practices, legal requirements, corporate culture, complex supply chains, and international politics.

This section tries to cut though a lot of the jargon and to identify issues that directly affect your Active Directory design. You can categorize some of these issues into the following categories:

- **Administrative concerns**—human resources, access control, and procedural requirements that come from business needs
- **Domain namespace concerns**—issues of corporate identity, branding, and internal marketing
- **Access to active directory content**—legal issues that necessitate particular actions on the part of the network designers
- **Schema concerns**—legal or other issues that require the addition or deactivation of particular objects and attributes
- **World trade concerns**—laws that might affect your security, encryption, and administration policies

In all of these considerations the best thing that you can do is formulate the questions and ask the business users who study these things to find the answers. Law, politics, and corporate culture are complex disciplines all their own, and unless you are adept at all of them, you will need outside help to sort through the issues.

Administrative Concerns

Every business has different legal requirements for auditing, storing, and providing in timely manner information about users, files, computers, inventories, and the like to relevant authorities.

The questions you need to ask include:

- What organizations require information from you, at what times, and in what format?
- What legal auditing and reporting requirements does your organization have?
- How long must you store historical directory data? Where does this requirement come from, and in what format should you store the data?
- Are there individuals within the IT organization who should not, for whatever reason, have the access typically permitted by their job function?
- Are there specific individuals in the business who require special treatment for legal, procedural, or political reasons?
- If you have international sites, do you have different data storage, auditing, and presentation requirements for each country?

With the answers to these questions, you can begin to formulate an understanding of what might be requested of you in the future.

4

PLANNING ACTIVE DIRECTORY

Domain Namespace Concerns

When you propose a namespace for your domain(s), you need to ask the following questions:

- Is the name in keeping with your internal corporate identity?
- Is the name trademarked by any other company?
- Does the name mean something in a foreign language that you would rather avoid saying? For example, the Chevrolet Nova automobile reportedly sold poorly in Spanish-speaking countries because "no va" means "no go" in Spanish.
- Is there a partnership or other agreement that affects your choices of namespace?
- How does the name you are proposing work with known and expected corporate internal marketing efforts?
- Have you unintentionally chosen a name that has negative connotations within your specific environment?
- Are there political or business needs within your organization that might require a new domain?
- Are there units within the organization that will split from the larger group within the next six months or year? If so, will they take their IT assets when they split from the company?

You also should be concerned with the perceptions of the highest levels of management when dealing with these issues. Unless you carefully explain what you are doing and why you want to do it, they are unlikely to listen to your "technical" concerns.

Access to AD Content Concerns

Access to the information contained in the Active Directory might need to be restricted based on legal, ethical, or procedural concerns. The questions that you need to ask are:

- What data is politically sensitive?
- What data are you legally bound to protect?
- What data is confidential to particular departments?
- What data is confidential to your company?

These concerns can play out in a number of ways. For example, in a hospital it might be tempting to put pointers to data about the patients assigned to a doctor into the Active Directory. The AD could act as a security broker, allowing access to various systems containing data about the patient. However, personal health information is protected by law, and accessing it without proper authorization can lead to fines, prison sentences, and dismissal from health-related positions. This is not data that should be stored in a directory that is available for public viewing.

Or take the example of a company that is responsible for cleaning up a waste site. They are working hard to contain the damage done by the waste, and also to protect both their reputation and the reputation of the company responsible for the dumping. Suddenly the name of the groups used to secure information about the site can become sensitive, because it is a reasonably trivial task to go in and look at someone's group memberships...even if the data is protected.

Schema Concerns

The Windows 2000 Active Directory schema is a bountiful source of information about your company, organization, or government branch if someone takes the time to look at it. What attributes have you populated? What attributes have you added? What objects? What ERP application do you run? What mail software? What other directories exist in your environment? A quick survey with a LDAP client can give any attacker the answer to these questions, and many more.

When thinking about access to your schema, you need to ask the following questions:

- Who should be able to view sensitive and important information?
- Who needs to know how you organize your information?
- What information do you need to expressly hide?
- Are there any human-resource related or legal concerns that you need to address when creating objects that represent people within your environment?

World Trade and Access Concerns

Once you cross an international border, the difficulties you face in determining your legal and business requirements expand exponentially. Not only do you have to worry about the laws in two (or more!) countries, but you also need to be concerned with trade agreements, international treaties, and organizations that use acronyms such as the WTO and the UN. And that's not counting the problems that you can run into just with the translation of procedural or process documents from one language into another.

Generally, you need to ask the following questions:

- How are your various international operations related to one another?
- Are there legal requirements in a specific country requiring a separation of your domain structures?
- Do you have any legal or security concerns related to trading possibly classified or restricted information with a particular site?

- Is there data in your systems that you do not classify as sensitive that is considered sensitive by international treaty?
- Is there data in your directory that is considered confidential or protected in another country?
- Are there financial or legal restrictions about where equipment must be purchased?
- Is your directory well suited for the reporting and auditing needs of another country?

Given the shear complexity of some of these issues, it would be easy to discard all of the questions and just run forward. Don't despair; just ask the questions and keep moving. Don't allow the work of the analysis to weigh down the project. You can always adjust the design, even after you get into production, if necessary.

Summary

This chapter was dedicated to the design and implementation aspects of Active Directory. Many of the considerations found in this chapter are based in political, logistical, and communications issues. These issues need to be properly understood and managed to create an AD design that is practical and functional.

The chapter covered migration considerations, such as how AD interacts with or affects other network services such as WINS, DNS, and DHCP. Administrative considerations such as OU, Group, and GPO structures were covered.

Other considerations included security and installation aspects. Security issues were covered to help you determine how to best protect your data, OU, Group, and GPO structures. Finally, the logistical and technical issues that could affect your AD implementation were discussed.

CASE STUDY

Learning by Example: The "Molly Pitcher Pharmaceuticals, Inc." Company

After reviewing the case study for Molly Pitcher Pharmaceuticals, Inc., there are some issues that need to be analyzed.

Migration considerations: In Molly Pitcher's case, one of your first design considerations is how to migrate from the current Windows NT 4 environment to a Windows 2000 Active Directory environment.

One of the requirements stated by Molly Pitcher is the elimination of the single master domain model. To accomplish this, you have two choices, migrate and reorganize the existing environment, or build a new environment. Because there is an existing master domain in place and all user accounts are located in this domain, you can choose to perform an in-place upgrade for the master domain. The resource domains can be migrated to Windows 2000 later and converted into OUs in the new domain.

Mixed or native mode: Because you are performing an in-place upgrade, you will initially be running in a mixed mode environment. It is important to note that Molly Pitcher deployed Windows 2000 Professional to all desktop and portable client computers. Because of this, you need to ensure that all domain controllers (the PDC and BDCs) have been upgraded to Windows 2000 before switching to native mode. If you switch modes before all domain controllers are migrated, you might end up with some clients that cannot log on to the domain.

Server migration: Molly Pitcher uses a number of servers to provide file and print services, messaging, and intranet services. They also have several varieties of application servers. Any servers that do not meet the hardware requirements for Windows 2000 need to be replaced. You must also verify that *all* applications used on these servers are compatible with Windows 2000. If they are not, you need to contact the software vendor about an upgrade or investigate other vendor solutions.

Client migration: Molly Pitcher deployed Windows 2000 Professional to all client computers throughout their environment. As such, there are no issues with client migration.

Administrative considerations: Finally, you need to consider the administrative issues and tasks that the Molly Pitcher IT department might face when your Active Directory design goes into production. The IT staff needs to be educated in Active Directory overall, including how OUs are utilized, how to delegate tasks and authority to other staff (such as departmental staff), and how to implement and manage group policies.

Interaction with Other Network Services

IN THIS CHAPTER

This chapter provides a view into the various network services found in a typical Windows 2000 and Active Directory-based network. Although some of these networking services are required, others are used to increase the functionality and usefulness of the network.

Domain Name System (DNS)

The Domain Name System (DNS) is a required component in a Windows 2000 network that utilizes Active Directory. And, of course, the Internet uses DNS. Whenever you are using the Internet, whether it is the World Wide Web or simply e-mail, you are using DNS.

DNS is a client/server based protocol that is used in TCP/IP-based networks to resolve host names (computer names) to IP addresses. DNS is the primary method for name resolution in Windows 2000. DNS also enables Windows 2000 clients to locate network services, such as domain controllers. Previous versions of Windows operating systems used NetBIOS computer names and as a result required the use of either NetBIOS broadcasts or Windows Internet Naming Service (WINS) servers.

Before the chapter gets into great detail about what DNS is and how it works, let's take a look back into the early days of the Internet.

As almost anyone who has worked on a TCP/IP-based network knows, trying to remember many IP addresses is nearly impossible for anyone, especially with the growth of the Internet during the past 10 years. Host names, or computer names, make lives easier by giving an IP address a memorable name. As one can see, remembering amazon.com is easier than remembering 168.2.12.48.

In the early days of the Internet and TCP/IP, host name resolution was left to a single text file, called a HOSTS file. Host names would be manually added to this file. The file would then be copied to each TCP/IP host. If your network is small, *HOSTS* files work fine and were manageable.

HOSTS files in Windows NT and Windows 2000 are stored in the %systemroot%\SYSTEM32\DRIVERS\ETC directory.

```
Sample HOSTS file
# Copyright (c) 1994 Microsoft Corp.
#
# This is a sample HOSTS file used by Microsoft TCP/IP for Chicago
#
```

```
# This file contains the mappings of IP addresses to host names. Each
# entry should be kept on an individual line. The IP address should
# be placed in the first column followed by the corresponding host name.
# The IP address and the host name should be separated by at least one
# space.
#
# Additionally, comments (such as these) may be inserted on individual
# lines or following the machine name denoted by a '#' symbol.
#
# For example:
#
#     102.54.94.97     rhino.acme.com        # source server
#      38.25.63.10     x.acme.com            # x client host

127.0.0.1       localhost
192.168.0.1     router
192.168.0.254   proxy
192.168.0.2     neall
```

As the Internet and other TCP/IP-based networks grew, the HOSTS file method of host name resolution became more cumbersome and inefficient. In 1984, two new RFCs (Request for Comments), 882 and 883, were released detailing DNS. These RFCs have since been replaced by RFCs 1034 and 1035.

DNS is a distributed database that allows local administrators to maintain and manage their portion of the DNS database, while allowing access for host name resolution across the entire Internet. DNS consists of two parts—DNS clients and DNS servers.

The server portion is driven by name servers. Name servers hold the segment of the DNS database (called a *zone*) that they have authority over. The DNS client is known as a *resolver*. This can be any TCP/IP client that supports DNS.

The DNS database structure can be described as an inverted tree. The top of the tree (or the trunk) is known as the root domain. It is shown as a single dot (.). Figure 5.1 shows the structure of the DNS database.

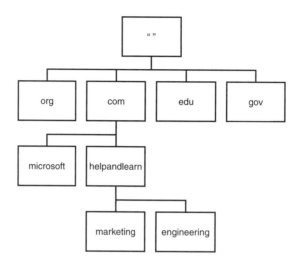

FIGURE 5.1
The structure of the DNS database.

Below the root domain are the top-level subdomains. Currently these include .com, .edu, .net, .org, .mil and country domains, such as .jp for Japan and .nz for New Zealand. However, in 1998, the United States government turned Internet addressing and naming duties over to a private organization called the Internet Corporation for Assigned Names and Numbers (ICANN). ICANN is currently developing and releasing a new standard for top-level subdomain naming. This standard will expand the top-level domains into more recognizable domain names. The new domain names will make it simpler for users to search the Web. This new domain naming standard will blur the line between the original top-level subdomains, such as .com, .net, and .org.

Subdomains are DNS-management structures. The local administrators for those domains are responsible for maintaining that portion of the DNS database. These subdomains can also be broken into additional subdomains, which can be delegated authority as well.

An absolute host name in DNS is called the *Fully Qualified Domain Name* or FQDN. A FQDN begins with the host name and proceeds to the root. For example, www.lucidnetworking.com describes a host with the name www in the subdomain lucidnetworking under the com top-level domain.

DNS Zones

As mentioned earlier, name servers have authority over one or more zones. Zones are simply a subset of the DNS database. Note that zones do not have to have any normal boundaries. A zone can contain a single domain, two subdomains, or multiple levels of the name space (see Figure 5.2).

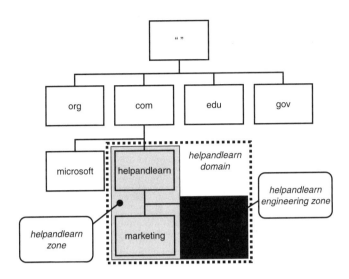

FIGURE 5.2

A DNS zone.

A zone file contains all necessary information for a DNS server to resolve host names and IP addresses.

Windows 2000 provides support for the two standard DNS zone types, as well as a new zone type found exclusively in Windows 2000, the Active Directory Integrated Zone.

Standard Primary

A standard primary zone is essentially a read-write copy of the DNS database stored in a text file on the DNS server's storage subsystem. The DNS server service loads the text file into memory when the service first starts. The text file holding the standard primary zone is copied to the DNS servers hosting the standard secondary zones during the zone-transfer process.

All updates to the DNS database must occur at the standard primary zone.

Standard Secondary

A standard secondary zone is a read-only copy of the DNS database. Again, like the standard primary zone, its data is stored in a text file on the DNS Server's storage subsystem.

The standard secondary zone is used for load balancing client queries as well as to provide for limited fault tolerance. If the standard primary zone is unavailable, the secondary zone can still be used to satisfy client queries.

It can only be updated via the DNS zone-transfer process.

Active Directory-integrated

With an Active Directory-integrated zone, all data in the zone, such as resource records, are stored within Active Directory. The Active Directory replication process, instead of the standard zone transfer process, handles replication of DNS zone data. This zone type provides for secure updates as well. This solution is also more fault-tolerant because it can take advantage of Active Directory's multiple master replication concept. Only DNS Servers that are also Windows 2000 Domain Controllers can host an Active Directory-integrated zone.

Reverse Lookup

A reverse lookup zone is a special zone type. Reverse lookup zones are used to resolve IP addresses to host names, the opposite function of the other zone types that resolve host names to IP address. Hence the name, reverse lookup. For example, if you needed to determine the host name of a particular IP address, you could query DNS with the IP address. The DNS server would examine its reverse lookup zones to return the host name.

Reverse lookup zones have a particular naming standard. This standard involves the domain name in-addr.arpa. This domain is reserved for reverse lookup zones. Because a reverse lookup consists of using a host name to resolve an IP address, a reverse lookup zone is configured per subnet. In other words, if the subnet is the class C network 192.168.1.0, the reverse lookup zone is 1.168.192.in-addr.arpa.

Using Non-Windows 2000 DNS Servers

The DNS server found in Windows 2000 is based on RFCs created by the Internet Engineering Task Force (IETF). As a result, it is also compatible with DNS servers found on other operating systems. Most of these other operating systems' DNS servers comply with the Berkeley Internet Name Domain (BIND) version 8.2.2.

If you want to use a non-Windows 2000 DNS server, you must ensure that the server is compatible with the following:

- **Support for SRV (service) records**—BIND 4.9.6 or later
- **Incremental zone updates**—BIND 8.2.1 or later
- **Dynamic Update**—BIND 8.1.2 or later

Microsoft recommends that DNS servers compatible with BIND 8.2.2 or later be used if necessary.

Installing the DNS Server

There are two ways to install the DNS server in Windows 2000.

The first method is to use the Add/Remove Programs applet in the Control Panel. Select the Add/Remove Windows Components option on the left side of the dialog box. The Windows Components Wizard dialog box is displayed. From the list of components, select the Network Services component and click on the Details button.

From the list of subcomponents, place a checkmark next to the Domain Name System (DNS) subcomponents (see Figure 5.3). Click OK to close the subcomponent dialog box. Click Next to view the Windows Components Wizard dialog box.

Windows 2000 will now install the files required to configure the Windows 2000 DNS server.

NOTE

You may have to insert the Windows 2000 Server CD-ROM if the binary CAB files are not located on your server's hard disk.

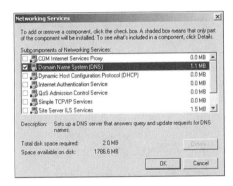

FIGURE 5.3
Installing the Windows 2000 DNS server.

The second way to install the DNS server in Windows 2000 involves the creation of a Windows 2000 domain controller.

The Active Directory Installation Wizard, also known as DCPROMO, will prompt you whether or not a DNS server has been installed and configured. If a DNS server is not installed, DCPROMO will automatically install and configure the DNS server.

To configure DNS, you must use the DNS MMC. To access the DNS MMC, select Start, Program Files, Administrative Tools, and then DNS.

The DNS MMC configures the DNS server, creates and manages the various zone types, and manages resource records (see Figure 5.4).

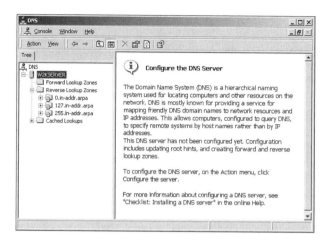

FIGURE 5.4
The Windows 2000 DNS MMC.

To begin configuring the DNS server, select Configure the server from the Action pull-down menu. The Configure DNS Server Wizard will start. Click Next.

The wizard will walk you through the general configuration of the server, such as creating forward and reverse lookup zones. Note that you do not need to create all zones at this time. Zones can be created at any time and will be addressed later in this section.

The Forward Lookup Zone screen will be displayed (see Figure 5.5). Select Yes to create a new forward lookup zone.

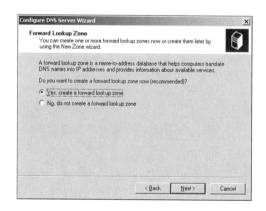

FIGURE 5.5
Creating forward lookup zones.

Next, the Zone Type screen is displayed. Here you need to specify whether the zone is Active Directory-integrated, standard primary, or standard secondary. Note that if the DNS Server is not also a Windows 2000 Domain controller, the Active Directory-integrated option will be ghosted (see Figure 5.6). Select Standard Primary and click Next.

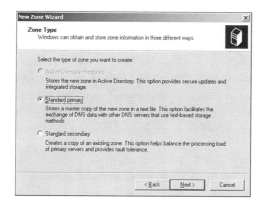

FIGURE 5.6

Selecting a zone type.

Enter the zone name. Typically this will be the name of the domain or subdomain. Enter helpandlearn.com and click Next (see Figure 5.7).

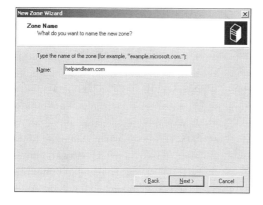

FIGURE 5.7

Specifying the zone name.

Now you need to specify the name of the zone file. Remember from earlier in the chapter that the standard primary and standard secondary zone types are stored in a text file. Windows

2000 will specify a default zone filename, which is usually sufficient (see Figure 5.8). However, you can change it if your requirements dictate a change is needed.

If you already have a zone file (such as when you are copying the file from another DNS server), you can specify the file that the DNS server should use to create the zone.

Accept the default filename and click Next.

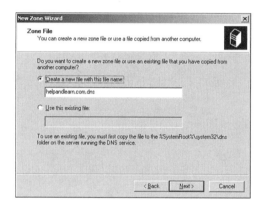

FIGURE 5.8
Specifying the zone file's filename.

The next screen asks you whether you want to create a reverse lookup zone. Reverse look-up zones are used to resolve IP addresses to host names. Select Yes and click Next (see Figure 5.9).

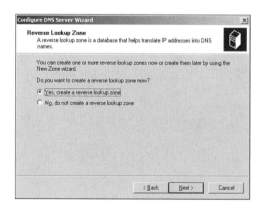

FIGURE 5.9
Creating a reverse lookup zone.

Just like normal forward lookup zones, you need to specify whether the zone will be Active Directory-integrated, standard primary, or standard secondary. Select standard primary and click Next (see Figure 5.10).

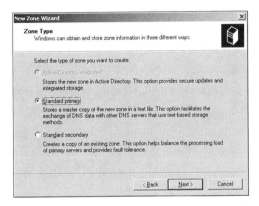

FIGURE 5.10

Selecting a zone type.

To name the reverse lookup zone, you must enter the IP subnet address for the network the zone will be servicing. For example, if your network is using the subnet 192.168.0.0, you enter that address in the network ID. The wizard will automatically convert the network ID into the reverse lookup zone's name, `0.168.192.in-addr.arpa`. As you can see, the network ID is reversed with `in-addr.arpa` added. The `in-addr.arpa` address tells the DNS server that this is a reverse lookup zone (see Figure 5.11).

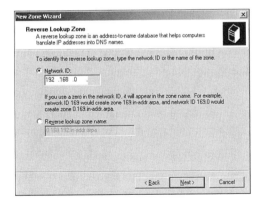

FIGURE 5.11

Naming the reverse lookup zone.

Again, just like the forward lookup zone, you must specify the file where the zone data is to be stored (see Figure 5.12). Click Next.

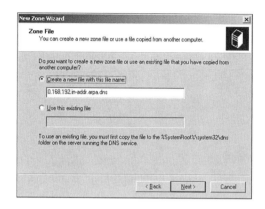

FIGURE 5.12
Specifying the zone file's filename.

Finally, the wizard has enough information to configure the DNS server initially. Click Finish to complete the wizard.

If you need to create more zones, you can now manually create them using the other wizards found in the DNS server.

Dynamic Host Configuration Protocol (DHCP)

Installing the TCP/IP protocol suite on a computer requires careful configuration of an IP address, subnet mask, and default gateway. The computer cannot communicate with other computers on the network if any of these parameters are incorrect. It is also important to correctly configure the computer with the IP addresses of DNS servers and WINS servers. If these items are incorrectly configured, the computer might not be able to perform name resolution correctly.

An administrator can maintain these IP addresses and configurations on each computer either statically or dynamically. When maintaining static configurations, you must visit each computer and enter the TCP/IP configuration. Also, if any part of the configuration changes, you need to revisit every computer.

It is a better use of your time to use a dynamic method. Dynamic Host Configuration Protocol (DHCP) allows administrators to automatically configure and control the TCP/IP configuration options on computers in their networks.

Using DHCP to distribute and manage IP configurations alleviates most of the problems associated with a statically maintained environment. Simple problems such as a wrong IP address, subnet mask, or default gateway are completely eliminated. Also, configuration information central to the operation of the network can automatically be updated. If the IP addresses of DNS or WINS servers change, you simply update the DHCP database and the changes are sent to the DHCP client upon next boot or when their lease expires.

The DHCP Conversation

DHCP, much like DNS, is a client/server based service. The two components, the DHCP server and a DHCP client, exchange a number of broadcast packets to provide the service. This exchange of packets is known as the DHCP conversation (see Figure 5.13).

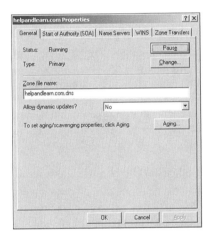

FIGURE 5.13
The exchange of messages during the DHCP conversation.

First, the DHCP client sends out a DHCPDISCOVER message. This message is broadcast on the client's subnet and any listening DHCP server can receive it.

Next, listening DHCP servers receive the DHCPDISCOVER message. Using information provided in the message, the DHCP servers respond with a DHCPOFFER message. This message contains the client's TCP/IP configuration parameters.

The client receives all DHCPOFFER messages and selects one to use. Usually the first offer received is selected. The DHCP client then sends a DHCPREQUEST message to all DHCP servers. This allows the selected DHCP server to complete the lease process. It also lets the client notify the other offering DHCP servers that the client selected a lease from another DHCP server.

Finally, the selected DHCP server sends a DHCPACK message to the client to acknowledge that the lease is valid and complete.

At this point the DHCP client initializes its TCP/IP configuration.

Before moving on to the next section, it's important that you understand that the entire DHCP conversation takes place with broadcast packets. Routers do not forward broadcast packets, so implementing DHCP is a routed environment and therefore must take the functions of routers into consideration. Some routers can be configured to pass BOOTP/DHCP broadcast packets. These routers are considered RFC-1542 compliant. If the router is not RFC-1542 compliant, Windows 2000 includes a DHCP relay agent. The DHCP relay agent allows a Windows 2000 server to listen for DHCP broadcast packets and automatically forward them to a DHCP server.

Defining DHCP Scopes

For DHCP clients to receive even a single IP address from the DHCP server, a DHCP scope needs to be created. A DHCP scope is a range of IP addresses to be distributed by the DHCP server. The range consists of contiguous IP addresses from the same subnet.

The range of IP addresses used to create the scope should not contain any static IP addresses of existing computers. If there are any static addresses in use, an administrator could either convert them into DHCP clients, use address reservations or exclusions, or shorten the scope range.

The DHCP scope also contains other information, such as a lease duration and DHCP options that will be distributed along with the IP address. The lease duration is the amount of time that a DHCP client can use an IP address before being required to renegotiate the lease. DHCP options are used to configure items such as the default gateway and the IP addresses for DNS servers.

Defining DHCP Options

To configure DHCP options, you need to consider the DHCP clients and which DHCP options they support and require. All Microsoft operating systems support the following DHCP options:

- **The subnet mask option (1)**—This option specifies the subnet mask to be used by the client.
- **The routers option (3)**—This option specifies the default gateway.
- **The domain name option (15)**—This option specifies the domain name to be used by the client.
- **The domain name servers option (6)**—This option lists the DNS servers to be used for host name resolution by the client.

- **The NetBIOS name servers option (44)**—This option lists the WINS servers to be used for NetBIOS name resolution by the client.

- **The NetBIOS node type option (46)**—This option determines the NetBIOS node type to be used by the client.

- **NetBIOS scope option (47)**—This option specifies the NetBIOS scope ID to be used by the client.

Taking into account the current network infrastructure, the administrator would need to determine which options are required and determine the correct values for these options.

Installing the DHCP Server

To install the DHCP server in Windows 2000, use the Add/Remove Programs applet in the Control Panel. Select the Add/Remove Windows components option on the left side of the dialog box. The Windows Components Wizard dialog box appears. From the list of components, select the Network Services component and click the Details button.

From the list of subcomponents, place a checkmark next to the Dynamic Host Configuration Protocol (DHCP) subcomponents (see Figure 5.14). Click OK to close the subcomponent dialog box. Click Next on the Windows Components Wizard dialog box.

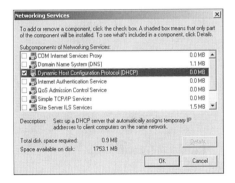

FIGURE 5.14

Installing the Windows 2000 DHCP server.

Windows 2000 will now install the files required to configure the Windows 2000 DHCP server.

> **NOTE**
>
> You might need to insert the Windows 2000 Server CD-ROM if the binary CAB files are not located on your server's hard disk.

To configure DHCP, you must use the DHCP MMC. To access the DHCP MMC, select Start, Program Files, Administrative Tools, DHCP.

Authorizing the DHCP Server in Active Directory

Windows 2000 provides a new feature for networks running Active Directory that allows administrators to authorize DHCP servers. An authorized DHCP server can deliver IP addresses and TCP/IP configuration data on a Windows 2000-based network. If the DHCP server is not authorized in Active Directory, the server's DHCP service will not start.

An unauthorized or badly configured DHCP server could wreak havoc on a network. It could lease incorrect IP addresses that cause the DHCP client to be unable to connect to the network. Another possibility is that the DHCP server could send negative acknowledgements to the clients when they attempt to renew their current IP address leases. As a result, the client loses IP connectivity.

To authorize a DHCP server in Active Directory, follow these steps:

1. To authorize a DHCP server in Windows 2000, you must be a member of the Enterprise Administrators group. If you are not a member of this group, log on with a user account that is a member or have an Enterprise Administrator add you to that group. Another option is to have an Enterprise Administrator delegate control to your account.

2. Open the DHCP MMC (Start, Programs, Administrative Tools, DHCP).

3. In the tree pane, pick DHCP.

4. Right-click DHCP and select Manage authorized servers. The Managed Authorized Servers dialog box appears (see Figure 5.15).

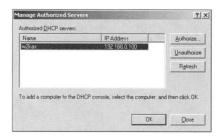

FIGURE 5.15

Managing authorized servers.

5. Pick Authorize and enter the name or IP address of the DHCP server you want to authorize.

Creating Scopes

Creating a DHCP scope is very simple once the design criterion is decided. Follow these steps to configure a DHCP scope:

1. In the DHCP MMC, right-click the DHCP server that will contain the scope. Select New Scope from the menu.

2. The New Scope Wizard starts. Click Next on the Welcome screen.

3. Enter a name and description for the new scope. This name identifies the scope. You can use descriptive names, such as the physical location of the scope, for example, Building 411, Third Floor, or simply the subnet it serves, for example, 192.168.1.0. Click Next.

4. Now define the scope address range. The range must be a set of contiguous IP addresses belonging to a single subnet. Enter the starting IP address and the ending IP address. Next enter the subnet mask traditionally (such as 255.255.252.0) or as a length (such as the number of bits that comprise the network address, 22).

5. Next, enter any address exclusions. An address exclusion is an IP address that is included in the scope range but the DHCP server is not to distribute.

6. Next, specify the lease duration to be used for this scope. Lease durations allow the DHCP server to reclaim IP addresses.

7. Now you have a choice of configuring DHCP options now or later. If you already determined which DHCP options to configure, select "Yes, I want to configure these options now" and click Next.

8. The New Scope wizard will prompt you to enter a router (default gateway) IP address. Enter the IP address for the router and click Add. Click Next.

9. Next you need to enter DNS configuration data. These configuration settings enable the DHCP clients to query DNS servers for host name to IP address resolution. First, enter the parent DNS domain. Next, enter the IP addresses for the DNS servers. If you are not sure of the IP address but you do have the host name of the DNS server, you can enter the server's name and click Resolve to find the IP address. Click Next.

10. Now it's time for WINS configuration. WINS servers resolve NetBIOS names to IP addresses. Enter the IP addresses for the WINS servers or enter the WINS server's name and click Resolve. Click Next.

11. Next you will be prompted to activate the scope. Activating the scope allows DHCP clients to obtain IP addresses from the scope. Select "Yes, I want to activate this scope now". There may be situations where you'll wait before activating a scope, such as when you are converting from one IP addressing scheme to another. Click Next.

12. Click Finish to create the scope.

Another important component in DHCP scopes is the *address reservation*. A reservation allows a particular DHCP client to always receive a particular IP address. The DHCP server reads the DHCPDISCOVER packet from the client and notes its MAC address. The DHCP server then looks in its database for any reservations that match that MAC address. If one is found, the client is configured with the reserved IP address. Reservations are useful for network devices that seldom change their IP addresses, such as network printers and servers. Reservations allow these devices to benefit from the use of DHCP options while still maintaining a static IP address.

Dynamic DNS: The Interaction of DNS and DHCP

A new feature in Windows 2000 is the ability for Windows 2000 clients to update their DNS records via DHCP. It's important to note that previous versions of Windows operating systems do not support this feature. To resolve this issue, you can configure the DHCP server to do the updating on their behalf.

Previously, whenever a computer's IP address changed, the administrator needed to manually go into the DNS database and update the computer's resource records to reflect the change. With DHCP, a computer's IP address could change whenever the computer's DHCP lease expired. As a result, the administrator would need to constantly make changes to DNS.

To alleviate this problem, the IETF released RFC 2136 for the Dynamic Update Protocol. This protocol allows a DHCP servers and DHCP clients to update DNS resource records automatically without the need of an administrator.

When a DHCP server leases an IP address to a Windows 2000 DHCP client, the following occurs:

- The client sends a DHCPREQUEST message to the DHCP server. This message includes the Fully Qualified Domain Name (FQDN) of the client.
- The DHCP server returns a DHCPPACK message to the client to acknowledge the lease.
- The client sends a DNS update request to the DNS server to update the client's forward lookup record (A record).
- The DHCP server sends a DNS update request to the DNS server to update the client's reverse lookup record (PTR record).

For operating systems that do not support dynamic updates (also known as down-level clients, such as Windows 95/98 and Windows NT), you need to configure the DHCP server to always update the A and PTR records on behalf of the client. In this situation, the following occurs:

- The client sends a DHCPREQUEST message to the DHCP server. Unlike Windows 2000, the FQDN is not included in the message.

- The DHCP server returns a DHCPACK message to the client to acknowledge the lease.

- The DHCP server sends DNS update requests to the DNS server to update the client's A and PTR records.

To configure the DNS server for dynamic updates, open the properties for the zone on the DNS server you need to configure. On the General tab, select Yes in the Allow Dynamic Updates list box (see Figure 5.16).

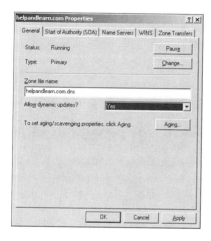

FIGURE 5.16
Configuring the DNS server for dynamic updates.

To configure the DHCP server for dynamic updates, open the properties for the DHCP server and click the DNS tab (see Figure 5.17). Select Automatically update DHCP client information in DNS and then select one of the following options:

- Update DNS only if DHCP client requests
- Always update DNS

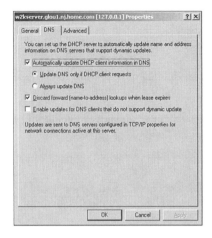

FIGURE 5.17
Configuring the DHCP server for dynamic updates.

Remote Installation Services (RIS)

Remote Installation Services makes it easier for administrators to automatically deploy Windows 2000 Professional and Windows XP Professional throughout an organization. With RIS, an administrator doesn't need to physically visit each computer.

With RIS, a computer can connect to a RIS server during its initial boot phase and remotely install the Windows 2000 Professional or Windows XP Professional operating system.

There are three primary components in RIS: the RIS server, the RIS client, and the client image.

The RIS server distributes the operating system to the clients.

The RIS client is the recipient of the remote install.

The client image is the installation that reflects the operating system configuration for the client computers. RIS supports two types of client images: CD-ROM images and RIPrep images.

RIS Requirements

For RIS to successfully deploy client images to RIS clients, certain services must be available on your network.

RIS requires the following Windows 2000 services:

- **Active Directory**—Active Directory locates client computer accounts and RIS servers. It also manages RIS configuration settings and installation options.
- **DHCP**—Client computers use DHCP to obtain their IP addresses.
- **DNS**—Clients use DNS to locate Active Directory and other resources.

In addition, the RIS server requires at lease 2GB of free disk space for the source installation files. The hard disk must have two volumes as well, one for the operating system and one for the client images.

RIS clients must meet the hardware requirements of the operating system to be installed, of course. They must also support Pre-Boot Execution Environment (PXE) boot ROM version .99c or later. This enables the client computers to boot from their network adapter.

For client computers that do not support PXE, Windows 2000 provides a utility called RBFG.exe. This utility enables you to create a floppy disk to boot the computer to the network and contact AD and a RIS server. It's important to note that there is a limited set of network adapter drivers supported by this utility.

Installing and Configuring RIS

To install RIS, in Control Panel, open the Add/Remove Programs. Select the Remote Installation Services check box and click Next.

Once RIS is installed, you need to run the RIS Setup wizard to configure and start RIS.

To start the RIS Setup wizard, open a command prompt and type RISETUP and press Enter.

The RIS Setup wizard will start.

On the Remote Installation Folder Location screen, specify the NTFS partition and folder on the RIS server where the operating system installation files and your first CD-based client image are to be located. If you do not have an NTFS partition, the installation will not continue.

On the Initial Settings screen, specify how the RIS server will respond to RIS clients. You can specify that the RIS server will respond to all requests by checking the Respond to Client Computers Requesting Service check box. You can also specify that the RIS server will not respond to computers that do not have computer account in Active Directory. To do this, select the Do Not Respond to Unknown Client Computers check box.

On the Installation Source Files Location, specify where the Windows 2000 Professional source files are located.

On the Windows Installation Image Folder Name screen, specify the name of the folder where the initial CD-based client image is to be created.

Finally, on the Friendly Description and Help Text screen, specify a description that will be displayed via the Client Installation wizard. This helps the user select the appropriate image.

Authorizing the RIS Server in Active Directory

A RIS server must be authorized in Active Directory before it can begin responding to clients and remotely deploying Windows 2000 Professional or Windows XP Professional.

To authorize a RIS server, follow the same procedure found in the DHCP section earlier in this chapter.

Prestaging Computers

You can prestage a RIS client computer by preconfiguring a computer account and assigning it to the RIS server. Prestaging is used primarily for security purposes. When you select the Do Not Respond to Unknown Client Computers check box, prestaging allows you to control which computers are authorized to use RIS. You can also load-balance your RIS servers by specifying different RIS servers for each prestaged computer.

To prestage a computer, you need to know the globally unique identifier (GUID) for the computer. Manufacturers of PXE enabled clients place a label on the computer case with the GUID. If using a RIS startup disk, the GUID is simply the MAC address of the network card along with enough leading zeros so that the GUID is 32 characters long.

To prestage a RIS client, open Active Directory Users and Computers. Right-click the OU where the computer account will reside. Select New then click Computer.

The Create New Object —Computer dialog box appears. Enter the name of the computer and click Next.

Select the "This is a managed computer" check box and enter the GUID. Click on Next.

Specify the FQDN for the RIS server that will perform the install for this RIS client.

Finally, click on Next and then Finish.

Summary

This chapter delved into the various network services that are used in an Active Directory implementation.

DNS provides the overall framework for Active Directory. AD uses DNS to locate resources and services on the network. DNS also provides its traditional network function: *hostname resolution*.

DHCP provides an automated and efficient method for providing TCP/IP configuration to network devices. Configuration information such as IP addresses, subnet masks, domain names, default gateways, and DNS server IP addresses can be automatically distributed and updated throughout the network. DHCP and DNS work together to dynamically update DNS records for Windows clients and servers.

RIS is an optional network service that provides a quick and efficient way to install Windows 2000 Professional and Windows XP Professional clients. RIS requires that AD, DNS, and DHCP be installed on the network.

CASE STUDY

Learning by Example: The "Molly Pitcher Pharmaceuticals, Inc." Company

After reviewing the case study for Molly Pitcher Pharmaceuticals, Inc., there are some issues that need to be analyzed.

DNS: Implementing DNS at Molly Pitcher is relatively straightforward. Because there are no other DNS servers in the environment, such as Unix-based servers, you can choose to implement Active Directory-integrated zones. These zones enable Active Directory's replication engine to replicate zone data throughout the environment. Active Directory-integrated zones also provide a multimaster capability to DNS. This provides better fault tolerance over the traditional standard primary/standard secondary zone method of fault tolerance because there will always be a read-writable copy of the zone available.

As far as the implementation of the domain namespace, it was already decided that the forest root for Active Directory will be placed in a subdomain off of the existing external Internet domain, `mollypitcher.com`. This domain is to be called `ad.mollypitcher.com`. This is the single DNS domain required for this implementation.

Molly Pitcher has 13 sites in its environment. DNS servers will be placed on all Active Directory domain controllers. The domain controllers are being placed close to users to make DNS queries and authentication more efficient.

DHCP: DHCP needs to be implemented into the Molly Pitcher environment. At a minimum, there are 13 sites in their environment. The case study does not state how many subnets are located at each site. After requesting more information, you are told that there are five subnets at headquarters and one subnet at each site. As a result, you need to create 18 DHCP scopes. Each scope will be configured with the correct IP address range and subnet mask for each subnet. Some of the DHCP options that need to be defined are the default gateway (the local router interface), the DNS domain name (ad.mollypitcher.com), and the DNS server IP addresses (the local DNS server).

DHCP servers should be placed throughout the environment for fault tolerance. Although you need to create 18 scopes to provide DHCP functionality, more scopes might be needed to create fault tolerance. At headquarters, two DHCP servers can be implemented. For each headquarters' subnet, two scopes need to be created (10 total, five on each DHCP server). Each scope would contain 50% of the available IP addresses for the subnet and should not overlap. If one of the servers fails, the remaining DHCP server can still respond to requests. For the remaining sites, two DHCP servers can be implemented with a split scope (50% of addresses) on each.

Another possibility for fault tolerance is the use of the clustering service found in Windows 2000 Advanced Server.

Molly Pitcher has already deployed Windows 2000 Professional to all of its desktops, so RIS is not required. However, RIS could be implemented to make existing redeployments easier or if the organization plans to upgrade to Windows XP Professional.

Creating the Components Within the Active Directory

IN THIS CHAPTER

There are many types of objects that you can create and manage in the Active Directory. This chapter covers the most common features and functions that are managed in the Active Directory. These items are the creation and management of Organization Units, User Accounts, Groups, Computers, Printers, Shared Folders, and Contacts. All these objects enable you to configure the Active Directory for your individual use. This chapter also looks at objects that are published in the Active Directory.

Managing the Active Directory Users and Computers

Active Directory's management tool is a *Microsoft Management Console* (MMC) snap-in called Active Directory Users and Computers (see Figure 6.1). From it, you can create and manage all the objects in the directory. It is automatically created in the Administrative tools folder in the Start menu.

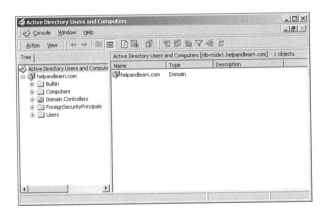

FIGURE 6.1
The Active Directory Users and Computers MMC.

Default Active Directory Configuration

After the first domain controller is installed, a default set of objects is created in the Active Directory. This is the starting place for the customization of Active Directory. These default objects are permanent and cannot be deleted.

You can create objects of any type in these containers: Computers, Domain Controllers, Foreign Security Principals, and Users. You can only create Computer, Group, and User objects in the Built-in container. These containers are described as follows:

- **Built-in**—This container stores all the default groups that are automatically created when you promote the server to a domain controller. These are the default set of groups that you can use to give permissions to users.

- **Computers**—This container is the default location for computers that are created in the Active Directory. This does not include domain controllers, which are stored in another container.

- **Domain Controllers**—This container is the default location for domain controllers that are created in the Active Directory. The first server you promote to install Active Directory is placed in this container.

- **Foreign Security Principals**—This container stores security access for objects outside the domain and forest. This is usually administered using the Active Directory Domains and Trusts MMC tool. You can still create the security principals in this container within the Active Directory Users and Computers.

- **Users**—This container is the default location for User and Group objects that are created in the Active Directory. User objects are security accounts that can be used to access resources within the Active Directory. When you promote the server to a domain controller, there are several default users and groups, including the Administrator User object and Domain Admin Group object.

However, using these default containers is not the best use of the Active Directory. The creation of organizational units is the preferred method of logically grouping objects together. Organization units are the basic building blocks of the Active Directory.

Active Directory Objects

There are many objects that you can create and manage using the Active Directory Users and Computers MMC. This is a list of the items that are covered in this chapter:

- **Computers**—This object controls information about a particular computer in the environment.

- **Contacts**—This object creates a directory entry that has information about a particular person who does not have a security principal in the environment. This is usually external people such as vendors, partners, and business associates.

- **Groups**—This object is a security principal that can contain other objects such as groups, computers, or users. They can be given security access to resources within the environment.

- **Organizational Units**—This object groups a logical set of objects together, such as computers, users, and organization units (OUs). This object can contain other objects, such as organizational units, which create a hierarchy within the domain. An important thing to remember about the OU object is that it is not a security principal. In other words, this object cannot be used to grant permissions to files, shares, and other objects. However, they do enable you to create administrative groupings by delegating control of the organizational unit. They also allow for group policies to be linked to the organizational unit, which enables you to manage the objects contained within.

- **Printer**—This object maps to a printer that is shared in the Active Directory so that users can easily search for and locate printers that match their requirements.

- **Shared Folders**—This object maps to server shares that have been published within the Active Directory so that users can more easily locate shared folders using the search capabilities.

- **Users**—This object describes users who access resources within the Active Directory. They are security principals that can be given access to resources such as shares and printers. The user object has attributes that are associated with the object, such as a password, an address, and group membership.

Organizational Units: Understanding the Concept

Organizational Units are a logical grouping of objects that have something in common. They might all be User objects for a particular location or objects that are used by the marketing group. One important thing about OUs is that they can contain other OUs. It is very much like a directory structure of a file system. Some of the more important benefits of using OUs are

- They can mirror the business effectively and more importantly change with the business as it changes.

- They can provide a hierarchy.

- They can link group policies to manage the objects contained.

- Objects within them can inherit security and configuration through their hierarchy.

- They can delegate administration.

Creating Organizational Units

> **NOTE**
>
> To run Active Directory Users and Computers (and other server-related functions) from a Windows 2000 Professional computer, you can install the Windows 2000 Administration Tools found on the Windows 2000 Server CD. Double-click admin-pak.msi.

You create Organizational Units using the Active Directory Users and Computers tool, as follows:

1. Open the Active Directory Users and Computers tool. You can do this by clicking the Start menu, and then clicking Programs, Administrative Tools. Then select the tool from the options.

2. Expand the domain similar to the way it's shown in Figure 6.2.

3. Right-click the domain and select New and click Organizational Unit (See Figure 6.2).

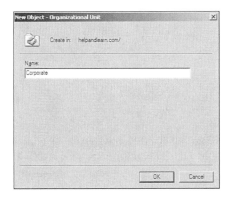

FIGURE 6.2

Creating an Organizational Unit.

4. Type the name of the OU corporate.

5. Click the OK button.

After the OU is created, you can find it in the Active Directory structure. This is the first step to creating the OU structure for the organization.

Organizational Unit Properties

After you create an OU, you can add other attributes to it. You can access these attributes by selecting the properties of the OU (right-click the OU and select Properties). It contains two main tabs:

• **General tab**—Here, you can enter the basic information about OU, including the address, city, state, ZIP, and country (see Figure 6.3).

FIGURE 6.3
Viewing an Organizational Unit's properties General tab.

- **Managed By tab**—Here, you can specify an owner or contact person who is responsible for the management of the OU. This information is linked to the user accounts information, including the office, street, city, state, and phone information (see Figure 6.4).

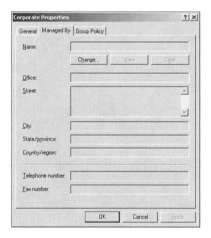

FIGURE 6.4
Viewing an Organizational Unit's properties Managed By tab.

Moving an Organizational Unit

The ability to move an organizational unit is very handy if your corporation reorganizes. This occurrence is quite common. Even when you move an OU, it retains the security and configuration items and doesn't take on the attributes of the new parent OU.

1. Open the Active Directory Users and Computers tool by clicking the Start menu, and then choosing Programs, Administrative Tools. Select the tool.

2. Expand the domain similar to Figure 6.5.

3. Right-click the OU then select the Move command.

4. Expand the containers and select the container to move the OU to (see Figure 6.5).

5. Click the OK button.

FIGURE 6.5
Moving an Organization Unit in Active Directory.

Renaming an Organization

How many times have you noticed that the names of departments change over time? Do you remember when Human Resources was called Personnel? Renaming OUs is as easy as renaming a file or directory.

1. Open the Active Directory Users and Computers tool by clicking the Start menu, and then choosing Programs, Administrative Tools. Select the tool.

2. Expand the domain.

3. Right-click the OU, and then select the Rename command.

4. Type the new name for the OU and press Enter.

Deleting an Organizational Unit

The permanent removal of OUs can happen from time to time. Be careful not to delete the objects that are contained within the OU, however. The objects will be deleted along with the OU and could cause you a headache. As a precaution, move the objects out of the OU before deleting it.

1. Open the Active Directory Users and Computers tool.

2. Expand the domain.

3. Right-click the OU then select the Delete command.

4. Click the Yes button to verify that you want to delete the OU.

5. If there are objects in the OU, you will be prompted to delete the objects inside the OU.

6. Click the Yes button.

Placement in Active Directory

The placement of OUs in the Active Directory is like the creation of folders and files on the file system. Instead of storing files, the OU contains objects such as Users and Groups. It is up to you how you want to organize the objects that will be created from users, computers, and many more. Organizational Units are the only objects that can contain other objects. So, think of the OU as the folder structure of the Active Directory. It enables you to create an administrative structure that best fits your organization.

Most often, companies break their OU structure into two main groups. The first is the alignment of objects based on location. This is useful for companies that tend to have groups that operate more on their own. An example of this is a plant where all the users have a common set of administrative and group policy requirements. This usually corresponds to an organization that has the manager of the plant that is responsible for all aspects of the production and financial goals.

The second is the alignment of objects based on function (see Figure 6.6). The function can include everyone in sales, for example, regardless of where they are located. The sales groups located around the country can be grouped together because they all have the same requirements from a management standpoint (such as laptops that need the same type of group policies).

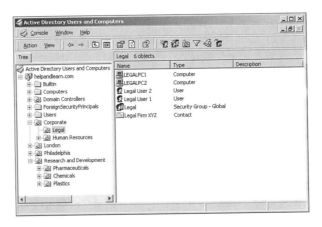

FIGURE 6.6

Organizing OUs based on function.

Planning Organizational Units

When designing the hierarchy of the OU, it's important to remember the basics of designing a system for use by an organization. There are three basic design principles to go by when working out the design.

The first principle is to bring to the table the key owners of the areas and to understand their requirements. This might be only the IT team or can include the sales director. It is also good to come to the table with many different designs. Be ready to listen and understand, and then design the users and administrators.

The second principle is to make the design simple. Don't overcomplicate the design with requirements that are not top priorities. This will skew the design in a direction that makes it impractical to use in the real world, no matter how good it looked on paper. Look for the simplest design that meets your needs. The more complicated the design the more work required to support the structure.

The final design principle is to make it consistent. The more consistent the design, the simpler it will be. There will always be exceptions to basic rules that you run across, but try to minimize them. Once there is a special situation for one group, then every group will want to have that special treatment. This can translate into simple concepts, such as having OUs that make logical sense (for instance, the OU called New Jersey is under the OU called United States).

Flexibility of OUs

One of the most important items about OUS is their ability to change as the organization changes. This morphing ability enables the system administrator to reorganize the structure quickly and efficiently. This is a much easier than having to redesign the domain, tree, or forest structure. This is why it is important to try to use the OU structure for the more volatile structure that changes rapidly. Most companies are reorganizing themselves very frequently within the current market of mergers and acquisitions. This process of changing the structure of the organization in the past has created many headaches for the IT departments.

When you move OUs from one location to another, their security is retained from the original parent OU. This is important to remember when restructuring the Active Directory.

Managing User Accounts

One of the most common tasks that will be done in the Active Directory is the management of User objects. This enables users to access resources in the domain. Without user accounts, this would be difficult.

Types of Logon Names

There are two types of logon names that you can use with Windows 2000 Server. The first is the User Logon Name method and the second is the new Windows 2000 User Principal Name. Both of these methods are valid to log in to the Active Directory but are used for different client platforms (see Figure 6.7). In Figure 6.7, you can see there is a field for User Logon Name. This is the new Windows 2000 logon method. There is also another field for User Logon Name (pre-Windows 2000). This is the backwards-compatible logon for clients who are not using Windows 2000.

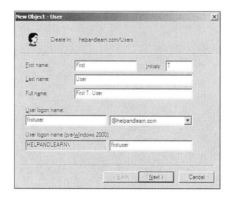

FIGURE 6.7
Displaying user account logon names in Active Directory.

User Logon Name Pre-Windows 2000

This method is a carry-over from the Windows NT domains, where users provided a username along with the domain that they are trying to log into. This method is required for clients using Windows 9x and Windows NT 4.0. In larger organizations with more than one domain, it was possible that domains could have the same user logon name. This made it sometimes troublesome when users tried to access resources contained in domains with the same name.

User Principal Names

This is the new method for logging in to the Active Directory. The new method looks like an e-mail address. An example of a User Principal Name is `firstuser@company.com`. The user can enter this information and a password and be authenticated in the Active Directory. There are two parts of the name. The first part (`firstuser`) is the prefix. The suffix (`@company.com`) comes from the root domain name when the account is created. You can have more than one suffix if you have a forest with other domain names. The User Principal Name must be unique within the forest. In other words, there cannot be more than one `firstuser@company.com`. This means you have a single sign-on to Active Directory.

Manipulating Users Accounts

Creating user accounts is one of the primary responsibilities of most system administrators. The accounts can be created quickly using the wizard within the Active Directory Users and Computers tool.

Creating a User

The following steps explain how to create a user account using the wizard. Later in this section, you'll learn about the user account's attributes.

1. Open the Active Directory Users and Computers tool.

2. Expand the domain.

3. Right-click the Built-in Users OU. Select the New option and then select the User object. The New object—User window will open (see Figure 6.8).

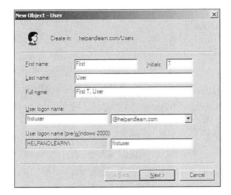

FIGURE 6.8

Creating a user account in Active Directory.

Fill in the following information:

First Name: First

Initials: T

Last Name: User

Full Name: Use the default

User Logon Name: firstuser

User Logon Name (Pre-Windows 2000): firstuser

4. Click the Next button to continue creating the user account (see Figure 6.9).

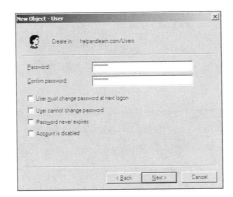

FIGURE 6.9
Specifying user account password requirements in Active Directory.

Fill in the following information:

Password: Type in a password

Confirm Password: Type in the same password again

5. Click the Next button to continue creating the user account.

6. This is the final step. Review the items in the window to verify that you have created the account with the correct information, and then click the Finish button.

Moving a User Object

The ability to move a user object is very handy when users move to new teams or locations. You can easily assign and move users to OUs within the same domain. To move objects between domains, you need the Windows 2000 Resource Kit tool (movetree.exe). This occurrence is quite common.

1. Open the Active Directory Users and Computers tool.

2. Expand the domain.

3. Right-click the user and then select the Move command.

4. Expand the containers and select the container you want to move the OU to.

5. Click the OK button.

Renaming a User Object

Like OUs, user objects can also be renamed. This can be very useful when a user is leaving the organization and someone is taking her place. Renaming the user object is much simpler than creating a new object along with its group assignments.

1. Open the Active Directory Users and Computers tool.
2. Expand the domain.
3. Right-click the OU then select the Rename command.
4. Type in the new name for the OU and press Enter.

Deleting a User Object

If a user leaves an organization, it is best to delete the user account for security reasons. It might be prudent to disable the account at first in case the account is needed at a later date.

> **NOTE**
>
> It is usually better to disable an account, and only delete the object when necessary. When you delete the user object it will delete the SID, and therefore lose all explicit permissions and group membership for the object. If this user were to come back you would have to reconfigure all permissions and group membership.

1. Open the Active Directory Users and Computers tool.
2. Expand the domain.
3. Right-click the OU and then select the Delete command.
4. Click the Yes button to verify that you want to delete the OU.
5. If there are objects in the OU, you will be prompted to delete them.
6. Click the Yes button.

Creating User Templates

Creating templates will quickly reduce the amount of time needed to create new accounts as long as there are similarities in the accounts that you are creating. Consider, for example, that each Human Resources user should be a member of the same few groups. By using a template you can automatically assign them the correct groups when the account template is copied. This saves you time and effort and ensures consistency across accounts.

User Account Basics

There are many more attributes associated with a User object than when you create an account. When you create an account in this chapter, you entered the minimum amount of information needed to create the account. This section reviews the other attributes you can store in the Active Directory by administering the account you just created.

1. Open the Active Directory Users and Computers tool.

2. Expand the domain to view all the built-in OUs.

3. Click the Built-in Users OU. Right-click the user account `firstuser` and select Properties.

Notice that there are quite a few tabs associated with this user object, most of which are discussed in the following sections.

General Tab

Using the General tab, you can associate more information with the user, including an account description, office location, telephone number, e-mail, and Web page (see Figure 6.10).

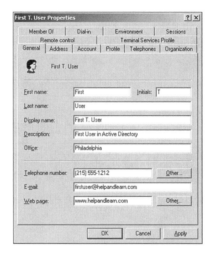

FIGURE 6.10

Viewing a user account's general information in Active Directory.

Address Tab

The Address tab allows you to store the address associated with the user.

Account Tab

This tab is similar to the account creation wizard used to create the account. You can control the account information, including user logon name, logon hours, where to log on to, account options, and account expiration (see Figure 6.11).

From this tab, you can disable the account or make the users change their passwords the next time they log on using the account.

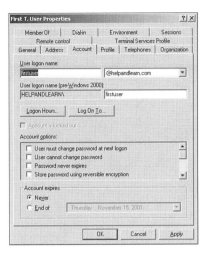

FIGURE 6.11

Viewing a user account's account information in Active Directory.

Telephones Tab

This tab lets you enter the associated contact information for the user account. This includes the home telephone, pager, mobile, fax, and IP phone. You can also specify more than one number for each of these. There is also an area for the administrator to enter notes about the account.

Organization Tab

This enables you to enter job-related information about the user associated with this account, including title, department, company, manager, and direct reports.

With this information you can create an organizational chart of the company using the manager and direct reports information contained within the Active Directory. The direct reports show up when you assign another user account that its manager was the firstuser (see Figure 6.12).

FIGURE 6.12
Viewing a user account's organization information in Active Directory.

Member Of Tab

This tab lists the groups that the user account is a member of (see Figure 6.13). This is where you can add users to groups to give them permission to resources in the environment.

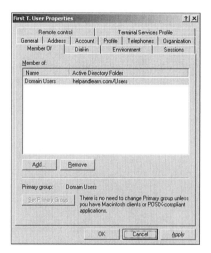

FIGURE 6.13
Viewing a user account's group membership information in Active Directory.

Profile Details

In the Profile tab, you can specify the location of the roaming or mandatory profile that a user can use when logging on to any computer in the organization (see Figure 6.14). Format this profile so that the server name, share and user name environment variable can be resolved to the actual name of the directory \\server\share\%username%. The roaming profile information is stored in this directory with all the information that is needed to make your settings travel from one computer to another. Items like your ntuser.dat file are stored here and are applied to the computer when you log on.

Mandatory profiles enable you to preconfigure a profile with specific settings, which are permanent settings for that user. The users cannot permanently change their profile's setting. To specify a mandatory profile, you need to rename the ntuser.dat file in the profile path to ntuser.man. This will prevent the users from making any permanent changes to the profile.

You also can specify a logon script in this area. Most likely the logon script will be assigned using a group policy that is associated with the OU. You can use batch files, command files, Visual Basic script files, JavaScript files, and executables for the logon script.

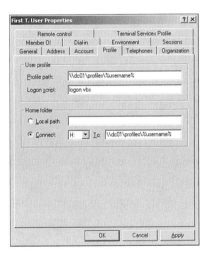

FIGURE 6.14

Viewing a user account's profile settings in Active Directory.

Home Directory Details

In the Profile tab you can specify the home path for personal data storage and application information. You should specify a drive letter to connect the home drive to along with the path location. This should be formatted, for example, like this \\server\share\%username%. You can connect to your home directory in your logon script by using the command `net use h:` `/home`. This will connect the H: drive to the path located in the Home folder To: section.

It's a good idea to provide users with a storage area on the server that is only usable by the users and not by any other account. This provides an area where users can store data that is regularly backed up.

Remote Access Services Details

The ability to access the network using a modem is a key feature for users who are working out of the office or permanently in an off-site environment. This enables such employees to access the resources on the network, like network share, printers, and electronic mail.

Dial-in Tab

The Remote Access Permissions enable you to set up the user account individually for access or denial of access to the remote access services (see Figure 6.15). The default is to control access through remote access policy, which is an easy way to set up many users for remote access. You can also override this policy if you do not want someone to be able to remotely access the network. You can specify a static IP address to such users when they dial in or can use DHCP to assign an address automatically every time users dial in. You can also specify static IP routes that will allow TCP/IP packets to transit remote networks.

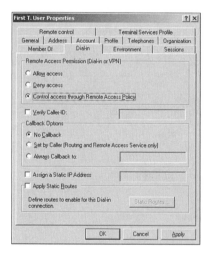

FIGURE 6.15

Viewing a user account's dial-in settings in Active Directory.

For more protection from individuals who might be trying to improperly access the dial-in capabilities of the server, you can require verification of the caller ID of the remote user. This prevents the users from using any other telephone line to dial in to the system. This also requires the modem to understand the caller-ID information passed by the telephone company. This is useful when the user dials from the same telephone line each time they access the network remote. You can also set up a callback option whereby the user dials in and is verified by the remote access server. The server calls back the user at a predetermined telephone number and connects the user remotely to the network. This also prevents the user from using any other telephone line to dial in to the system.

Terminal Server Details

Terminal services is a vital component in Windows 2000 that delivers the Windows graphical user interface via a client/server model. Terminal services can be used as an application server or used to remotely administer other servers in the network.

As an application server, administrators do not have to install Windows-based 32-bit applications on each desktop computer. Instead, the application is installed once on the server, and the clients automatically have access to the new or upgraded software package through the terminal services client software. This allows desktops that might not meet the application's hardware or software requirements to utilize the application.

For remote administration, administrators can connect to the server or workstation via terminal services. The administrator sees the server's desktop. At that point, he or she can monitor or configure the server as needed.

Terminal Services Profile Tab

In the Terminal Services Profile section, you can specify a specific roaming or mandatory profile path for terminal services to utilize. This should be formatted so that the server name, share, and user name environment variable can be resolved to the actual name of the directory \\server\share\%username%. The roaming profile information is stored in this directory with all the information that is needed to make your settings travel from one computer to another. Items like your ntuser.dat file are stored here and are applied to the terminal connection when you log on.

The Terminal Services Profile uses the information specified in the Profile Tab for the profile path if the Terminal Services Profile is not specified.

The Terminal Services Home Directory is used for personal data storage and application information.

The Terminal Services Home Directory uses the information specified in the Profile Tab for the home directory if the Terminal Services Home Directory is not specified (see Figure 6.16).

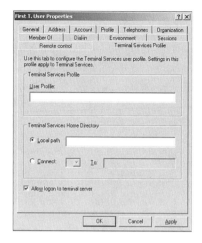

FIGURE 6.16

Viewing a user account's Terminal Services Profile settings in Active Directory.

Remote Control Tab

The ability to control a terminal session remotely is a very efficient way to help users who might be facing issues or problems. This can be enabled or disabled using the Enable Remote Control check box (see Figure 6.17). The Require User's Permission check box prevents someone from connecting to a session without the users knowledge. You can also specify the level of the control you'll have over the user's session. You can either view it or actively interact with the session. The view capability enables you to remotely control, but not actively use, the session. The active interact option enables you to work with the user in the session and use the session.

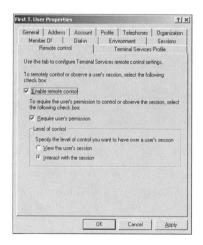

FIGURE 6.17

Viewing a user account's remote access settings in Active Directory.

Environment Tab

From the Environment Tab, you can configure the Terminal Services startup environment (see Figure 6.18). The environment controls how the users can start an application at logon. This is specified within the program's filename and can be started in a specific directory. This enables a terminal service user to connect to a specific application every time they connect.

The Environment tab also provides for some client device items to be connected, such as the client local drives, client printers, and default printer. The Connect to the Client Local Drive option is only available using third-party terminal services like Citrix Metaframe. The connection to the local printers is available for the Microsoft Terminal Services client. The ability to utilize the local printers is a great benefit from setting up the printers on the server.

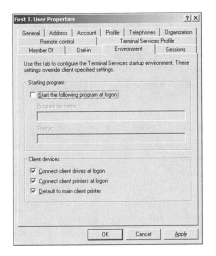

FIGURE 6.18
Viewing a user account's terminal services environment settings in Active Directory.

Sessions Tab

The Sessions tab controls how long a session will be available if the user gets disconnected from the session for any reason (see Figure 6.19).

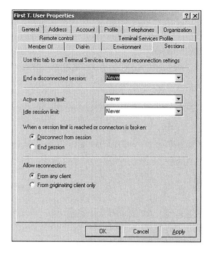

FIGURE 6.19

Viewing a user account's terminal services session settings in Active Directory.

Placement in Active Directory

User accounts can be placed in any of the built-in containers in the Active Directory. But in actual practice you will find that creating OUs to organize the users, groups, and computers will make the administration of the Active Directory more efficient.

All the objects in the Active Directory can be easily moved between OUs depending on the business's requirements. This enables the quick and easy reorganization of the administrative model depending on changes in the business. The one rule is to keep the structure simple and effective for the environment that it is supporting. The more complicated the design, the more difficult it is to support.

Take for example Figure 6.20, which shows OUs for the Corporate and Research areas of this company. Under the first level are the departments that make up those different groups. The Legal group has users, computers, groups, and contacts contained within one OU. This could have easily been created without the Legal and Human Resources OUs and had all the Corporate objects under the Corporate OU. This is where the structure has to fit the organization.

Creating the Components Within the Active Directory

CHAPTER 6

139

6

CREATING THE
COMPONENTS
WITHIN THE ACTIVE
DIRECTORY

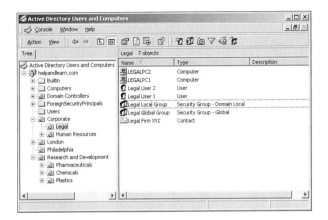

FIGURE 6.20
Viewing a user account's terminal services session settings in Active Directory.

You might have a need to set the structure via location. This is another strategy that works well for organizations. The logical grouping of objects based on the location and then the groups at those locations allows for another easy administrative model. In this case, all the objects for both Human Resources and Legal are contained in one OU.

Understanding Groups

Why are groups so important in Active Directory? The obvious reason is that they make administration much easier. Consider having to give permissions to each user for a specific resource. With the use of groups, this task can be greatly reduced. For example, the Research group could have a file share on the network that they all need access to. The creation of a group and assignment of permissions to this resource then makes the addition and removal of permissions to the Research team much easier. There always seems to be someone coming and going from any company all the time. Without this administration would be a nightmare.

Group Types

There are two types of groups that can be created. They are both similar in that they can contain other objects like users, contacts, and groups. Security Groups can be used to assign permissions to resources within the Active Directory or file system. Distribution groups are not security principals and cannot be used to assign permissions to resources. This is the fundamental difference between the two groups.

Security

These groups are security principals and can be used to assign permissions to resources within the Active Directory and file system. This will be the most common group used for administrative purposes. These groups are most often used to enable a team to access a resource like a share or printer.

There is also the ability to send e-mail to the group as long as the e-mail attribute is set on the members of the group.

The Contacts object can also be placed within a security group; however, the permissions will not apply to the contact because a contact does not have a security principal.

Distribution

These groups are not security principals and cannot be assigned to resources within the Active directory or file system. They are used as distribution lists like their counterparts in pervious versions of Exchange. They can contain user and contacts and can be easily used to send e-mail.

When the Active Directory is running in mixed mode, you cannot convert groups from Security to Distribution and vice versa. However, if you run in native mode, you can then exchange the groups between the two.

Group Scope

The second part of a group is the scope in which it can work. The scope determines which objects can be members of the group and the level of security applied to the group. There are three group scopes: domain local, global, and universal.

Domain Local

The scope of a local group is restricted to the domain in which it was created. These groups should be used to assign access to file-system resources. It allows for one layer of abstraction so that the use of global and universal groups can be easily added and removed from the local resources. They can contain global groups, universal groups, and user accounts.

Global

The scope of the global group is restricted to the domain in which it was created. These groups are commonly used to assign permissions for specific jobs like a recruiter. The group can be used to give permissions to the recruiting group by nesting the group within a domain local group that has permission to the file system.

Universal

The scope of a universal group is not restricted by domain and can contain groups from multiple domains along with other universal groups. Universal groups will not be available for use until the Active Directory is in native mode. Using universal groups has some impact on the

Creating the Components Within the Active Directory
CHAPTER 6

141

6

CREATING THE
COMPONENTS
WITHIN THE ACTIVE
DIRECTORY

Active Directory replication, because the group needs to be replicated to all domains along with the members of the group.

Group Changes

When the Active Directory is in native mode, the following rules apply to modifying the scope of a group.

- Domain local groups can be converted to universal groups as long as the domain local group does not contain any other domain local groups.

- Global groups can be converted to universal groups as long as they are not members of any other groups.

Creating Groups

The following steps enumerate the procedure of creating a group using the wizard. The attributes of a group object are covered later in this section.

1. Open the Active Directory Users and Computers tool.

2. Expand the domain to view all the containers.

3. Right-click on the user container and select New Group.

4. Type in the Group Name Executives (see Figure 6.21).

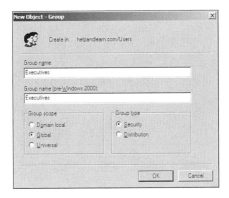

FIGURE 6.21

Creating a group in Active Directory.

5. Type in the Group Name (Pre-Windows 2000).

6. Select the Group Scope Global.

7. Select the Group Type Security.

8. Click the OK button.

Group Basics

This section reviews the group attributes you can set in the Active Directory.

1. Open the Active Directory Users and Computers tool.

2. Expand the domain to view all the built-in OUs.

3. Click the Built-in Users OU. Right-click the group object Executives and select Properties.

You will notice there are quite a few tabs associated with this group object, described here:

- **General Tab**—The general tab enables you to change the pre-Windows 2000 group name; however, you cannot change the group name for Active Directory (see Figure 6.22). The description better describes the purpose of the group and its function. You can add an e-mail address for the group, which allows messages to be sent to the members of the group. Because the domain is in native mode, you can change the group scope and group type. These options would not be present if the domain was in mixed mode.

FIGURE 6.22

Viewing the General tab of a group.

- **Members Tab**—This tab lists the members of this group. Currently there is only one user account that is a member but the membership can contain any object that is permitted for the scope and type of the group. You can use the Add or Remove buttons to modify the membership of this group (see Figure 6.23).

Creating the Components Within the Active Directory

CHAPTER 6

143

6

CREATING THE
COMPONENTS
WITHIN THE ACTIVE
DIRECTORY

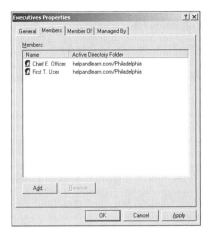

FIGURE 6.23
Viewing the Members tab of a group.

- **Member Of Tab**—This tab lists the groups that this object is a member of (see Figure 6.24). Membership can include any object that is permitted for the scope and type of the group. You can use the Add or Remove buttons to modify the membership of this group.

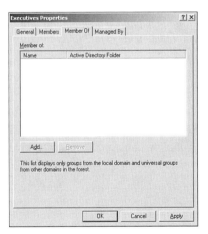

FIGURE 6.24
Viewing the Members Of tab of a group.

- **Managed By Tab**—From here, you can specify an owner or contact person who is responsible for the management of the group. This information is linked to the user account's information, which includes office, street, city, state, and phone information.

Group Nesting Capabilities

The ability to nest a group depends on the mode that the Active Directory is currently in, whether it be mixed or native.

Mixed Mode

In Active Directory mixed mode, the following rules apply to the objects that can be contained within the group scope:

- **Global**—User accounts within the same domain
- **Domain Local**—User accounts and global groups from any domain in the forest
- **Universal**—Only support the group type distribution. Does not support the group type security

Native Mode

In Active Directory native mode, the following rules apply to the objects that can be contained within the group scope.

- **Global**—User accounts and global groups
- **Domain Local**—User accounts, domain local groups from the same domain, global groups, and universal groups from any domain in the forest

Group Placement in Active Directory

Group objects should be placed according to the OU planning that was performed. The careful consideration of the objects and their locations should be done when the OU structure is discussed. This will make administering the system much more efficient. The principles for keeping the design simple still apply. Many organizations group the objects together based on the location or by functionality. For example, if there was a New Jersey OU, all the objects from users, computers, and groups would be contained within this container for the users who meet the criteria of working in New Jersey.

Planning Groups

When using groups in the Active Directory, it takes some time to address the needs of the organization along with using the preferred method of using the domain local, global, and universal groups.

Mixed Mode

Use the practice of granting security access to resources with domain local groups, and then placing global groups in domain local groups, and finally placing users in global groups.

The following reflects how groups should be planned in mixed mode: Resources <- Domain Local Groups <- Global Groups <- Users

Native Mode

The same rule applies in native mode, as it does in mixed mode for assigning permissions to resources. With native mode, there is another option that is similar: Universal groups. Universal groups allow you to assign permissions for users in a forest-wide basis.

Use the practice of granting security access to resources with domain local groups, and then placing global groups in domain local groups. Next, place universal groups in global groups and finally users in universal groups.

The following reflects how groups should be planned in native mode: Resources <- Domain Local Groups <-Global Groups <- Universal Groups <- Users

Using good naming standards also helps to organize your groups.

Understanding Computers in Active Directory

Computers objects are created in the Active Directory so that actual computers can be installed and joined to the domain. You can create the accounts before the computer joins or while it is joining. When using remote installation services, it's very helpful to create the computer accounts before the computer is installed. Computer accounts enable you to manage the computer from any location in the domain as long as the user has permissions to perform the tasks.

Creating Computers

These steps enumerate the procedure of creating a computer Account using the wizard. The attributes related to this account are covered later in this section.

1. Open the Active Directory Users and Computers tool.
2. Expand the domain to view all the containers.
3. Right-click the Computers Container and select New Computer.
4. Type in the Computer Name PC01 (see Figure 6.25).

FIGURE 6.25

Creating a computer account in Active Directory.

   5. Type in the Computer Name (pre-Windows 2000).

   6. Do not check Allow pre-Windows 2000 computers to use this account. This is for backwards-compatible computers to utilize the computer object.

   7. Click the OK button.

Computer Basics

This section reviews the computer-related attributes that you can store in the Active Directory.

   1. Open the Active Directory Users and Computers tool.

   2. Expand the domain to see all the built-in OUs.

   3. Click the Built-in Computer OU. Right-click the computer object PC01 and select Properties.

Notice there are quite a few tabs associated with this computer object, as follows.

- **Computer General tab**—Here, you can describe the function of the computer (see Figure 6.26), as well as set up the computer to access other computers in the environment (so it can request services from other computers).

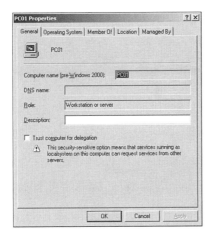

FIGURE 6.26

Viewing the General tab of a computer account.

- **Operating System tab**—This tab contains the name of the operating system, its version, and service pack (see Figure 6.27).

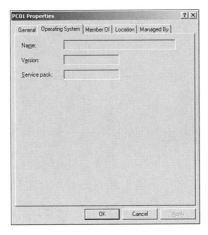

FIGURE 6.27

Viewing the Operating System tab of a computer account.

- **Member Of tab**—This tab displays the groups of which the Computer object is a member (see Figure 6.28). You can assign a computer with security privileges. Computer can have rights like User and Group objects.

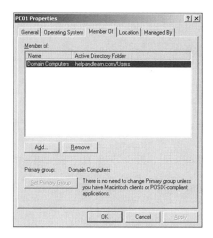

FIGURE 6.28

Viewing the Member Of tab of a computer account.

- **Location tab**—This tab enables you to set a particular administrative-designated location for the computer (see Figure 6.29).

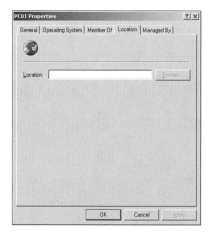

FIGURE 6.29

Viewing the Location tab of a computer account.

Placement in Active Directory

Computer objects should be placed in the OU structure that best fits the design previously described in the Organization Unit considerations.

Managed Computers

You can specify how specific objects will be managed within the Active Directory. By setting the Managed By information, you can determine who is responsible for the management of the computer (see Figure 6.30).

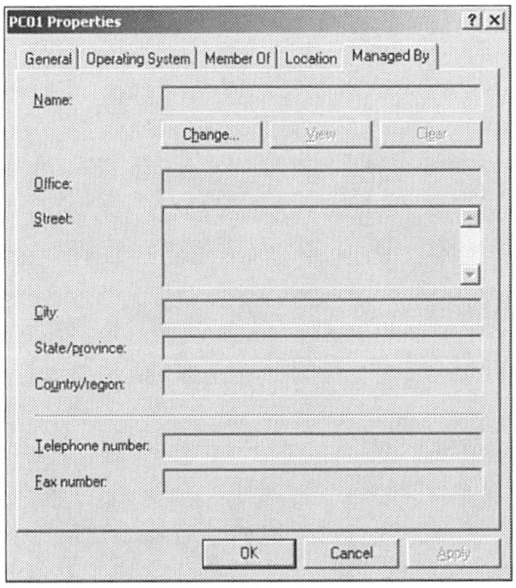

FIGURE 6.30

Viewing the Managed By tab of a computer account.

The ability to manage computers is defined by the local administrators group. By placing a global group into the local administrator group in the computer, you can remotely administer many features in Windows 2000 without having to go to the computer. This is very effective and has been used extensively by companies to reduce the amount of desktop support required. Windows 2000 includes support for Windows Management Instrumentation (WMI). WMI an initiative to establish standards for accessing and sharing management information over an enterprise network. Through WMI the computer is remotely manageable more than ever before.

To manage a desktop remotely within Active directory, you right-click the computer and select Manage. The Computer Management MMC will allow you to manipulate the key local computer objects (see Figure 6.31).

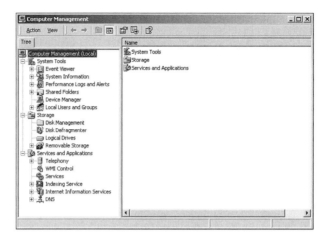

FIGURE 6.31

Accessing the Computer Management MMC.

Using Printers in Active Directory

So, why would you place a printer in Active Directory? This is a very good question. The main reason is that it makes finding a printer easier. In the past, printers were sometimes difficult to locate in the domain. You needed to know the server it was attached to, but that did not always mean that you knew where the printer was located in the building. When you place a printer in the Active Directory, you can now search more easily using the printer's attributes, such as location, model, or other features.

Publishing a Printer

These steps enumerate the procedure of creating a computer account using the wizard. The printer attributes are covered later in this section.

1. Open the Printers control panel from the Start menu.
2. Open a Printer currently created.
3. Click the Sharing tab.
4. Check the List in the Directory check box (see Figure 6.32).

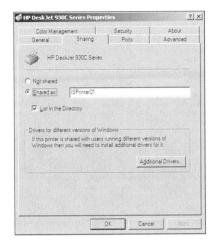

FIGURE 6.32
Publishing a Printer object in Active Directory.

5. Click the OK button.

Printer Search in Active Directory

These steps enumerate the procedure of searching for a printer in the Active Directory.

1. Open the Find Printers Search items from the Start menu search.

   Printer Tab: The ability search on the model or location of a printer is vital when there are hundreds of printers in an organization. A quick and easy searching by floor can yield a list of printers located near the user. The ability to search by the model of the printer is helpful if you know the model of the printer you're looking for. More importantly, the combination of these two pieces of information can narrow down the options quickly (see Figure 6.33).

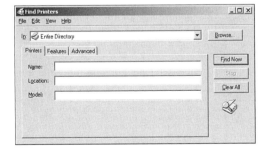

FIGURE 6.33
Searching for printers in Active Directory.

The ability to search for printers based on the features the printer possesses is important. Trying to locate a color printer or one that prints a specific paper size is now easy. Trying to locate these printers the old way could take significantly more time. The features of the printer appear in the Active Directory to make the life easier for all (see Figure 6.34).

FIGURE 6.34

Searching for printer features in Active Directory.

2. After entering the criteria for the search, Click the Find Now button.

Security of Printers in Active Directory

A printer's security permission determines who can print to the printer and who cannot. The default printer security is set up so that everyone can print to the printer and the printer operators and server operators can manage the printer and its documents (see Figure 6.35). This might not be the case for all printers shared in the organization. There are many cases where you might want to restrict who can print to certain printers, such as color or high-volume printers dedicated to specific groups.

FIGURE 6.35

Modifying printer security settings.

Planning Printers

Printer planning in the Active Directory is mostly focused around properly identifying the printers and their associated information. The quick ability to search the directory for printers that match the criteria is the key to planning for printers.

Using Shared Folders

Shares are an important resource that seems to be lost very easily. In organizations with hundreds of shares, it's imperative that they be easily located. Active Directory makes this easier by enabling users to look at items not by server but by an intuitive OU structure.

Creating a Share

These steps enumerate the procedure of creating a share using the wizard. The share attributes are covered later in this section.

1. Open the Active Directory Users and Computers tool.

2. Expand the domain to view all the containers.

3. Right-click the User Container and select New Share.

4. Type the Name of the Share (see Figure 6.36).

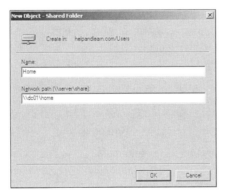

FIGURE 6.36

Creating a share.

5. Type the network path of the share.

6. Click the OK button.

Security of Shares in Active Directory

You set the security for a share on the local computer that uses the share. The existence of the share in the Active Directory no way influences the ability of a security principal to access the share. The configuration will continue to be done by managing the local computer, and then publishing the share within the Active directory.

Planning Shares

Using shares to access resources on a server will evolve in the coming years. The introduction of Windows 2000 and the fully aware DFS client has helped to centralize all shared resources in the environment. Also, the merging of the Exchange Web Store to utilize the network protocol has helped to blur the line of file services. Using publishing shares in the directory makes resources more company wide but also adds some confusion in the naming of the share. A company-wide look at resources might show that there are many items with the same name. A good standard will help to clarify the data contained within.

Using Contacts in Active Directory

Contacts in the Active Directory allow for the population of external resources that do not have security privileges within the current environment. These are key to be able to identify vendors, business partners, and external contacts. The feature is implemented to support Exchange 2000, which has moved its directory services to the Active Directory away from its own services. The ability to enter the information means better support for virtual organizations.

Creating a Contact

These steps enumerate the procedure of creating a contact using the wizard. The contact-related attributes are covered later in this section.

1. Open the Active Directory Users and Computers tool.
2. Expand the domain to view all the containers.
3. Right-click the Users Container and select New Contact.
4. Type the following information

    First Name: Hardware

    Initial: T

    Last Name: Vendor

Full Name: Hardware T. Vendor

Display Name: Hardware T. Vendor

5. Click the OK button (see Figure 6.37).

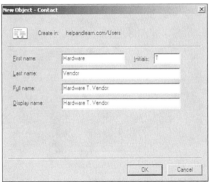

FIGURE 6.37
Creating a contact in Active Directory.

Contact Basics

This section reviews the various contact-related attributes you can store in the Active Directory.

1. Open the Active Directory Users and Computers tool.

2. Expand the domain to see all the built-in OUs.

3. Click the Built-in User OU. Right-click the Contact object Hardware T. Vendor and select Properties.

Notice there are quite a more few tabs associated with this contact object, which are described as follows:

- **Contact General tab**—From here, you can add descriptive information for the contact, including the office location, telephone number, e-mail address, and Web page (see Figure 6.38). Although these fields aren't required, it is recommended that you fill them out so the contact can be more easily reached.

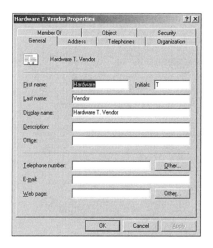

FIGURE 6.38
Viewing the General Tab of a Contact object

- **Address tab**—Contains the contact's address and other methods of communication (see Figure 6.39).

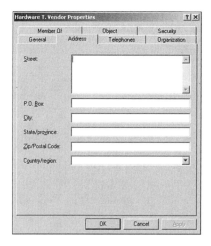

FIGURE 6.39
Viewing the Address tab of a contact object.

- **Telephones tab**—The Telephones tab contains the contact's various phone numbers (see Figure 6.40). You can include home, mobile, pager, fax, and IP phone numbers.

Creating the Components Within the Active Directory

CHAPTER 6

157

6

CREATING THE
COMPONENTS
WITHIN THE ACTIVE
DIRECTORY

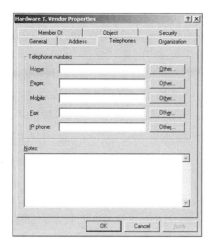

FIGURE 6.40

Viewing the Telephones tab of a contact object.

- **Organization tab**—The Organization tab contains the key information about the contact, including title, department, and company name. You can also specify a hierarchy for the contact (see Figure 6.41). This can be a user object or another contact object. Either would enable the reader to understand the reporting structure of the company.

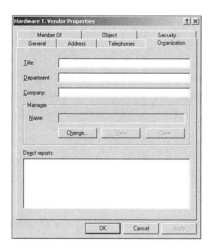

FIGURE 6.41

Viewing the Organization tab of a contact object.

- **Member Of tab**—The Member Of tab provides information about the groups that the contact is a member of (see Figure 6.42), whether it be a Distribution or Security group.

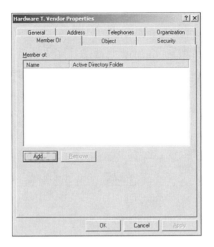

FIGURE 6.42
Viewing the Member Of tab of a contact object.

Contacts are not security principals and do not have access to resources in the environment. They can become members of either Security or Distribution groups but retain none of the permissions.

Planning Contacts

Using contacts in the directory, which is nothing new within e-mail systems, is changing the way partners, vendors, and business contacts affect the planning for the extended work force. Using contacts in the directory will only continue to grow and expand the capabilities of connectivity for all systems.

When planning contacts, you should keep all the contacts in one location that can be easily identified as external to the company. Or, you can place the contacts where the resource is playing a role in the organization. Managing contacts is a complex process. The most important point to remember is to assign a person who is responsible for the contained information to these contacts and to periodically review the continued need for the directory entry.

Summary

This chapter provided a walk-through for creating and managing the various objects found in Active Directory. Many of these objects comprise the heart and soul of Active Directory, such as Organizational Units, Users, Groups, and Computer Objects. Through these objects, you can use Active Directory to centrally manage an organization's IT infrastructure.

Creating the Components Within the Active Directory

CHAPTER 6

159

6

CREATING THE
COMPONENTS
WITHIN THE ACTIVE
DIRECTORY

CASE STUDY

Learning by Example: The "Molly Pitcher Pharmaceuticals, Inc." Company

After reviewing the case study for Molly Pitcher Pharmaceuticals, Inc., there are some issues that need to be analyzed.

Organizational Units: Organizational Units provide a method for the logical grouping of objects, such as departments. At Molly Pitcher, there are several departments located at headquarters, as well as 12 remote offices. You have several ways to create the organizational unit structure. First, you can create high-level OUs for headquarters and the remote offices. In the headquarters OU, you can create the department OUs. Another option is to create OUs for the departments and the remote offices.

To determine which structure is better, you need to determine whether there are any policies and where they need to be implemented. For example, if there are separate policies for each site and headquarters, the former structure makes better sense. If policies are defined domain-wide, the OU structure will not be as critical. In the case of Molly Pitcher, there will be a single domain policy. Also, all employees at the remote offices are from the Sales and Marketing department. You can simply create OUs for the various departments, ignoring the various sites.

Users: User objects will be created within the user's respective department OU. You must decide on a naming standard for users, such as first initial, last name (for example, `nalcott` for the user Neall Alcott).

Groups: It's important to realize the difference between groups and OUs in Active Directory. Although both are used to organize users with similar needs, groups are used to assign permissions to resources. OUs are used to organize AD, administer policies, and delegate authority.

So, in the case of Molly Pitcher, groups need to be created to provide access to resources. At the least, one group should be created for each department. This will allow department users to be given permissions to department resources.

Groups should be administered in the following order: Resources <- Domain Local Groups <- Global Groups <- Users.

Let's take a moment to walk through this process, where you will provide access to a server in the IT department to IT users.

First, you need to create a global group called "IT Users". Place user accounts for members of the IT department into the IT Users group.

Next, create a domain local group called "IT Server Access". Place the IT Users global group into the "IT Server Access" domain local group.

Finally, on the IT server, assign the appropriate permissions to the IT Server Access group for any resources.

Supporting Active Directory Environments

IN THIS CHAPTER

Chapter 6 discussed how to create the various objects in an Active Directory. This chapter discusses how to use those objects to support an active production environment.

This chapter focuses on practical operations techniques. It discusses:

- **Flexible Single Master Operations (FSMOs)**—what they are and why and how you should use them
- **Delegation of control**—Why and how you do it, as well as why you might consider making changes to your system's basic security authorizations
- **Group policy objects**—What you really set in them and why you set them at the various levels
- **Scripting**—What you should use it for and why
- **Interoperability services**—Which services are available and what functional role do they serve on your network

Throughout this chapter, you will learn about specific reasons and conditions that force you to "draw outside the lines" of the tools Active Directory has to offer.

Using Flexible Single Master Operations (FSMOs)

In any multimaster database design, there are a few functions that you want one machine to be responsible for. Things like granting ranges of SIDs or answering downlevel requests for a PDC. These single master operations are assigned to the various Flexible Single Master Operations (FSMO) services.

This section discusses:

- What these services are
- Where you should locate them
- How do you plan around them

FSMOs are fortunately rather simple in both function and design. They also require very little in the way of operational assistance, because almost everything about them is handled within the normal operations of the operating system.

What Are FSMOs?

FSMOs are services that perform specific functions that must be done by a single system in either a domain or a forest context. They use up very little memory, almost no processor power to speak of, and are usually inactive except under specified circumstances. They fail over automatically when their server is not operational, are self-healing in case of software disasters, and even back their data up on a fairly regular basis without intervention.

In short, they are very nearly the perfect infrastructure service—quiet, functional, redundant, and most importantly—hands off.

> **CAUTION**
>
> It is highly unlikely that the average administrator could do enough damage to a FSMO service to jeopardize the network. However, don't try it. FSMOs do important things that you want your network to continue doing, so don't go around randomly "optimizing" them out of service.

What do they do that's so important?

There are two FSMOs with a forest-wide scope:

- **Schema Master**—Holds information about the forest-wide schema. All schema changes happen on this server, before they are propagated to any other DC.
- **Domain Name Master**—Holds information about the forest-wide namespace. This server is the only one that can add a domain to the forest, and there it must be available when adding or removing domains.

There are three FSMOs with a domain-wide scope:

- **RID Master**—Allocates RID pools to all of the domain controllers in the domain. RIDs (relative Ids) are combined with the domain SID to create unique SIDs for every object.
- **PDC Emulator**—Acts as the central timeserver, the central point of contact for verifying bad passwords, and as authoritative information provider for account lockout information. It also responds to downlevel client and BDC requests for information.
- **Infrastructure Master**—Used to access GUIDs in other domains. It should not be run on a global catalog server.

Where Should You Locate FSMOs?

Now that you know what FSMOs are, what do you do with them? The answer, honestly, is as little as possible. They don't need you to do much with them, and you don't want to start playing around with them and accidentally shut down your network.

That being said, all of your network servers need to get access to the FSMOs at one time or another. This means that wherever you locate the FSMO services, it needs to be:

- Highly available to all network sites
- Quickly available to all network sites
- Quickly available to other servers in case of failover

In other words, take two of those low-end servers that you're going to replace and turn them into FSMO servers. Your users will thank you. Your FSMOs will thank you.

Typically, you will take these two servers, place them in your data center, and ignore them. This is actually a perfectly fine way to handle the "FSMO problem."

It is important to realize that the FSMO services demonstrate such a low utilization pattern that, for that most part, putting them on their own servers (even low-end ones you were going to throw in the closet) is probably a waste of electricity. It's easy enough to save the couple of dollars it costs to run the things every month by running the services off of, say, a file and print server instead.

Planning for Your FSMOs

Given how easy these things are to deal with, you might wonder what kind of planning is really required for FSMOs. You can simply throw them up and forget about them, right?

Mostly, it is that simple. Unless you've decided to go with the so-called "empty root" forest design. In this case (in which you have a single root domain called something like corp.root and your actual domain), you do need to be a bit more careful about where you place your FSMOs and what you decide to do with them. Specifically:

- You need to have at least two servers in the root domain (both domain controllers). This allows for failover of both the schema-wide FSMOs and the root domain's AD structure.
- You need to make sure that the root domain's schema FSMO roles are available to the entire forest. This means that you cannot just shut the root domain down and put the machines in a closet. You can, however, put them into a quiet (but not dusty) corner of your data center.
- You need to decide what you are going to do with the domain-wide FSMOs for your usable domain. Typically, this means taking another low-end server or two and making sure that they stay somewhere safe. Perhaps next to the domain controllers for the root domain is a good choice.

In the case of an empty root forest structure, you will probably end up putting the domain-wide FSMOs on a file and print server located in your data center. There is no harm in this at all. In fact, in a reasonably small network (say less than 10,000 nodes), it's probably the most sensible idea in the first place.

Delegating Control

In most IT organizations there are a variety of administrative, security, and organizational levels. These levels tend to correspond to job functions, so people who administer print servers have one profile, whereas those who answer front line support questions have another.

In Windows NT, it is difficult to granularly allocate administrative privilege. You either have to resort to third-party utilities, complex ASDI scripting, grant almost no privileges whatsoever, or simply accept the fact that one in every two of your help desk employees was going to have domain administrator rights.

With the coming of a real relational database for your directory service in Windows 2000, you have more choices. Specifically, you can actually assign rights to particular user attributes. Thus, you can give one person the ability to update ZIP codes, and another person the ability to change passwords. You can assign these rights by individual or by security group. This gives you a level of administrative granularity that you simply did not have in previous Microsoft products.

Using the Wizard

However, you don't just go into the schema and start assigning rights. That would be overly complex for most of your needs. In fact, Microsoft has created a Delegate Control wizard that can handle most common tasks for you.

The Wizard is accessible through the Active Directory Users and Computers MMC (see Figure 7.1). Just open it and right-click on any of the OUs.

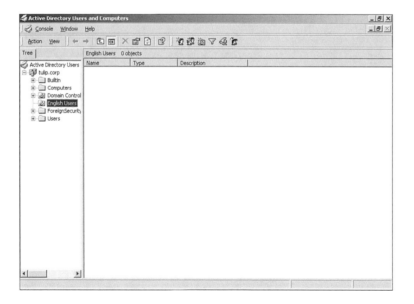

FIGURE 7.1
Active Directory users and computers MMC.

Then select Delegate Control (see Figure 7.2).

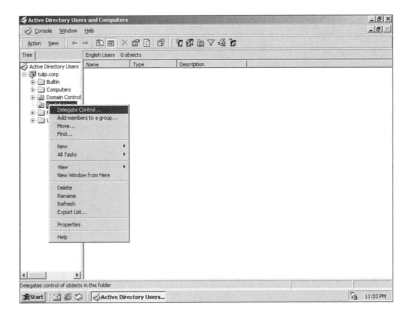

FIGURE 7.2

Activating the Delegate Control wizard.

After the screen telling you what the wizard does (see Figure 7.3) and selecting a delegate (Figure 7.4), you can either delegate the common tasks listed (see Figure 7.5), or select Custom, press Next, select the targets, and then select a more complex delegation (see Figure 7.6).

FIGURE 7.3

The Delegate Control Wizard explanation screen.

Supporting Active Directory Environments

CHAPTER 7

167

7

SUPPORTING
ACTIVE DIRECTORY
ENVIRONMENTS

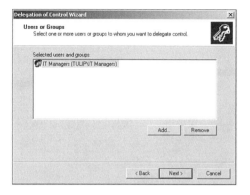

FIGURE 7.4

Selecting a group to grant permissions to—in this case IT managers.

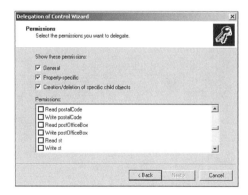

FIGURE 7.5

Selecting from the common task list.

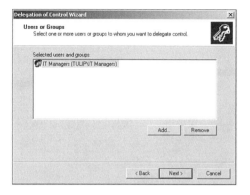

FIGURE 7.6

Creating your own permissions for delegation.

Whichever you choose, you will eventually reach a screen that summarizes the changes that you have requested (see Figure 7.7). Read this screen carefully; you don't want to make changes that you didn't intend to make.

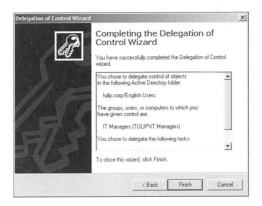

FIGURE 7.7
Accepting the delegation options you previously specified.

Viewing the Delegation Results

To review what you've done, open the Security settings on the OU you delegated control in. Figure 7.8 shows the security permissions before you delegated control; Figure 7.9 shows the permissions after you executed the wizard. If you want to view these settings on a live system (rather than on paper), you need to use the Active Directory Users and Computers MMC, with the View Advanced Features enabled.

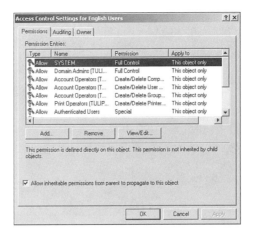

FIGURE 7.8
Looking at a normal OU.

FIGURE 7.9

Viewing the results of your delegation.

As you can see, the ACL for the OU has changed.

You can also see any changes you made to objects in the OU by selecting the Properties of an object in the OU and examining the Security tab. Figure 7.10 shows an object before delegation; Figure 7.11 shows an object after delegation.

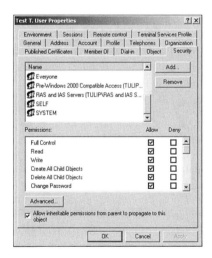

FIGURE 7.10

Looking at an object before delegation.

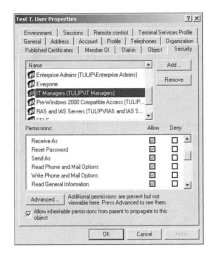

FIGURE 7.11

Viewing the results of your delegation on an object.

Deleting Delegate Control

Although the Delegate Control wizard is good for adding permissions, it is unfortunately not written to actually remove the permissions. This means that if you make a mistake when using the wizard, you have to go in by hand and remove the entries.

It also means that, from a practical standpoint, you do not want to grant access to specific users. Always grant administrative rights to groups. Therefore, as employees come and go, you can shuffle them in and out of the appropriate groups as required.

Using Group Policy Objects (GPO)

Group Policy Objects (GPOs) are one of the most powerful tools for administering workstations and users in the Windows 2000 environment. They allow you to control user and computer settings with surprising detail, and enable you to control your user's environment to an unprecedented degree.

This impressive level of control comes at a price. The price is complexity, the bane of network administrators everywhere. Although you can configure your environment in nearly any way you want, and apply unique settings for each user if you want, the complexity of such arrangements makes it difficult (if not impossible) to actually administer the network afterwards.

Understanding GPOs

Group Policy Objects (GPOs) are text files that contain information about specific Registry key settings. In this, they are much like the old NT policy files. However, GPOs are much larger, and cover a far wider range of behaviors and configurations.

The other thing that you need to realize is that, despite their name, Group Policy Objects are actually linked to organizational units, sites, and domains. They can be filtered by security groups (as they have ACLs like any other object), but are not directly related to them in any way.

Your best resource for GPOs is actually the help files written by the developers. Most GPO settings have comprehensive explanations built into them that describe how they function.

However, you should always be careful with GPO settings. Remember that every option you configure, in every GPO, increases the complexity of your design. The most effective way to proceed is to apply only those policies that you need, so that you don't have to wade though dozens of irrelevant entries trying to find what you are looking for.

Creating a Group Policy

Creating a Group Policy is simple enough:

1. Open the Active Directory Users and Computers MMC.
2. Select an OU.
3. Select Properties.
4. Open the Group Policy Objects tab (see Figure 7.12).
5. Click the New button.

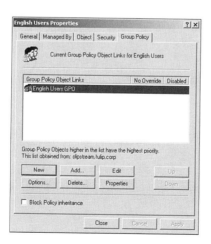

FIGURE 7.12
The GPO tab of the Users OU.

If you want to edit the GPO, you use the same process, but highlight a GPO you want to Edit and click the Edit button instead.

User and Computer Application

One of the things that you need to realize about GPOs is that every setting that is processed adds a fraction of time to the login process. So, if you have a large number of GPOs, each with a large number of settings, you can substantially add to your users login time. For example, one client of mine successfully increased his login time to a little over five minutes.

One of the things that you can do to prevent this kind of fiasco is simply to not apply a large number of GPOs. But what if you have an honest need to apply three, four, or even five GPOs to a single workstation/user combination? What then?

You can significantly decrease your login times by selectively telling Windows 2000 not to process portions of the GPO. Specifically, the settings in a GPO are divided into two broad categories:

- **Computer settings**—Settings that control the configuration settings on the workstations.
- **User settings**—Settings that control the user's environment.

If you have established your OUs based on functional lines (as described in Chapter 4, "Planning Active Directory"), you can open the properties of the Group Policy Object and select "Do not process" for the section that does not apply to the OU. You can see these options in Figure 7.13.

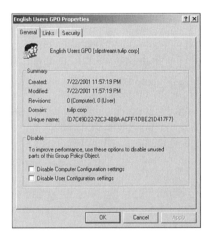

FIGURE 7.13

Setting options on the initial page of the GPO properties.

Parts of the Group Policy

Rather than going through all of the hundreds of options, this section talks briefly about the categories of settings within each of the GPO sections. You can see those sections in Figure 7.14.

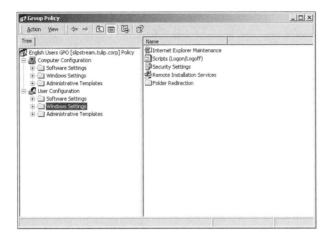

FIGURE 7.14
The anatomy of a GPO.

Within the Computer Section are three main sections: Software Settings, Windows Settings, and Administrative Templates. Software settings contains the programs you have assigned or advertised to computers receiving this GPO. Windows Settings contains information about how the workstation behaves as a member of the environment. Administrative Templates by default contains information about various Windows settings and printers.

In the Windows Settings section are two subsections; Scripts and Security. Scripts indicates which scripts run during the computer's start up and shut down processes. Security has a variety of subsections, including

- **Account Policies**—Details password requirements, lockout policies, and how Kerberos is configured for computers that receive this OU.

- **Local Policies**—Details the auditing, user rights, and security options for a specific computer.

- **Event Logs**—Details how the event logs will be recorded, how large they can become, and how they are retained.

- **Restricted Groups**—Details which accounts are allowed to be part of restricted groups on systems with this GPO.

- **System Services**—Details which services start, which are set to manual, and which are disabled on the system.

- **Registry**—Details specific Registry keys that the administrator sets for all computers receiving this GPO.

- **File System**—Details settings for how the workstation handles its local disks.

- **Public Key Policies**—Details the way in which the computer interacts with the Enterprise Certificate Authority.

- **IP Security Policies**—Details the levels of secure communications required by the computer before it is willing to communicate with another workstation or server.

In the Administrative Templates section, you find:

- **Windows Components**—Machine-based configurations for various Windows programs, including Net Meeting, Explorer, and Windows Installer.

- **System**—Settings for the computer that specify how disk quotas, the DNS Client, and Group Policy, and Windows File Protection (among other services) are configured.

- **Network**—Details about how the computer shares network connections and how it deals with offline folders.

- **Printers**—Details about how the printers are configured and advertised on computers receiving this GPO.

In the User section, you see three sections: Software Settings, Windows Settings, and Administrative Templates. Software Settings contains all of the software you have advertised or assigned to the users who receive this GPO. Administrative Templates contains some default .adm files that control the behavior of the operating system.

In the Windows Settings section, you find:

- **Internet Explorer Maintenance**—Details the settings of Internet Explorer, including title bars and default behaviors.

- **Scripts**—Details the user's login and logoff scripts.

- **Security Settings**—Details the users individual security preferences.

- **Remote Installation Service**—Details the users server of choice for the RIS service.

- **Folder Redirection**—Indicates where the user's Applications Data, Desktop, My Documents, and State Menu reside.

By default under the Administrative Templates section, you find:

- **Windows Components**—Contains a more extensive list than the one provided in the Computer Section, detailing exact functions and operations in NetMeeting, Internet

Explorer, Windows Explorer, Microsoft MMC Snap-Ins, Task Schedule, and Windows Installer.

- **Start Menu and Task Bar**—Configures the users environment in terms of what appears in the Start menu and task bars.

- **Desktop**—Details the users shell, active desktop, and active directory-searching configuration.

- **Control Panel**—Provides basic configuration of the Control Panel applet, and detailed configurations for Add/Remove Programs, Display properties, Printers, and Regional settings.

- **Network**—Details the configuration of a users Off-line folders and Network/Dial-up sharing configurations.

- **System**—Contains information about login and logoff and group policy settings.

Editing a Group Policy

It's fairly simple to edit a Group Policy Object. In the Active Directory Users and Computers MMC, you follow these steps:

1. Select an OU linked to the GPO you want to edit.
2. Right-click on the OU and select Properties.
3. Select the Group Policy Objects tab.
4. Highlight the GPO you want to edit.
5. Click on the Edit button.

However, before you go running off and editing every GPO, you need to consider what you are doing. Changes are made to GPOs as they are edited, so it's better to plan your changes before you get in there and start whacking. Especially in a production environment, you need to be careful not to accidentally make changes that you do not intend to.

In other words, before you fire up the console to start editing the GPO, let's take a look at the Help files, be sure that you know what you are doing, and record the reasons for your change before you start. You should also consider editing the GPOs to be a maintenance task; therefore, you should only do it during appropriately designated maintenance times.

Security of a Group Policy

The concept of filtering a Group Policy Object can seem more complex than it really is. The long and the short of it is this: Just like every other object in Active Directory, Group Policy Objects can have Access Control Lists (ACLs) associated with them. You can access these ACLs on the Security tab of the GPO's Property page (see Figure 7.15).

FIGURE 7.15
Setting security on a GPO using the MMC.

Your options are:

- The standard Windows options (read, write, and so on)
- Apply Group Policy, which indicates which groups should be allowed to apply the group policy

As with any Windows 2000 ACL, there is a strong difference between not setting a permission and explicitly denying it. If permission is not specified for one group, the account has permission as long as it is a member of a group with permissions and is denied access otherwise. If permission is explicitly denied to a group, that account cannot access the function.

When you think about this, it means that there are two ways that you can filter GPOs:

- You can use groups to explicitly deny permission to certain users (say people in the sales department) from receiving a particular GPO.
- You can remove all permissions to the GPO and grant read and apply permissions to those who need it (by removing the Everyone Group from the GPO's permissions and then adding a group called, say, Sales).

The first technique is useful if you have only one or two special GPOs in the organization. The second is useful if you have multiple GPOs bound to the same OU.

Application of the Group Policy in AD

Okay, so now you have all of these Group Policy Objects, and you've linked them to various sites, domains, and OUs. How are you going to tell if something was actually applied?

Supporting Active Directory Environments

CHAPTER 7

177

7

SUPPORTING
ACTIVE DIRECTORY
ENVIRONMENTS

The order of application goes like this:

- Site GPOs
- Domain GPO
- First Level OU
- Second Level OU
- Third Level OU

And so on. Each container is applied in order, changing the settings of the computer to match the settings specified on the container. The word *specified* is important—if you configure a value at the Site level, and do not specify a different value for it at any point farther down the GPO chain, the value will not be changed in the final, resultant set of policies on the workstation. However, if at any point in the process, you specify another value, the Site's value is overwritten.

In practical terms, what does that mean? Consider this example:

- Site Holland sets A=2, B=3, C=1
- Domain Tulip.com sets B=2, C=2
- OU Users sets A=1

The resultant set of policies is A=1, B=2, C=2.

What does this tell you?

Accounts will typically have the GPO setting that is applied directly to their containers. Anything that is not configured by the GPO linked to the account's container will be configured by another container somewhere in the container chain.

There are two ways that you can change this chain:

- **Block inheritance at the OU level**—This prevents the OU from processing any GPOs except for those that are directly linked to it. You use this trick when you are trying to create a specific, managed (or unmanaged) workspace for specific accounts. This is set in the OU's Property page, on the GPO tab (see Figure 7.16).

- **No override at the GPO level**—This forces the container's GPO settings down on every container below it in the chain. The values that the container sets cannot be overwritten by GPOs applied later. You use this trick to ensure that certain important settings (like the security message users get before login) are consistent across the enterprise. You can set this by right-clicking on the GPO you want to enforce, and then selecting No Override from the context menu that appears (see Figure 7.17).

FIGURE 7.16
Setting an OU to block inheritance.

FIGURE 7.17
Preventing a GPO from being overridden.

With all these options, you need to be careful not to get lost in the confusion. If you keep your GPOs to a minimum and only apply those settings that you need to apply, you can greatly reduce your complexity and therefore your troubleshooting headaches.

Also, realize that a GPO retains its No Override setting no matter which container it is connected to. Therefore, if the GPO is linked to multiple containers, you have to track which settings are being applied to which users and in what order.

Custom Group Policies

Even after looking through all of the GPO options, you still may not be satisfied. Perhaps you have custom applications written to read registry values, or perhaps you just need to set something that isn't included in the GPO standard template.

To create custom Group Policies, you need to:

1. Create an .adm in Notepad following the syntax found in the other .adm files and described in the Microsoft Help files.
2. Open the GPO you want to apply the new .adm template to.
3. Open the Administrative Templates section of either the Computer or the Users section of the GPO.
4. Right-click on the Administrative Template section.
5. Select Add Template.
6. Find and select the template that you want to add.

A word of warning about adding .adm templates to active GPOs: GPOs are text files that are replicated according to the domain/site replication schedule. Don't expect your changes to appear automatically in every site on the network. It will take time for the GPO to be changed in every site across your domain.

Setting User Rights

In Windows NT, you had the concept of User Rights, which are a set of permissions to particular operating system functions that you could change if you absolutely had to. Generally, you only worked with these rights when creating service accounts or when trying to create a highly privileged account for some specific reason.

Windows 2000 has the same concept, only with more rights and greater opportunities for configuration. Furthermore, some of the rights are now relevant to the day-to-day operations of a network.

So where are they? In NT, you fired up User Manager for Domains, and got right to them. Now where did your friends at Microsoft hide them?

User Rights are located in the Group Policy Objects.

Does that mean that you can set the User Rights for each OU? That, in fact, you can set different user rights for every GPO you create?

Yes, it does. It's as easy as editing any other GPO property. With a little work, you can make it as customized as you want.

But hold on for a moment. You don't really want to have different rights for different OUs, do you? In fact, looking at a lot of the user rights, these seem like things that you should decide on an enterprise level, or at the very least at the domain level.

In fact, that's probably a very good idea. If you set user rights at a domain level you can most likely more easily control the rights assigned to various groups and users.

The only reasons you violate these rules are:

- You have an OU that requires a special security assignment (like servers or domain controllers).
- You have an OU that requires separate administration (it represents a part of the company that has its own IT group).
- Some number of servers requires a very specific set of rights and policy assignments for legal or political reasons.

When you are planning your user rights assignments, you should be careful to apply the Principle of Least Access (discussed in Chapter 4) to avoid accidentally granting too many permissions.

Scripting

In Windows NT, your scripting choices are limited. You could use batch files that run native Windows NT commands, or you could go out and download/purchase various third-party scripting tools. Sometimes this is the only way that you can get access to the functions that you need to.

All Windows 2000 computers come with the Windows Scripting Host, a runtime compiler for Visual Basic Script, JavaScript, or (with additional modules) any other language. The Windows Scripting Host is a powerful new tool in your administrative toolkit.

Windows Scripting Host

The Windows Scripting Host is a runtime compiler for various scripting languages. It is associated with various file extensions, including .vbs. When a file with one of these extensions is called, WSH compiles it and runs the script just like a program.

WSH enables you to use a much more sophisticated set of tools for administering your computers. Rather than being limited by the third-party offerings, you can write simple scripts that can do anything from create printers to configure workstations, servers, and print queues.

Any function in the operating system can now be scripted for execution when, where, and how you need it to be. You can also cause the script to act just like a macro, acting on programs that are not part of the OS (like backup software or antivirus agents) as if you're at the keyboard.

Some examples of tasks accomplished in real-world environments using scripts include:

- Verifying that your antivirus software's .dat file is up to date and forcing an update if it is not.
- Recreating printer queues on a restored server.
- Scanning the files in a secured directory and reporting if any of their checksums have changed in the last four hours.
- Adding users who request access to a specific directory to group and sending e-mail to the Helpdesk announcing the change.

Whole-scale applications created using scripting include:

- A Web site that enables any user with appropriate access to move, add, or change a user, workstation, or group in the domain.
- A user interface that disables an account, moves it to the disabled OU, removes the user from his or her groups, deactivates the user's mail box, sets up a task to monitor the account's attempts to access enterprise resources, and then sends an update to the security administrator about the change.

It gets better though. WSH is available on all Microsoft platforms—you don't have to install Windows 2000 to gain the benefits of open scripting. You can even build entire applications on Windows NT, and then later port them over to Windows 2000 if that is what you need to do.

ADSI

Active Directory Service Interface (ADSI) is a common set of objects that enable administrators to write scripts that access or change information in the directory (or on a server in the directory).

What? Okay, let's try that again in English (rather than *Developer*, a somewhat related dialect of English).

ADSI is a common (as in standard) set of commands that you can use to interact with the information in your directory and on your client workstations. It enables you to use scripts written to those commands that can read and alter whatever information is exposed.

Because the ADSI set is standard, it doesn't really matter what scripting language you use to pass information to the commands or get information from them. So long as you send the requests in the right syntax, ADSI doesn't care if you are using Perl, VBS, Java, or a C program.

As an administrator, what this means for you is

- All those administrative tools that you spend money on will finally have a single, reliable way to access information about your Windows networks.

- You can stop using third-party scripting tools and start writing your scripts in something resembling a normal language.
- You can leverage the ability to access any information in the directory for any application so that you can use reporting tools to generate exactly the reports you need, when you need them.

ADSI is frankly more exciting for developers than for administrators. With it, developers can finally get access to and use all of that information that you keep in your directories.

Interoperability with Other Systems

Despite all of its great features, Windows 2000 would not be of much use in a real, production environment if it didn't have stable, reliable ways to work with other operating platforms. Most enterprises contain at least two platforms (Microsoft and Unix), and many have three or more.

Windows 2000 addresses interoperability on a number of fronts:

- **Downlevel clients**—How Windows 2000 deals with previous Microsoft client operating systems.
- **Downlevel servers and domains**—How Windows 2000 deals with previous Microsoft server operating systems.
- **NetWare and NDS**—Scripted directory interactions and tools for interoperating with Novell.
- **Services for Unix**—Tools for interacting with enterprise Unix environments.

The goal of all of these services and features is to enable Windows 2000 to integrate seamlessly into whatever environment you're using.

Downlevel Clients (Windows 9X and Windows NT Workstation)

By default, you can authenticate any downlevel client (Windows 9X or Windows NT Workstation) into a Windows 2000 domain. Windows 9X clients do not need to be members of the domain to authenticate against it. Windows NT Workstation clients, on the other hand, should be members of the domain: You have to add them by hand so that a computer account is set up properly for them (see Figure 7.18).

FIGURE 7.18
Setting up a computer account for a NT 4.0 Workstation.

However, this does not mean that the workstation has access to Active Directory, or to any of the features that Windows 2000 professional takes for granted.

Fortunately, Microsoft has written Active Directory extensions for Windows 9X and Windows NT 4.0 Workstation. These extensions enable client computers to:

- Use NTLM 2 for authorization
- Be aware of Active Directory Sites (thereby enabling site-based scripting as well as local DC lookup and DFS redirection)
- Browse the Active Directory

These extensions do not, however:

- Allow downlevel workstations to use Kerberos
- Apply Group Policies
- Enable the use of IPSec
- Allow for mutual authentication (where both client and server are verified as to their identities before information is exchanged)

These extensions are available for free from Microsoft. They can add to the functionality of your downlevel clients, especially during long or particular difficult migrations during which you will, by simple logistical necessity, run multiple client operating systems in your environment for some length of time.

Windows NT 4 Servers and Domains

When it comes to interoperating with Windows NT 4.0 servers and domains, you have two choices:

- Join the server to the new Windows 2000 domain
- If the computers are in a domain, create a trust between the Windows NT domain and the Windows 2000 domain

You can move servers into the Windows 2000 domain when they hold applications that you will not have time to test or upgrade, or when there is a particular business need to keep them as Windows NT servers. These servers must either be part of a workgroup, or member servers in the Windows NT domain.

You can establish trusts with Windows NT domains for a variety of reasons. For example, most migration tools require that a trust be set up between the Windows 2000 domain and the Windows NT domain being migrated from.

You might want to establish a trust between NT and 2000 domains for other reasons as well. The most common reasons are

- You have a NT domain that you will have to coexist with for a period of time during the migration.
- You have a NT domain that you must interoperate with temporarily (for legal or political reasons with your organization).

Trusts with an NT domain must be explicit. These trusts are considered explicit because they follow the old NT model—you trust only the domain you have targeted, not all of the domains that the target domain trusts.

To create an explicit trust, you must:

1. Open the Active Directory Domains and Trusts MMC.
2. Right-click on the appropriate domain node.
3. Select Properties.
4. Select the Trusts tab.
5. Add either domains trusted by this domain (you will use their account information) or domains that trust this domain (they will use your account information).
6. Click Add.
7. Enter the NetBIOS name of the domain you are trying to establish a trust with.

As with any trust, remember that you have to build both sides of the trust or the connection will not work.

NetWare and NDS

Novell NetWare retains a strong presence in the enterprise market space. NDS 5.0 in particular is a powerful, robust, and mature directory service with sophisticated deployment and management tools.

To leverage the NDS market space and to play well in environments where NDS is the primary directory service, Microsoft has invested in Services for NetWare v5.0. This product (available for under $200 from resellers) is an unlimited license tool that incorporates the following:

- **Microsoft Directory Synchronization Service (MSDSS)**—A set of rules, services, and tools that enable synchronization between Active Directory and NDS 5.0.
- **File Migration Utility**—A tool allowing administrators to quickly migrate files from Novell to Windows 2000 servers.
- **File and Print Services for NetWare 5**—A tool that mimics the NetWare interfaces, allowing administrators to work with a familiar interface while using Windows 2000 servers.

These functions are in addition to the following native Windows 2000 tools:

- **Client Services for NetWare (CSNW)**—A service that enables Windows 2000 Professional to log into an NDS tree.
- **Gateway Services for NetWare (GSNW)**—A service that enables a Windows 2000 server to share file and print resources from a Novell server.

All of these tools require that IPX run on both the Novell and the Windows 2000 sides of the network. This means that in Novell 5.0 environments, the administrators will have to establish an IPX/IP gateway, so that the Microsoft resources can access their native IP servers.

With all of these tools, you really need some way of knowing what to use and when. Generally, you can divide your choices into four interoperability scenarios:

- **Windows 2000 Point Coexistence**—In this case, Windows 2000 servers are brought into an existing NDS tree for specific reasons. The spread of the servers is limited, and Active Directory is either not implemented or very limited in scope. You use File and Print Services for NetWare, Gateway Services for NetWare (GSNW) and potentially the Microsoft Directory Synchronization Service (MSDSS) to administer the servers and ensure that data gets from one resource to another. The majority of the client computers will run either the Client Services for NetWare (CSNW) provided by Microsoft or Novell's client software.
- **Novell Point Coexistence**—In this case, a small number of Novell servers remain in an otherwise native Windows 2000 environment. There might be a legacy application that does not run on Windows 2000 that is business critical, or perhaps a particular critical

7

SUPPORTING ACTIVE DIRECTORY ENVIRONMENTS

application simply runs in a more stable fashion on Novell. In any case, you install Client Services for NetWare on select Professional workstations, and Gateway Services for NetWare on one or two Windows 2000 servers to ensure that any file/print resources are shared with the users who need them. In some cases, GSNW is used to facilitate the transfer of data via automated processes from legacy database applications to newer, more robust N-tiered databases.

- **Windows 2000/Novell Integration**—In this case, both Windows 2000 and Novell have a significant presence in the environment. Both AD and NDS are in full use, although each holds authority for different users and/or data fields in those users. In this case, you use Microsoft Directory Synchronization Service (MSDSS) to ensure that data is consistent throughout the enterprise. Workstations run either Client Services for NetWare or the Novell Client. Some administrators (especially those trained in NetWare) might find value in the File and Print Services for NetWare 5.0 product.

- **Replacement**—In this case, Windows 2000 is replacing an existing NDS structure. NDS is subordinate to AD, and will eventually be removed from production. All resources on the Novell servers (including directory information) must be migrated to the new environment. In this situation, you use Gateway Services for NetWare to bridge the gap between the time the migration starts and the time the NDS tree is removed, Microsoft Directory Synchronization Service to gather the NDS data, and the File Migration Utility to move data in a coherent and reasonable fashion between the two systems.

The bottom line is that you have a variety of options to choose from when establishing your environment. Microsoft has provided a set of tools that can help you to ease your pain before, during, and after the installation of Windows 2000, no matter which of the options you end up accepting.

Services for Unix

Although Windows NT has long had tools to interoperate well with Novell environments, moving into the Unix space has taken longer. Unix is a robust, powerful, mature, highly configurable, and stable technology with dozens of flavors. The only thing you can be absolutely sure about any given version of Unix is that the man pages will be difficult to understand.

That being said, Microsoft has taken great strides in enhancing Unix compatibility in recent years. The latest version of the Services for Unix (SFU 2.0) is a strong step in the right direction.

SFU contains

- **Services for the Network File System (NFS)**—Gateway services to access NFS shares from Windows computers, Server services to share Windows 2000 resources to Unix computers, and services to tie user authentication together for both Windows 2000 and NFS.

- **Services for Administrators**—Unix commands and shells, Perl compilers, and even a Telnet server with reasonable functionality to enable Unix administrators to leverage their existing experience on the new platform.

- **Services for Administration**—Network Information System (NIS) to AD translation (both as an export and as an active participant in an NIS network), password synchronization, and a user mapper that allows you to match usernames across platforms. These tools enable you to administer your network as though it were one system, rather than as multiple unconnected systems.

Natively, Windows 2000 also contains

- **Basic Telnet and Web functionality**—Many Unix services are available via either Telent clients or HTTP interfaces. Windows 2000 has both functions out of the box.

- **LPD functionality**—Windows 2000 servers can share Unix printers using the Print Services for Unix that comes built into the system.

Unix is, and remains, the dominant player in the highest end of the enterprise market. These functions allow you, as a Windows 2000 deplorer, to present a way that you can work with your friends in the Unix space, leveraging their information without giving up your own bids to take over their functions.

Summary

This chapter described the various components and methods used in supporting an Active Directory.

First, it discussed the role of Flexible Single Master Operations (FSMOs), including what they are, and why and how you should use them.

Next, it discussed delegation—why and how you delegate, as well as why you might consider making changes to your system's basic security authorizations.

You also learned how group policy objects (GPOs) are set up and why you use multiple levels of GPOs.

Finally, the chapter concluded with a discussion on the various forms of Windows 2000 scripting and also how Active Directory can interoperate with other directory services from Novell and Unix.

CASE STUDY

Learning by Example: The "Molly Pitcher Pharmaceuticals, Inc." Company

After reviewing the case study for Molly Pitcher Pharmaceuticals, Inc., there are some issues that need to be analyzed.

FSMOs: Because Molly Pitcher is a true distributed computing environment, you can place the FSMO roles on various domain controllers throughout the enterprise. That said however, you really want to make sure that they are located on a network that is accessible to most users. At Molly Pitcher, this is the headquarters. You can place some of the roles out at the remote sites, but it would be very inefficient because they would need to be accessed across a WAN link (for headquarters) or two WAN links (for other remote sites). It's best to keep them centralized.

Delegation: To determine whether you need to delegate control for any tasks or permissions, discuss the organizations needs with the appropriate personnel. For example, if the R&D department does not want IT personnel to manage their OU, you can delegate control of the OU to a designated R&D member. You can also delegate individual capabilities, such as creating computer objects to the person who installs new computers in the environment.

Group Policy Objects: GPOs allow you to control the user and computer settings in the Molly Pitcher environment. You should consult with the appropriate personnel to determine how GPOs are configured and how they should be implemented.

In the previous chapter, you used a relatively flat OU structure for Molly Pitcher based on the company's departments. If each department had different security policies, you could assign separate GPOs for each. Also, GPOs can be assigned at the site level. This would allow each remote office to be assigned a separate GPO. If Molly Pitcher has a single GPO, it can simply be applied at the domain level. No GPOs would be needed at the department and site levels.

Migration Planning and Migration Tools

IN THIS CHAPTER

The first step in upgrading to Windows 2000 is to architect your new Windows 2000 Active Directory domain structure. The next piece of the puzzle is to determine how you will successfully migrate to your envisioned Windows 2000 Active Directory environment. There are many tools available to help you facilitate your Active Directory domain migration. This chapter covers an array of Microsoft supplied tools and third-party migration utilities that assist in your migration efforts. Which tools you use depends on the complexity of your domain structure and the availability of resources, such as hardware and team members.

The first thing you need to determine is which type of migration you'll perform. Migration falls into one of two categories:

- *In*-place upgrade: A migration where the existing Windows NT 4.0 domain controllers are upgraded to Windows 2000.
- *Domain restructure*: A migration where a new, pristine Windows 2000 environment is built. Objects from the old environment, such as users and groups, are migrated to the new environment.

Depending on your resources and the size of your environment, you might even find it necessary to combine these methods to accomplish your migration plan.

Migration Preparation

The first step in assuring a successful Windows 2000 Active Directory migration is to have a well-documented plan of attack. By putting your plan in project form, you can be sure that you have not neglected any phase of the migration process. This will give you an opportunity to determine whether there are any services that might not have been considered in your initial plan.

Server Hardware Upgrades and Server Replacements

The requirements to run Windows 2000 Server are not that intensive. Failure to meet these requirements can dictate the need for replacement servers. The minimum requirements set by Microsoft are listed here:

- Pentium 166MHz
- 64MB RAM
- 1GB of hard drive space
- One partition formatted with NTFS for an upgrade
- TCP/IP

It is highly recommended that you compare your server hardware to the hardware that is supported by Microsoft's hardware compatibility list. You can also run the `/checkupgradeonly` switch to determine whether there are any hardware-related issues. This helps ensure a smooth transition process. There is nothing worse than losing a server due to lack of preparation. In addition, you must make sure that if you are to perform an in-place upgrade, your current server has an upgradeable operating system and is at the appropriate service pack level. Otherwise, the upgrade will fail. The operating system and service pack requirements are listed here:

- Windows NT Server 3.51: SP 5
- Windows NT Server 4.0: SP 4 or later

Note that Windows NT 3.5 cannot be upgraded to Windows 2000. If you have Windows NT 3.5 Server in your environment, you will need to upgrade it to Windows NT 3.51 or 4.0 before upgrading it to Windows 2000.

TIP

Although you can perform a direct upgrade from Windows NT Server 3.51 to Windows 2000, Microsoft does not recommend it. Instead, you should perform an upgrade to Windows NT Server 4.0 and then proceed to upgrade to Windows 2000.

A preferable method of migration to Windows 2000 Active Directory is to have a parallel installation to your current Windows NT 3.51/4.0 environment. This is usually accomplished by securing replacement servers to phase out the old servers. This gives you more flexibility when you perform the migration and in how you phase in the new environment.

8

MIGRATION PLANNING AND MIGRATION TOOLS

Analyzing Your Active Directory Design

The administrative objective should drive your Active Directory design. After all, your users will be oblivious to the context in which they reside. Your goal is to design a directory services infrastructure that facilitates ease of administration while providing the network services your users require. Therefore, some of the decisions you'll face include

- Will you have multiple trees in a forest?
- Will you collapse multiple Windows NT 4.0 domains into a single Windows 2000 Active Directory domain?
- How will you determine the organizational unit structure within those domains?

There is no doubt that organizational structure, resources (money), and politics all contribute to your final design.

In-Place Upgrade or Domain Restructure

Migration provides you with an opportunity to reevaluate your company's administrative model. In a single domain environment, you may simply choose to perform an *in-place upgrade*. This type of upgrade—in which you overwrite your existing operation system—is risky if you have a failure. It is also the most cost efficient.

If you have an environment that contains many trusts, you might decide that some of these domains can be more efficiently administered at an organization unit level rather than a domain level. In this type of scenario, you can perform an in-place upgrade to convert each domain to a Windows 2000 domain that mirrors your current Windows NT 4.0 domain and trust structure. Then, after that process is complete, you can collapse security principals from various domains into organizational units in your root domain. You can then decommission the old domain controllers. This process also enables you to consolidate servers, thus reducing total cost of ownership for the environment.

> ### Outlining a Disaster-Recovery Plan
>
> Although this might not be your favorite subject, the disaster-recovery plan can save your job. Make sure that you have developed a sound disaster-recovery plan in case of hardware, software, or user error. I suggest that before you perform any upgrade procedure, you synchronize the entire domain and take a backup domain controller offline. When I say offline, I mean disconnect it from the network and secure the server where no one will accidentally "help" you by reattaching it to the network. This way, if the upgrade fails, it is possible to quickly reinstate your NT account database from the Backup Domain Controllers (BDC) that was offline.
>
> In addition, I suggest securing a full backup of the servers you plan to upgrade with a disaster recovery option. If your organization cannot afford such a backup solution, an operating system reinstall with a full data backup should suffice.

Mixed Mode Versus Native Mode

Depending on the timeframe that the upgrade will cover, you might have to consider the possibility of a mixed mode environment. A mixed mode environment has a mixture of both Windows 2000 domain controllers and Windows NT 3.51/4.0 domain controllers. You must take special care to account for the policies, scripts, and replication issues that can arise.

Policy Support

A compelling reason to switch to native mode as soon as possible after the migration process is the issues that arise with support of policies. If a Windows 2000 domain controller authenticates a user who is on a Windows 2000 client, that client will have a Group Policy Object applied at logon. This is a desired method of application for policies. To provide backward compatibility, if that same Windows 2000 domain controller authenticates a user who is a Windows NT 4 client, the user will have the ntconfig.pol file applied to the workstation. Again, this would be the desired application of policies in this scenario, as shown in Figure 8.1.

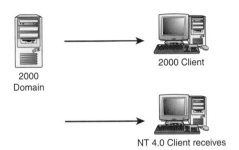

2000 Domain

2000 Client

NT 4.0 Client receives

FIGURE 8.1

Policy support with a Windows 2000 domain controller.

The problem arises when you have a mixed mode environment. In a mixed mode environment, a Windows NT 4 domain controller can authenticate a client on a Windows NT 4 workstation. In this scenario, the ntconfig.pol file will be applied to the workstation. This is still the desired result. However, if that same Windows NT 4 domain controller authenticates a Windows 2000 client, the Windows 2000 client will receive the ntconfig.pol policy applied to the workstation, as shown in Figure 8.2.

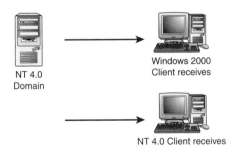

NT 4.0 Domain

Windows 2000 Client receives

NT 4.0 Client receives

FIGURE 8.2

Policy support with a Windows NT 4 domain controller.

This improper result is due to the fact that the Windows NT 4 domain controller does not understand the Group Policy Object concept. To make matters worse, the ntconfig.pol file will *tattoo* the Windows 2000 workstation with the policy. This means that even after you remove the Group Policy object from the container in which the workstation resides, the policy will remain. It will now take much more effort to remove the policy from the workstation.

Therefore, your client type as well as the type of domain controller you log in to will dictate whether you receive a GPO or ntconfig.pol file.

File Replication Support

Another compelling reason to move to native mode as soon as possible is the administrative overhead present to maintain file replication. The files replicated usually include the aforementioned policies and logon scripts. In Windows NT 4.0, the Directory Replication Service handled file replication. This was performed generally from the primary domain controller, which copied the contents of its export directory to the import directory of the other import servers. The other import servers were generally backup domain controllers although they could have been member servers. This is an example of a master-slave solution, as illustrated in Figure 8.3.

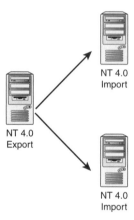

NT 4.0
Import

NT 4.0
Export

NT 4.0
Import

FIGURE 8.3

The Windows NT 4 file-replication process.

However, Windows 2000 replicates the *SysVol* directory via Active Directory replication. In Active Directory Replication there is no designated master server; therefore, Windows 2000 servers can receive their updates from any other domain controller. This is an example of a multi-master solution, as illustrated in Figure 8.4.

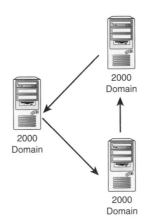

2000
Domain

2000
Domain

2000
Domain

FIGURE 8.4

The Windows 2000 file-replication process. A Windows 2000 environment is a multi-master environment. Therefore, replication is handled by Active Directory Replication of the SysVol, and it is accomplished in a ring manner.

To facilitate file replication between domain controllers, you need to adopt one of the following policies:

- Impose a freeze on all changes to items that replicate until you can migrate to a native mode environment.
- Designate an NT server as the export server for your NT servers. Configure your import servers to receive replication updates from your export server via Server Manager, as shown in Figure 8.5. Once this is accomplished, you can implement one of the following replication strategies based on the volatility of your file replication environment:
    - Manually copy the contents of the `Repl$` directory to the Netlogon of the Windows 2000 server and vice-versa.
    - Use a script utility to automate the copy of the contents of the `Repl$` directory to the Netlogon of the Windows 2000 server and vice versa.

Resorting to either of these policies will provide you with a consistent Netlogon share, but the recommended procedure is to move to native mode as soon as possible.

The Windows NT 4 Export Server acts as the master in a master-slave relationship with the import servers in a Windows NT 4.0 environment. This process uses the Directory Replication Service to govern replication between the Export and Import servers.

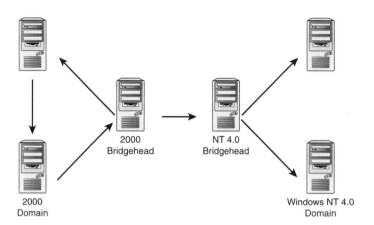

FIGURE 8.5
Supporting Windows NT 4 file replication in Windows 2000.

In Figure 8.5, note that it uses a server acting as a bridgehead server for both the Windows 2000 and NT 4.0 environments. Each of these servers is responsible for propagating the associated files to its environment via its replication mechanism. The replication between the two servers is set up manually by you via a script utility.

Post Migration Cleanup

You will want to verify that you have a successful migration by parsing the domain controller's event logs for errors. Then you can proceed with your object migration utility's log files. It is possible that you might choose a combination of migration utilities to meet the needs of your organization. After this task is complete, you should analyze how to approach the by-products of the migration, such as SID History. Your game plan on how to attack this issue will be governed by the type of migration you performed, whether it is an upgrade, intra-forest migration, or inter-forest migration. An *intra-forest* migration is the restructuring of single Active Directory forest. An *inter-forest* migration is the restructuring of two or more Active Directory forests.

Finally, at this point, you might want to consider optimizing placement of your master operations roles in your Windows 2000 environment.

Before you do an actual migration, you need to set up a lab area to proof of concept our migration plan. Failure to do so may result in lack of future employment.

The following sections examine each possible scenario more in depth.

In-Place Upgrade

This type of upgrade is generally reserved for a small to medium size company that has a simple domain structure. As implied in its name, you upgrade the current primary domain controller to host the root of the Windows 2000 Active Directory domain. This process, in effect, overwrites your current Windows NT 4 installation. As with most other Microsoft upgrades, this type of upgrade supplies you with the added benefit of user, group, computer, security, application, and environmental setting retention from your old domain to your new Active Directory environment. In addition, this method will usually be the least expensive because additional equipment is not required to complete the upgrade process unless your current hardware does not meet the minimum requirements for the upgrade procedure. It is also advisable to verify that Windows 2000 supports your current hardware.

The primary domain controller is the first domain controller you should upgrade. You do so by executing the WINNT32.exe program from the Windows 2000 Server media. You will find that the procedure mimics many of the other Microsoft-based upgrades you have completed in the past. Before you begin this process, you should review the following checklist to make sure that the PDC is prepared for the upgrade process:

- Windows 3.51 Server with Service Pack 5
- Windows NT 4.0 with Service Pack 4
- Pentium 166MHz with 64MB of RAM
- Have at least one partition formatted as NTFS
- Verify the compatibility of third-party disk utilities
- Verify the compatibility of applications
- Disable virus engines
- Disable third-party services
- Disconnect the UPS

It is *strongly* recommended that you synchronize the domain and take a BDC offline during the migration upgrade process. This will enable you to recover your account database in the event of a failed upgrade. Next, DCPromo will launch automatically and place your Windows 2000 domain in mixed mode. You will then upgrade your BDCs to domain controllers and follow in the same manner with the member servers. Note that the member servers will not run DCPromo. You can then convert to native mode, as shown in Figure 8.6.

8

MIGRATION PLANNING AND MIGRATION TOOLS

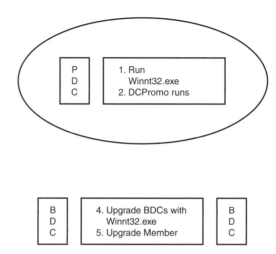

FIGURE 8.6
Procedure for performing an in-place upgrade.

Domain Restructure

You can use a Domain Restructure when you feel that your organization's administrative model is no longer efficient and requires an overhaul. For example, if your organization's domain structure consists of a complex web of trusts, it can get difficult to manage global groups and their permissions to resources.

Domain Restructure provides you with the opportunity to reorganize the domain structure to a more efficient model. There are two basic types of restructures—an upgrade then restructure model and a parallel restructure model.

Upgrade and Restructure

In the upgrade and restructure model, you perform a series of upgrades on existing Windows NT servers. After you have completed the upgrades, you analyze your environment and determine which domains should merge or collapse into another domain. When you do this, you generally move the security principals into an organizational unit for administrative purposes.

This process eliminates the sometimes-confusing array of trusts, which was present in the previous versions of Windows NT. This is possible due to the enhanced scalability built into Windows 2000. A Windows 2000 Active Directory design can support millions of objects. It also provides you with greater control over the administrative model deployed in your organization through the use of organizational units.

When dealing with a multiple domain upgrade and restructure, you must decide on the upgrade order. The following list enumerates a few guidelines you need to follow in your upgrade and restructure plan:

1. Upgrade the user account domain.

2. Upgrade resource domains.

3. Merge the resource domains into organizational units in a consolidated domain.

Parallel Restructure Model

In a parallel restructure model, you can deploy new servers and have the environment up and running before you officially switch over from your old environment. This should give you the time to optimize and tweak your Active Directory design for peak performance. In this environment, you can deploy new servers and start with a pristine Active Directory environment. From there, you use the Active Directory migration tools discussed in the rest of this chapter to help facilitate the migration of security principals to the new environment.

The Domain Upgrade and Restructure consists of the following phases. Phase one includes the upgrade of the existing NT 4.0 domain structure to Windows 2000. This upgrade will keep the existing domain structure in place, as shown in Figure 8.7.

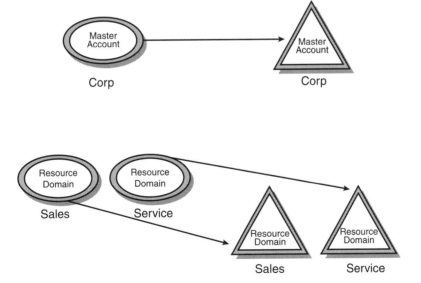

8

MIGRATION PLANNING AND MIGRATION TOOLS

FIGURE 8.7
The domain upgrade portion of a Domain Upgrade and Restructure.

Phase two is the actual restructure portion of the migration. After the master account domain and the resource domains are upgraded, the security principals can be moved or cloned into organizational units in the Windows 2000 domain structure, as shown in Figure 8.8. After the security principals are moved from the old domains, you can decommission the domains.

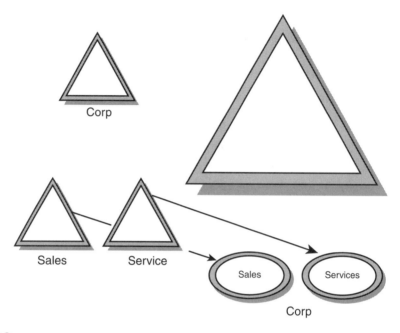

FIGURE 8.8

The restructure portion of a Domain Upgrade and Restructure.

Figure 8.9 shows an example of a parallel restructure, whereby you can move you security principals from the source domains to the organizational units in the destination Windows 2000 domain at your leisure. You can phase in the security principals over to the new structure a few at a time or a whole domain at a time, depending on your migration plan. This type of migration gives you the most security and flexibility in terms of the migration structure and time frame.

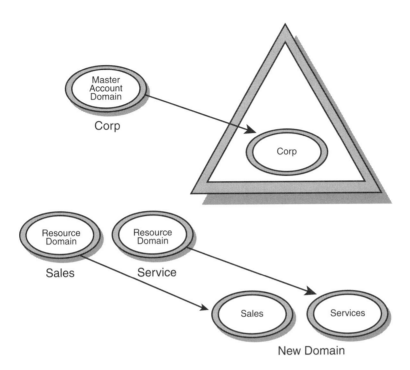

FIGURE 8.9

Performing a parallel restructure.

Using Active Directory Migration Tool

The Active Directory Migration Tool is a GUI-based migration utility provided by Microsoft. The tool relies heavily on wizards, as does the rest of Windows 2000. The tool, which works as a MMC snap-in, can provide the following functionality:

- Inter-forest clones and intra-forest moving of objects
- Migration of users, groups, computers, and service accounts from one domain to another
- Migration of the SID from the object in the source domain to the target object's SIDHistory attribute
- Use of Exchange Directory accounts to create accounts in the destination domain
- Trust creation so that the destination domain will have the same trusts that the source domain had

- Security policy migration from the source domain to the destination domain
- Ability to translate roaming profiles
- Ability to perform a test migration to determine whether any problems might prevent the migration from completing successfully
- Undo support to roll back a migration process that you have attempted

Before you run the Active Directory Migration Tool, you must meet the following minimum requirements:

- Source domain must be Windows NT 4.0 SP 4 or Windows NT 3.51 SP 5
- Two-way trust must be in place
- Must have administrative rights in both domains
- The destination domain must be in native mode to support `SIDHistory`
- The source domain requires a local group named `SourceDomainName$$$` for auditing
- Auditing must be enabled in both domains
- A Registry edit on the source primary domain controller of HKEY\Local Machine\System\Current Control Set\Control\LSA with a value of `TcpipClientSupport REG_DWORD 0x1`
- Enable auditing of both the source and destination domains for both success and failure of account management

Because the Active Directory Migration Tool relies heavily on wizards, the next section takes a look at the wizards offered by the utility.

Reporting Wizard

The Reporting Wizard provides you detailed reports that evaluate the migration process and the potential impact on your envisioned domain structure. You need to configure the Reporting Wizard before attempting to proceed with your domain migration. After you open the Active Directory Migration Tool, you will see only a Reports object within the tree. Select the Active Directory Migration Tool object and then, from the Action menu, click Reporting Wizard as shown in Figure 8.10.

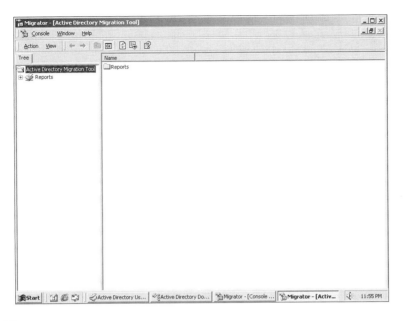

FIGURE 8.10

Viewing the Active Directory Migration Tool.

The Welcome screen will appear. Click the Next button to proceed, as shown in Figure 8.11.

FIGURE 8.11

The Welcome screen for the Reporting Wizard.

The Domain Selection page appears, as shown in Figure 8.12. Select the appropriate source and destination domains. If you have met all of the prerequisites for the migration, you will be prompted to select the Next button to continue. If there are any criteria that you have not met, an error box appears prompting you to perform the necessary corrective action.

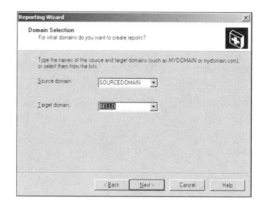

FIGURE 8.12

Selecting source and destination domains.

Next, you are prompted to select a location to store the report information. Provide this information and click the Next button to proceed to the Folder Selection page, as shown in Figure 8.13.

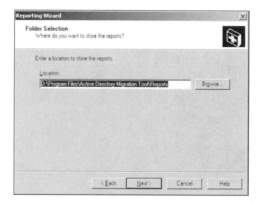

FIGURE 8.13

Specifying the report location.

The Report Selection page presents you with a list of report types available. Select the reports that you want to create and then click the Next button to proceed, as shown in Figure 8.14.

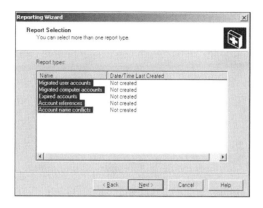

FIGURE 8.14

Selecting report types.

The User Account page asks you for the credentials to access the source domain. Click the Next button to proceed, as shown in Figure 8.15.

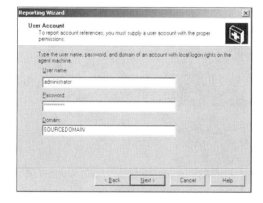

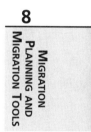

FIGURE 8.15

Specifying an administrative account to the source domain.

On the Computer Selection page, you are prompted to identify the computer that stores the accounts that you will migrate. Click the Next button to proceed, as shown in Figure 8.16.

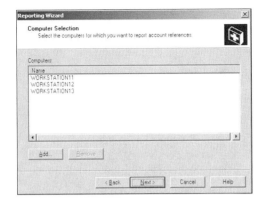

FIGURE 8.16
Specifying the source domain controller.

Finally, the Reporting Wizard Summary page appears (see Figure 8.17). It summarizes the selections you have made during the wizard process. Click the Finish button to return to the Active Directory Migration Tool window.

FIGURE 8.17
Completing the Reporting Wizard.

User Account Migration Wizard

The User Account Migration Wizard enables you to migrate a single account or multiple accounts from the source domain to the target domain. During the setup of this process, you are presented with many options, which are covered in this section. From the Action menu, select User Migration Wizard and then click Next on the Welcome page, as shown in Figure 8.18.

FIGURE 8.18

The Welcome screen for the User Migration Wizard.

First you must decide whether you will test the migration process for errors or actually per-form the migration. If it is your first attempt, I suggest you perform a test run. The Active Directory Migration Tool is actually quite helpful in identifying problems and helping you determine how to resolve the issue. Click Migrate Now and then the Next button, as seen in Figure 8.19.

FIGURE 8.19

Specifying whether to perform a test migration or an actual migration.

Next you select the source domain and the target domain for the migration process. Then click the Next button, as shown in Figure 8.20.

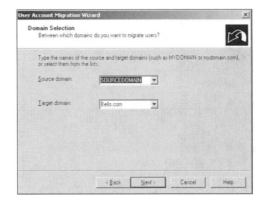

FIGURE 8.20

Specifying source and target domains.

Now you see the Select Users dialog box. Here you can select single or multiple users to proceed with the migration by highlighting the users and clicking the Add button. After you have added all of the user accounts you deem necessary, click the OK button to proceed, as shown in Figure 8.21.

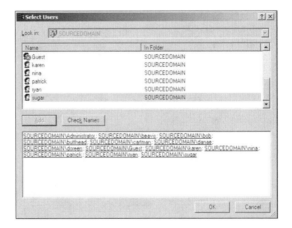

FIGURE 8.21

Selecting users to migrate from the source domain.

The Organizational Unit Selection dialog box now appears and prompts you to select the organizational unit that should be the destination for the account that you are migrating. You can browse to the destination organizational unit by clicking the Browse button. Once selected, click OK to return to the Organizational Unit Selection dialog box. Now you can click Next to proceed, as shown in Figure 8.22.

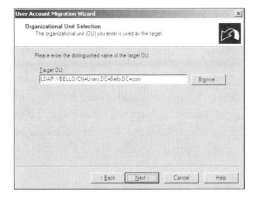

FIGURE 8.22
Selecting the destination organizational units.

On the Password Options page, you can select from one of two options for users' passwords. Do you want the user's password to be a complex password that you must supply to each user, or do you want the password to be the same as the username? Select an option and specify the location of the password file that will contain the associated usernames and passwords. Then click Next to proceed, as shown in Figure 8.23.

> **NOTE**
>
> I feel that the inability to retain the user's current password is one of the shortcomings of the Active Directory Migration Tool, which may persuade you to look at third-party alternatives. Note that this limitation is for inter-forest only; intra-forest can retain the user's current password.

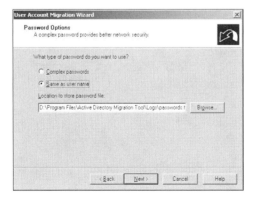

FIGURE 8.23
Specifying password options.

The Account Translation Options page prompts you to select how you want to handle the migrating accounts. First, you must decide whether you want to disable the source or destination account after the migration. If not, you can leave both accounts active.

Second, you have an option to set when you want the source accounts disabled. This will set the appropriate value in the user's account expiration date attribute. Finally, and most importantly, you can select to migrate the user's SID to the SIDHistory attribute in the target domain. Failure to select this option prevents the destination account from accessing resources in the source domain. Click Next to proceed, as shown in Figure 8.24.

FIGURE 8.24
Specifying that SIDHistory *be retained.*

You are next prompted for administrative credentials for the source domain. Enter the requested information and click Next, as shown in Figure 8.25.

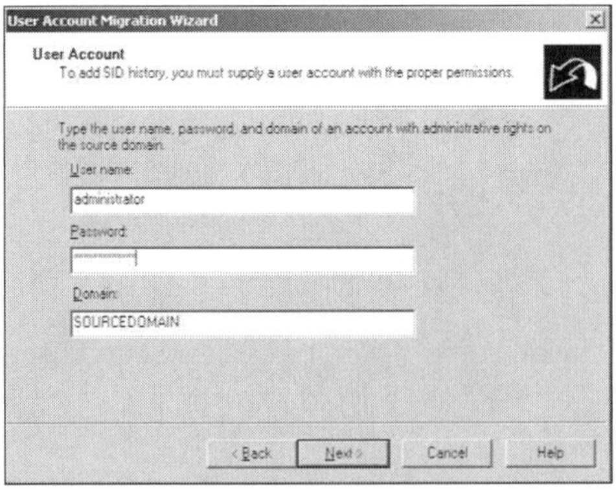

FIGURE 8.25
Specifying an administrative account to the source domain.

The User Options page provides you with an array of options. You must decide whether to translate the user's roaming profile. This can present you with issues when the user is logging in between Windows NT 4 workstations and Windows 2000 professional computers. You have to decide whether to update the user's rights from the source domain to the destination domain.

Next, you need to decide whether to migrate the user's associated groups. In addition, you need to decide whether you want to update any groups that have been already migrated with this user's information. Finally, you are prompted to select if you want to rename the user accounts or append them with a prefix or suffix. Click Next to proceed, as shown in Figure 8.26.

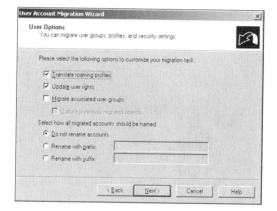

FIGURE 8.26

Specifying user options.

8

MIGRATION PLANNING AND MIGRATION TOOLS

The Naming Conflicts page appears to allow you to select how to handle accounts that conflict with an existing name in the destination domain. You can select to ignore the account and not migrate it, to replace the account that already exists in the destination domain with the account you are migrating from the source domain, or to rename conflicting accounts by appending a prefix or suffix to the account name. Select Next to proceed, as shown in Figure 8.27.

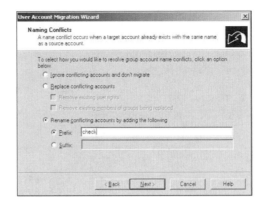

FIGURE 8.27
Specifying how user naming conflicts are resolved.

Click Finish to begin the migration process, as shown in Figure 8.28.

FIGURE 8.28
Completing the User Account Migration Wizard.

The migration process begins and presents you with a progress screen that alerts you to any errors that might have been encountered during the migration process. When the status is complete, you can click Close to end the process, as shown in Figure 8.29.

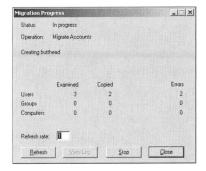

FIGURE 8.29
The User Migration Wizard progress screen.

Group Migration Wizard

From the Action menu, select Group Migration Wizard and you will be presented with the Group Migration Wizard Welcome screen. Select Next, as shown in Figure 8.30.

FIGURE 8.30
The Welcome screen for the Group Migration Wizard.

Next you are prompted to select if you will perform a test migration or proceed with the actual migration. Make your selection and click Next, as shown in Figure 8.31.

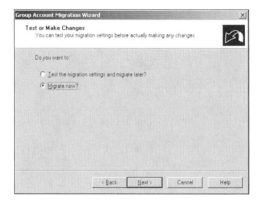

FIGURE 8.31

Specifying whether to perform a test migration or an actual migration.

As in the user account migration process, select the source and destination domain for the migration process. Then click the Next button to proceed, as shown in Figure 8.32.

FIGURE 8.32

Specifying source and target domains.

From the Group Selection page, select the groups that you want to migrate to the destination domain by highlighting the group name and clicking the Add button. Click the Next button when you're done to proceed, as shown in Figure 8.33.

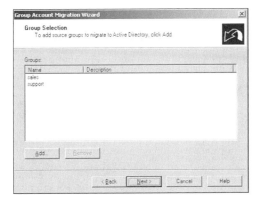

FIGURE 8.33

Selecting groups to be migrated.

On the Organizational Unit Selection page, supply the distinguished path for the organizational unit in which you want the group accounts to reside. If you do not know the distinguished name, you can click the Browse button to drive to the destination organizational unit. After this is complete, click the Next button to proceed, as shown in Figure 8.34.

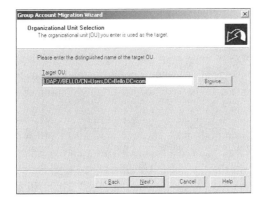

FIGURE 8.34

Selecting destination organizational units.

On the Group Options page, you have an array of options. You can update the account rights assigned in the source domain to the destination domain. You can copy the group members along with the group during the migration. You can select Update Previously Migrated Objects if some accounts that were members of the group have been previously migrated and you want to update those accounts also. There is also an option to migrate the group SIDS to the target domain. Keep in mind, that if you do not select this option, the destination accounts cannot access resources in the source domain. Finally, you are prompted to select if you want to rename the group accounts or append them with a prefix or suffix during the migration. Click Next to proceed, as shown in Figure 8.35.

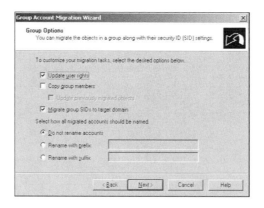

FIGURE 8.35

Specifying group options.

If you do decide to migrate the group members to the destination domain, you will be prompted to select the password and account transition options. These are very similar to the options covered in the user account migration. On the Password Options portion of the page, you can select from one of two options for the user passwords: The user password is a complex password that you must supply to each user, or it's the same as the username. Select an option and specify the location of the password file that will contain the associated usernames and passwords.

From the Account Translation portion of the page, select how you want to handle the migrating group member accounts. First, you must decide if you want to disable the source or destination account after the migration. If not, you can leave both accounts active. Second, you have an option to set when you want the source accounts disabled. This will set the appropriate value in the group member account expiration date attribute. Finally, you must decide whether to translate the roaming profiles.

From the Naming Conflicts page, you are prompted to select how to migrate group accounts that will conflict with existing accounts in the destination domain. You can select to ignore the account and not migrate it, replace the conflicting account, or rename the conflicting account with an appended prefix or suffix, as shown in Figure 8.36.

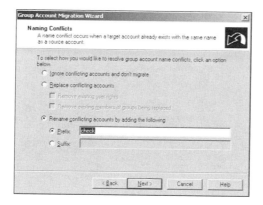

FIGURE 8.36

Specifying how group naming conflicts are resolved.

On the Completing the Group Account Migration page, select Finish to perform the migration, as shown in Figure 8.37.

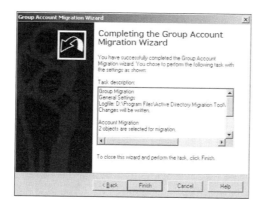

FIGURE 8.37

Completing the Group Account Migration Wizard.

The migration process begins and presents you with a progress screen that alerts you to any errors that came up during the migration process. When the status is complete, you can click Close to end the process, as shown in Figure 8.38.

FIGURE 8.38

The User Migration Wizard progress screen.

The Active Directory Migration Tool (ADMT) includes many other wizards for use such as

- Computer Account Wizard: Migrates computer accounts from the source domain to the destination domain.

- Security Translation Wizard: Translates security policies from the source domain to the destination domain.

- Service Account Migration Wizard: Migrates account used for services.

- Exchange Directory Migration Wizard: Allows you to parse an Exchange server for accounts. You then can migrate the Exchange accounts to the destination domain. However, keep in mind that Exchange accounts do not have the same attributes that a domain account contains.

- Undo Wizard: Removes the accounts from the destination domain and places them back into the source domain.

- Retry Tasks Wizard: Allows you to continue a migration process that was aborted due to user or computer error.

- Trust Migration Wizard: Allows you to procure the same trust relationships to the destination domain that the source domain had established. This will alleviate any failed permission errors between the trusts.

- Group Mapping and Migration Wizard: Assists you in preparing the source group accounts for migration into the target domain.

Active Directory Migration Tool Version 2

Microsoft will soon release Active Directory Migration Tool v2, which will ship with Windows 2002. However, it will run on Windows 2000 and can be used to migrate a Windows NT 4 domain to Windows 2000. It will include the following added functionality:

- Password migration
- Scripting interface
- Command-line interface
- Extensions for re-ACLing
- No need to be an administrator in the target domain
- Delegation at the OU level

The interface is fairly similar because NetIQ also developed it. Keep in mind that these are nice additions; however, if you are in a large enterprise, you will want to consider some of the third-party tools discussed later in the chapter.

ClonePrincipal

The ClonePrincipal tool is used in inter-forest restructures along with Visual Basic script files provided by Microsoft to control how your security principals are cloned. Security principals can be a user, shared local group, domain local group, global group, or universal group. The Visual Basic scripts can be edited to accommodate your environment's specific requirements.

This functionality differs from the Active Directory Migration Tool in that ClonePrincipal actually *copies* the source security principal into the destination domain, whereas the Active Directory Migration Tool *moves* the source security principal into the destination domain.

You can install the ClonePrincipal utility and Visual Basic script files from the Windows 2000 Server CD-ROM by executing setup.exe in the Support Tools folder. The ClonePrincipal tool uses a COM object a Visual Basic scripts to facilitate your migration efforts. The clonepr.dll contains the DSUtils.Clone.Principal COM object, which supports three methods:

- Connect—Creates authenticated connections between the source and destination domain controllers.
- AddSIDHistory—Copies the SID of the source security principal to the destination security principal.
- CopyDownLevelUserProperties—Copies the source security principal properties to the destination security principal.

Table 8.1 includes descriptions of these files.

TABLE 8.1   ClonePrincipal Scripts

File	*Description*
sidhist.vbs	Copies the SID of the source security principal to the SIDHistory of the destination security principal.
	Syntax: `cscript sidhist.vbs /srcdc:<source domain controller> /srcdom:<source domain> /srcsam:<source account name> /dstdc:<destination domain controller> /dstdom:<destination domain> /dstsam:<destination account name>`
clonepr.vbs	Clones a source security principal and properties to the destination security principal. Also appends the source SID to SIDHistory of the destination security principal.
	Syntax: `cscript clonepr.vbs /srcdc:<source domain controller>> /srcdom:<source domain> /srcsam:<source account name> /dstdc:<destination domain controller> /dstdom:<destination domain> /dstsam:<destination account name> /dstdn:<destination distinguished name>`
clonegg.vbs	Clones all global groups.
	Syntax: `cscript clonegg.vbs /srcdc:<source domain controller> /srcdom:<source domain> /dstdc:<destination domain controller> / dstdom:<destination domain> /dstou: <destination organizational unit>`
cloneggu.vbs	Clones all global groups and users.
	Syntax: `cscript cloneggu.vbs /srcdc:<source domain controller> /srcdom:<source domain> /dstdc:<destination domain controller> / dstdom:<destination domain> /dstou: <destination organizational unit>`
clonelg.vbs	Clones shared local groups.
	Syntax: `cscript clonelg.vbs /srcdc:<source domain controller> /srcdom:<source domain> /dstdc:<destination domain controller> / dstdom:<destination domain> /dstou: <destination organizational unit>`

Benefits of ClonePrincipal

The main benefit of ClonePrincipal is that you can control the migration process without affecting your source domain. Because ClonePrincipal copies the security principals, your source domain is still intact, unmodified. This provides the user the ability to log in with the old account and provides you with a fault-tolerant migration solution in the event there is a problem with the cloning process. Because the source security principal still exists and has not been modified, you still have a security principal to revert to without any additional administrative effort. During the cloning process, the following properties are applied to the destination security principal.

- Callback options
- Description
- Dial-in properties
- Full name
- General properties
- Home directory
- Password set to Null
- Profile properties
- RAS properties
- Static IP address
- Terminal services properties

> **NOTE**
>
> By default, user accounts created by ClonePrincipal are disabled and the "user must change password at next logon" property is selected. In addition, properties unique to Windows 2000 are not migrated even if the source domain is a Windows 2000 domain.

Because the source security principal is not modified during the cloning process, you can apply a phased approach to your migration. You can therefore clone small groups of users to the destination domain as you see fit. In addition, ClonePrincipal allows you to merge multiple groups from a source domain into the destination domain. These various groups can even be merged into a single group if that fits the administrative model.

Finally, ClonePrincipal has support for SIDHistory. SIDHistory provides you with the capability to have a user authenticate with the destination account, yet still access resources in the source domain. This is accomplished by appending the SID from the old domain to the security principal in the destination domain. This does not replace the existing SID on the destination security principal; it acts as a secondary SID for the security principal.

Prerequisites for ClonePrincipal are as follows:

- Administrative credentials in both the source and destination domains
- Appropriate trusts to facilitate the security principal cloning
- The cloning must be between two forests with different SIDs
- The source primary domain controller must be running Windows NT 4.0 with Service Pack 4 or higher or Windows 2000
- The source domain requires a local group named SourceDomainName$$$ for auditing
- A Registry edit of the source primary domain controller of HKEY\Local Machine\ System\Current Control Set\Control\LSA with a value of TcpipClientSupport REG_DWORD 0x1
- The source primary domain controller or PDC Emulator must be the focus
- The destination domain must be in native mode to support SIDHistory
- You must enable auditing of both the source and destination domains for both success and failure of account management

Disadvantages of ClonePrincipal

ClonePrincipal is not a GUI-based tool. It therefore might be a bit confusing for those who are not familiar with Visual Basic. Although syntax is documented in the clonepr.doc, which is installed in the Support Tools folder, you must be very comfortable working with Visual Basic scripting. ClonePrincipal does not support cloning of local groups on workstations or stand-alone servers. ClonePrincipal only supports cloning of local groups on domain controllers. In addition, ClonePrincipal does not clone computer accounts or preserve profiles. Finally, you must verify that the following prerequisites are in place in order to use ClonePrincipal:

If you do encounter problems, you will want to examine the %windir%\debug\clonepr.log file, which is the progress and error log file for the ClonePrincipal tool.

MoveTree

MoveTree is a command-line utility that enables you to move users, groups, and organizational units from one domain to another in a single forest. This means the source domain must be a Windows 2000 domain to use this tool. MoveTree cannot move computers or *populated* local or global groups. Therefore, you have to recreate local or global group membership to maintain resource access. Generally, this tool is used at the final stages of your migration. It assists you in moving objects from one domain to another or collapsing multiple domains in to a single domain.

The defining characteristics between MoveTree and ClonePrincipal are that ClonePrincipal *copies* objects *between* forests. MoveTree is an intra-forest utility, whereas ClonePrincipal is an inter-forest utility. In addition, because MoveTree actually moves the object, the source object is destroyed once the operation is complete. This functionality differs from ClonePrincipal because it does not affect the source object. Table 8.2 compares these two utilities.

TABLE 8.2   Comparing MoveTree to ClonePrincipal

MoveTree	*ClonePrincipal*
Moves objects	Copies objects
Destroys source object	Leaves source object intact
Intra-forest utility	Inter-forest utility
Retains user's current password	Assigns user new password
Retains object's Global Unique Identifier (GUID)	Destroys object's GUID

MoveTree is installed when you install the support tools.

Benefits of MoveTree

MoveTree also preserves permissions on files and links to group policy objects when you move organizational units. However, if you plan to decommission the source domain or want increased performance, you should re-create the group policy in the destination domain. In addition, MoveTree provides support for SIDHistory. As described within the ClonePrincipal section, this allows the destination object to still access resources in the source domain.

Prerequisites of MoveTree

To use the MoveTree command-line utility, you need to have several prerequisites in place. These are listed here:

- Source domain must be Windows 2000.
- Destination domain must be in native mode.

8

MIGRATION PLANNING AND MIGRATION TOOLS

- Error log.
- Password.
- Guid.

Now that you have seen the necessary prerequisites, let's explore the syntax of this command-line utility. The MoveTree command syntax is as follows:

```
movetree {/start | /startnocheck | /continue | /check} /s SrcDSA /d DstDSA
➡ /sdn SrcDN /ddn DstDN [/u [Domain\]Username /p Password] [/verbose]
➡ [{/? | /help}]
```

Because this is a rather long syntax, let's explore the parameters seen in the MoveTree utility further. Table 8.3 highlightes the different parameters in more detail.

TABLE 8.3   MoveTree Command-Line Parameters

Parameter	Function
/start	Initiates a MoveTree operation with a /check operation by default.
/startnocheck	To start a MoveTree operation with no check, use /startnocheck.
/continue	Continues the execution of a previously paused or failed MoveTree operation.
/check	Performs a test of the MoveTree operation without moving any objects. The /check command returns an error if any of the following issues arise:
	The user does not have the necessary permissions to create objects in the destination container.
	The destination server does not have sufficient disk space.
	A relative distinguished name conflict exists on the destination.
	There is a samAccountName conflict for any object that would be moved.
	Any objects cannot be moved because they are built-in accounts or they are a domain local or a global group.
	Any computer objects would be moved.

Parameter	Function
/s SrcDSA	Identifies the FQDN of the source server.
/d DstDSA	Identifies the FQDN of the destination server
/sdn SrcDN	Identifies the distinguished name of the source subtree.
/ddn DstDN	Identifies the distinguished name of the destination subtree.
/u [Domain\]Username /p Password	Credentials in which to perform the MoveTree operation.
/verbose	Displays detailed information about the MoveTree operation to the screen.

Netdom

Netdom is a command-line utility that provides functionality in two administrative areas; trust management and computer account management.

Computer Account Management

Netdom provides you with extensive management options on how to administer computer accounts. Netdom can move, remove, and rename computer accounts. The Netdom computer account administrative options are as follows:

- Adds a computer account to the domain—Netdom add /d:<domain name> <computer account> ou:<ou path>

- Joins a computer account to the domain—Netdom join /d:<domain name> <computer account> ou:<ou path>

- Removes a computer account from a domain—Netdom remove /d:<domain name> <computer account> /ud:<domain name\user name> /pd:<password>

- Moves a computer account from one domain to another—Netdom move /d:<domain name> <computer account> /ud:<destination domain user> /pd:<destination password>

Trust Management

Netdom also enables you to perform trust management. The most commonly used parameters, which include removing a computer account, verifying/resetting a secure channel, querying for trusts, and establishing, verifying, and resetting trust relationships, are discussed here.

8

MIGRATION PLANNING AND MIGRATION TOOLS

- Removes a workstation or computer from a domain—`Netdom remove /d:` `<domain name> /ud:<user name> /pd:<password>`
- Verifies the secure channel between a computer and a domain controller— `Netdom verify /d:<domain name> <computer account>`
- Resets a secure channel between a computer and a domain—`Netdom reset /d:` `<domain name> <computer account>`
- Queries for all trusts of a domain—`Netdom query trust /domain:<domain name>` `/ud:<user name> /pd:<password>`
- Establishes, verifies, or resets a trust relationship between domains—`Netdom trust` `<trusting domain name> /d:<trusted domain name> /ud:<user name> /pd:` `<password> uo:<user name> /po:<password> [/Verify] [/Reset]` `[/PasswordT:new realm trust password] [/Add] [/Remove [/Force]] [/Twoway]` `[/Kerberos] [/Transitive[:{yes | no}]]`

There are a handful of other parameters you can access by viewing the support tools help file.

ADSI MMC Snap-in

After you have completed your migration and your users no longer need access to the source domain, you will want to clean up the `SIDHistory` for your users and groups. This can be accomplished by using the Active Directory Service Interface Edit MMC snap-in. This will prevent the possibility of the access token growing too large (in excess of 1,023 SID entries), which can prevent your users from being able to log in or access resources. You will then create a query to locate the `SIDHistory` attribute. Then you can use either ADSI scripts or third-party scripts to actually perform the `SIDHistory` cleanup.

NetIQ Suite of Migration Tools

If you feel comfortable with Microsoft's Active Directory Migration Tool, you will also feel comfortable with the NetIQ (`www.NetIQ.com`) suite of tools. The reason is that NetIQ is the company that developed Microsoft's Active Directory Migration Tool. Therefore, it has the same look and feel as Microsoft's Active Directory Migration Tool with quite a bit more functionality built into the product.

The major difference is that NetIQ Domain Migration Administrator is specifically targeted for a medium-to-large corporation. It has many of the bells and whistles that Microsoft's Active Directory Migration Tool lacks. This section takes a look at some of the significant differences you will find between Microsoft's Active Directory Migration Tool and NetIQ Domain Migration Administrator.

- Password migration from Windows NT 4 to Windows 2000.
- The ability to create project plans to help track the progress of the migration.
- Status, rollback, full event logging, detailed discovery, assessment, impact analysis, action history, and detailed reporting.
- You can import data about your source and target domain into the database as a part of your initial discovery and analysis. Then you can model the data of the source domain as you see fit, such as changing IDs of migrated users or the target OUs.
- The ability to use either VBScript or JScript to automate migration tasks via an ActiveScript trigger.
- Clean up of Active Directory's SIDHistory. You can replace references to an account's SIDHistory with references to the account's primary SID.
- Migration and consolidation of server data, shares, connection limits, and permissions.
- Ability to exclude disabled and expired accounts from the migration process.
- Migration of profiles.
- Migration of Windows Terminal Services profiles.
- Remote computer renaming and rebooting.

In addition to the Domain Migration Administrator, NetIQ offers the following migration utilities that I have found to been efficient, easy to use, and helpful in addressing some of the other issues that arise in a large enterprise environment.

NetIQ NetWare Migrator

This tool will assist you in migrating from Novell NetWare binderies to Windows NT 4.0 or Windows 2000. It migrates users, groups, and OUs from the Novell structure to your Windows 2000 implementation. If you are migrating multiple binderies, you can merge multiple accounts into a single Windows account. In addition, you can maintain the file permissions of your current Novell environment. Finally, there is support for incremental migrations, which enables you to migrate only the files that have changed on the source server since the last migration task.

Server Consolidator

This tool assists you in migrating files, shares, permissions, and printers between Windows NT 4.0 and Windows 2000 servers. This product also provides additional support for clustered environments and network attached storage devices.

Migration Assessor

This tool assists you in assessing and reporting efforts associated with both Active Directory and Exchange 2000 migrations. It generates reports detailing a variety of information, including existing infrastructure, computers/workstations, printer and share permissions, and file systems.

Exchange Migrator

This tool lets you move Exchange mailboxes, distribution lists, public folders, and custom recipients from one Exchange organization or site to another. It supports Exchange 5.5 to Exchange 5.5 consolidation and from Exchange 5.5 to Exchange 2000. It assesses your current Exchange 5.5 organization and automatically discovers mailboxes, distribution lists, custom recipients, and public folders. It also migrates and keeps intact calendar and public folder permissions. As with all of the NetIQ products, it uses wizard-driven interfaces and a project-based migration.

Now let's take a look at the NetIQ Domain Migration Administrator interface. This section walks through various screens and explains the various options you will be asked during the migration process.

Figure 8.39 shows the opening screen of NetIQ Domain Migration Administrator. From here, you can select the step in the migration project you want to perform.

FIGURE 8.39
NetIQ Domain Migration Administrator.

You can begin by running the Project Object Selection Wizard, as shown in Figure 8.40.

FIGURE 8.40
The Welcome screen for the Project Object Selection Wizard.

Click Next, and the Project Object Types page displays, as shown in Figure 8.41.

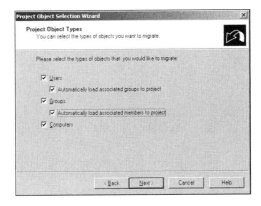

FIGURE 8.41
The Project Object Types page.

The Project Object Types page specifies the objects you want to migrate. The fields are defined as follows:

- Users—Specifies that you want to include users in this project.
- Automatically add users' associated groups to project—Specifies that group memberships associated with the selected user accounts are loaded into the project.

- Groups—Specifies that you want to include groups in this project.
- Automatically load associated user members to project—Specifies that users associated with the selected groups are loaded into the project.
- Computers—Specifies that you want to include computers in this project.

Click Next to continue to the Account Selection page, as shown in Figure 8.42.

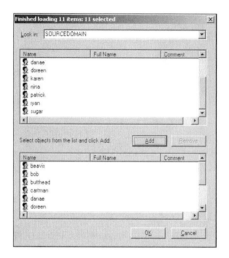

FIGURE 8.42
The Account Selection page.

In the Account Selection page, you specify which user accounts in the source domain should be migrated. To add user accounts, click Add and follow the instructions on the Select Users window.

The Group Selection page specifies which groups in the source domain will be migrated. To add groups, click Add and follow the instructions on the Group Selection window, as shown in Figure 8.43.

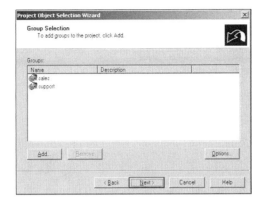

FIGURE 8.43

The Group Selection page.

The Computer Selection page specifies which computers Domain Migration Administrator will migrate (see Figure 8.44). To add computers, click Add and follow the instructions on the Select Computers window. Domain controllers cannot be migrated.

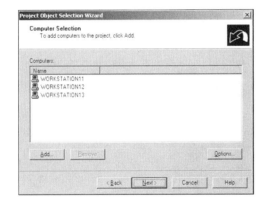

FIGURE 8.44

The Computer Selection page.

To migrate a computer that is operating as a Windows 2000 domain controller, you must first demote that domain controller to a member server or standalone server. Windows NT domain controllers cannot be migrated. You must either upgrade them to Windows 2000 server or reinstall Windows NT. Click Next, and the Data Modeling page displays, as shown in Figure 8.45.

FIGURE 8.45
The Data Modeling page.

The Data Modeling page allows you to specify whether you would like to do data modeling for this project. Data modeling allows you to review potential migration results and adjust some properties for the accounts that are created in the target domain. If you do not enable it, the modeling tasks will not be available for this project. Click Next to view the results page. From the NetIQ Domain Migration Administrator, select the Migration Settings Wizard and you will be presented with the Migration Settings Wizard welcome screen.

FIGURE 8.46
The Welcome screen for the Migration Settings Wizard.

Through the Migration Settings Wizard, you can specify the settings to be used for the migration process. Click Next, and the Organizational Unit Selection page displays as shown in Figure 8.47.

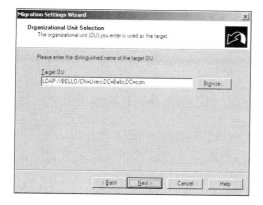

FIGURE 8.47

The Organizational Unit Selection page.

The Organizational Unit Selection page specifies the target container, such as an organizational unit, to which Domain Migration Administrator will migrate the selected user accounts, groups, or computer accounts. Click Next, and the Scripting page displays as shown in Figure 8.48.

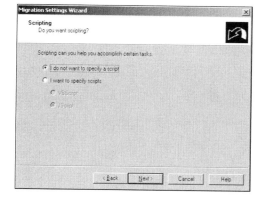

FIGURE 8.48

The Scripting page.

The Scripting page specifies whether you want to use VBasic or JScript scripts during migration. Make your selection and click Next, and the Settings Options page displays, as shown in Figure 8.49.

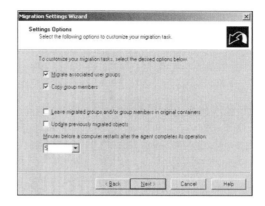

FIGURE 8.49
The Settings Options page.

The Settings Options page allows you to specify options to use for the user, group, and computer migration tasks performed using this project. These options globally apply to migrations performed using this project. Setting these options can reduce steps required when performing the actual user, group, and computer migration tasks. Click Next, and the Rename Options page displays as shown in Figure 8.50.

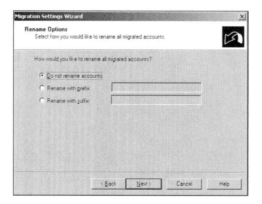

FIGURE 8.50
The Rename Options page.

The Rename Options page specifies options to use for the user, group, and computer migration tasks performed using this project. These options globally apply to migrations performed using this project. Setting these options can reduce steps required when performing the actual user, group, and computer migration tasks. Click Next, and the Naming Conflicts page displays as shown in Figure 8.51.

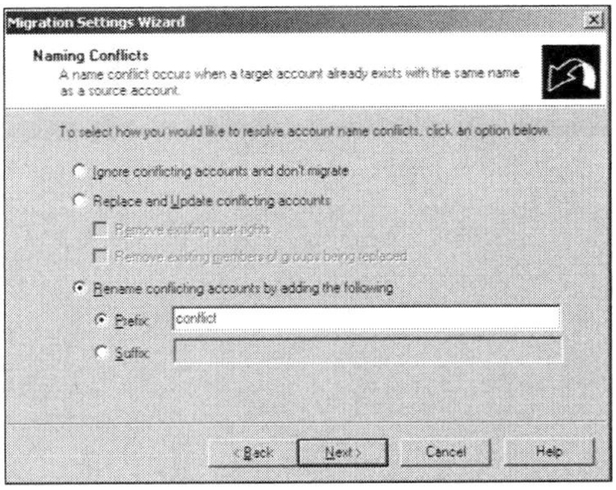

FIGURE 8.51

The Naming Conflicts page.

The Naming Conflicts page specifies how the Domain Migration Administrator handles accounts in the target domain that have the same name as a copied account in the source domain. Click Next, and the Password Options page displays as shown in Figure 8.52.

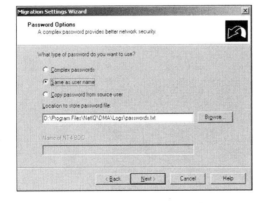

FIGURE 8.52

The Password Options page.

The Password Options page specifies how the Domain Migration Administrator assigns passwords to migrated user accounts. Click Next, and the Account Transition page displays as shown in Figure 8.53.

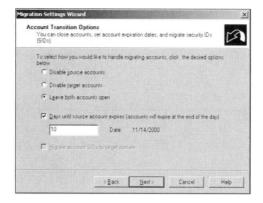

FIGURE 8.53

The Account Transition Options page.

The Account Transition Options page specifies how the Domain Migration Administrator handles migrated user accounts in both the source and target domains. Click Next, and the Advanced User Options page displays as shown in Figure 8.54.

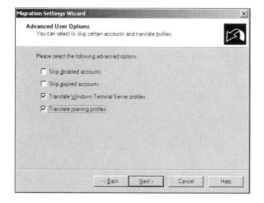

FIGURE 8.54

The Advanced User Options page.

The Advanced User Options page specifies advanced options. These options allow you to skip certain accounts or translate profiles in the source domain, as follows:

- Skip disabled accounts.
- Skip disabled user accounts in the source domain.

- Skip expired accounts.
- Skip expired user accounts in the source domain.
- Translate Windows Terminal Server profiles
- Copy the Windows Terminal Server profiles from the source domain to the target domain for the selected user accounts. This process associates the Windows Terminal Server profile with the new user account in the target domain.
- Translate roaming profiles.
- Copy roaming profiles from the source domain to the target domain for the selected user accounts. This process associates the roaming user profile with the new user account in the target domain.

Click Next, and the Translate Options page displays as shown in Figure 8.55.

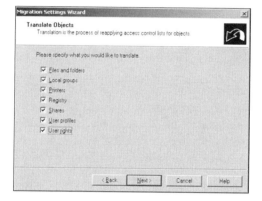

FIGURE 8.55

The Translate Objects page.

The Translate Ojects page specifies the types of objects for which you want Domain Migration Administrator to translate security. Click Next, and the Security Translation Options page displays, as shown in Figure 8.56.

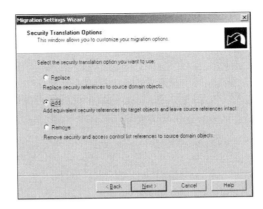

FIGURE 8.56

The Security Translation Options page.

The Security Translation Options page specifies how the Domain Migration Administrator handles the security translation process.

Replace

Replaces the SID for the account in the source domain with the SID for the account in the target domain. This is done in the access control lists (ACLs) and system access control lists (SACLs) in the security descriptors of the selected objects. This option gives the account in the target domain the same permissions to the selected objects as the account in the source domain. This option also removes these permissions from the account in the source domain.

When performing an intra-forest migration, SID history is migrated and the source object is deleted. So, when performing an intra-forest migration, the Domain Migration Administrator only allows security translation in Replace mode.

Add

Adds the SID for the account in the target domain to the ACLs and SACLs in the security descriptors of the selected objects that contain the SID for the account in the source domain. This option gives the account in the target domain the same permissions to the selected objects as the account in the source domain.

Windows 2000 only recognizes the first 30 entries in Registry key ACLs. If security translation is performed in Add mode, more than 30 entries can exist at the end of the process. The large number of access control entries (ACEs) on certain Registry keys might result in users being locked out of the effected system.

To prevent this, if the wizard encounters an ACL with more than 15 ACEs while running in Add mode, the system registry security translation process skips the Registry. This will not occur if the security translation is run in Replace or Remove mode. This is not a problem if you have not manually changed any Registry key ACEs on the effected computers.

Remove

Removes the SID for the account in the source domain from the ACLs and SACLs in the security descriptors of the selected objects. This option removes the permissions to the selected objects from the account in the source domain. Click Next and the Completed Migration wizard will appear here. The next wizard in the list is the Reporting Wizard. Select it and the Reporting Welcome screen displays as shown in Figure 8.57.

FIGURE 8.57
The Welcome screen for the Reporting Wizard.

Click Next, and the Folder Selection page displays as shown in Figure 8.58.

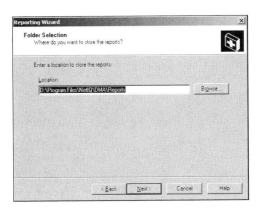

FIGURE 8.58
The Folder Selection page.

The Folder Selection page specifies the folder where Domain Migration Administrator stores the generated reports. Click Next, and the Report Selection page displays as shown in Figure 8.59.

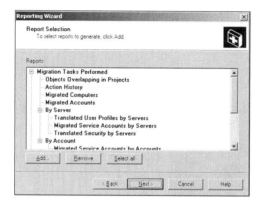

FIGURE 8.59
The Report Selection page.

The Report Selection page specifies the reports you want Domain Migration Administrator to generate. Click Next, and the User Account page displays as shown in Figure 8.60.

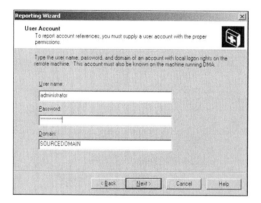

FIGURE 8.60
The User Account page.

The User Account page allows you to specify the user account name and password that the Domain Migration Administrator uses to collect the information for the reports. The specified user account must have the required access permissions to collect the required information. Click Next, and the Computer Selection page displays as shown in Figure 8.61.

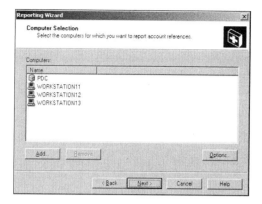

FIGURE 8.61
The Computer Selection page.

The Computer Selection page specifies which computers Domain Migration Administrator will migrate. To migrate computers, click Add and follow the instructions on the Select Computers window. Click Next and the Completed Migration wizard appears. Click Finish to complete the wizard. The next Wizard in the list is the Import wizard. Select it and the Import Wizard Welcome screen displays as shown in Figure 8.62.

FIGURE 8.62
The Import Wizard Welcome screen.

Click Next, and the Database Persistence page displays as shown in Figure 8.63.

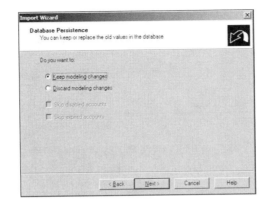

FIGURE 8.63

The Database Persistence page.

The Database Persistence page allows you to specify whether the previously imported data in the modeling database should be kept or replaced. You can also specify whether to collect data about disabled or expired accounts.

You can run the Edit Wizard of Model Data for Users (as shown), Groups, and Computers. When you run this wizard, the data will appear similar to Figure 8.64.

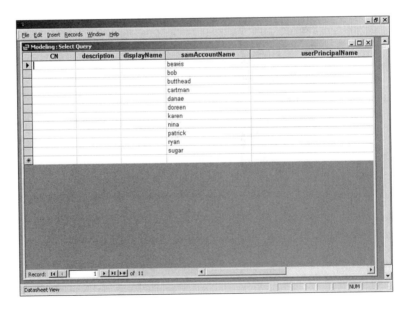

FIGURE 8.64

Specifying a data query.

The next wizard in the list is the Map and Merge Groups Wizard. Select it and the Group Mapping and Merging Wizard Welcome page displays as shown in Figure 8.65.

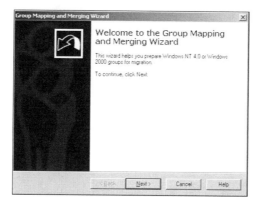

FIGURE 8.65

Welcome screen to Group Mapping and Merging Wizard.

Click Next and the Test or Make changes page displays, as shown in Figure 8.66.

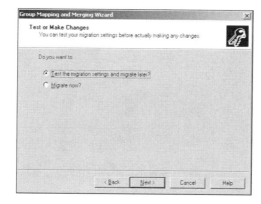

FIGURE 8.66

The Test or Make Changes page.

The Test or Make Changes page specifies whether Domain Migration Administrator writes the specified changes to the source and target domains. Click Next, and the Source Group Selection page displays as shown in Figure 8.67.

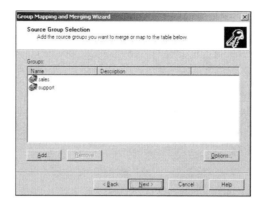

FIGURE 8.67
The Source Group Selection page.

The Source Group Selection page specifies which groups in the source domain will be migrated. To add groups, click Add and follow the instructions on the Select Groups window. Click Next, and the Target Group Selection page displays as shown in Figure 8.68.

FIGURE 8.68
The Target Group Selection page.

The Target Group Selection page specifies the target group that will contain all the members of the selected source groups. Specify the name of the desired target group. If the group does not exist, Domain Migration Administrator can create the specified group. Click Next, and the Organizational Unit Selection page displays as shown in Figure 8.69.

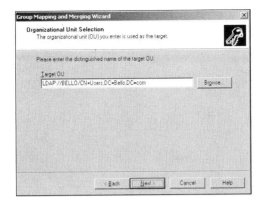

FIGURE 8.69

The Organizational Unit Selection page.

The Organizational Unit Selection page specifies the target container, such as an organizational unit, to which Domain Migration Administrator will migrate selected user accounts, groups, or computer accounts. Click Next, and the Group Options Selection page displays as shown in Figure 8.70.

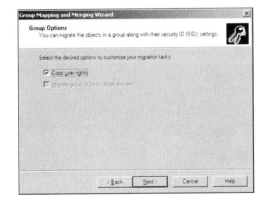

FIGURE 8.70

The Group Options page.

The Group Options page specifies how Domain Migration Administrator handles the group migration. Click Next, and the Scripting page displays as shown in Figure 8.71.

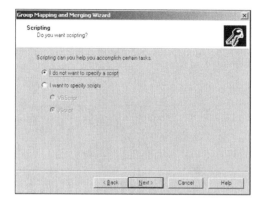

FIGURE 8.71

The Scripting page.

The Scripting page specifies whether you want to use Visual Basic or JavaScript scripts during migration. To specify scripting and the type of scripts to use, click the appropriate radio button. Click Next and the Completed Migration wizard will appear here. Click Finish to complete the wizard.

The next wizard is the Migrate User Account Wizard. Select it and the User Account Migration Wizard Welcome screen displays as shown in Figure 8.72

FIGURE 8.72

The User Migration wizard welcome screen.

Click Next, and the Test or Make Changes page displays as shown in Figure 8.73

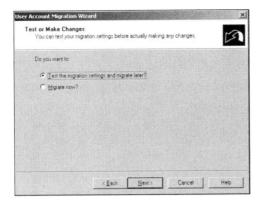

FIGURE 8.73

The Test or Make Changes page.

The Test or Make Changes page specifies whether Domain Migration Administrator writes the specified changes to the source and target domains. Click Next and the Data Source page appears.

The Data Source page allows you to specify whether to use the modeling data and the options specified for the project. They are described as follows:

- Migrate data using modeling database as source Uses the data specified in the modeling database. This database allows you to specify values for several properties of accounts you are migrating. You must have previously imported and edited the modeling data.

- Use migration settings defined in the Migration Settings wizard Applies the options specified through the Migration Settings task to the objects being migrated. If you select this option, some windows are not displayed during the migration process. You should review the values specified through the Migration Settings task before selecting this option. Click Next, and the User Selection page displays as shown in Figure 8.74.

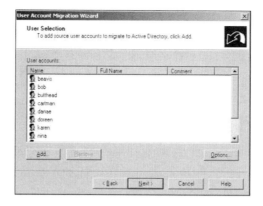

FIGURE 8.74

The User Selection page.

The User Selection page specifies which user accounts in the source domain will be migrated. To add user accounts, click Add and follow the instructions on the Select Users window. Click Next, and the Organizational Unit Selection page displays as shown in Figure 8.75.

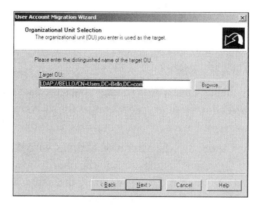

FIGURE 8.75

The Organizational Unit Selection page.

The Organizational Unit Selection page specifies the target container, such as an organizational unit, to which Domain Migration Administrator will migrate selected user accounts, groups, or computer accounts. Click Next, and the Password Options page displays as shown in Figure 8.76.

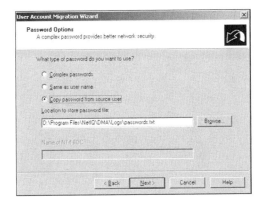

FIGURE 8.76

The Password Options page.

The Password Options page specifies how Domain Migration Administrator assigns passwords to migrated user accounts. Click Next, and the Account Transition Options page displays as shown in Figure 8.77.

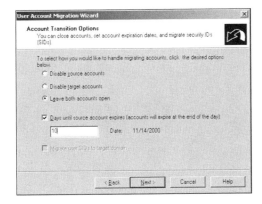

FIGURE 8.77

The Account Transition Options page.

The Account Transition Options page specifies how Domain Migration Administrator handles migrated user accounts in both the source and target domains. Click Next, and the User Options page displays as shown in Figure 8.78.

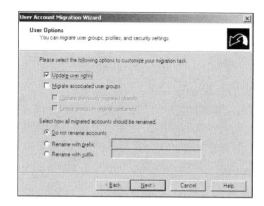

FIGURE 8.78

The User Options page.

The User Options page specifies how Domain Migration Administrator handles the user account migration. Click Next, and the Naming Conflicts page displays as shown in Figure 8.79.

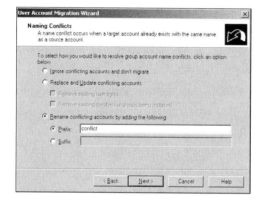

FIGURE 8.79

The Naming Conflicts page.

The Naming Conflicts page specifies how Domain Migration Administrator handles accounts in the target domain that have the same name as a copied account in the source domain. Click Next, and the Advanced User Options page displays as shown in Figure 8.80.

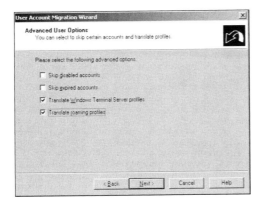

FIGURE 8.80

The Advanced User Options page.

The Advanced User Options page specifies advanced options allowing you to skip certain accounts or translate profiles in the source domain. Click Next, and the Scripting page displays as shown in Figure 8.81.

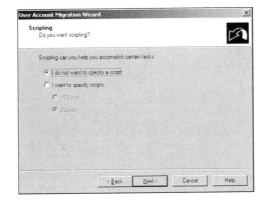

FIGURE 8.81

The Scripting page.

The Scripting page specifies whether you want to use VBasic or JScript scripts during migration. Click Next and the Wizard complete dialog box appears. The next wizard is the Computer Migration Wizard. Select it and the Computer Migration Wizard Welcome displays as shown in Figure 8.82.

FIGURE 8.82

The Computer Migration wizard Welcome screen.

Click Next and the Test or Make Changes page displays as shown in Figure 8.83.

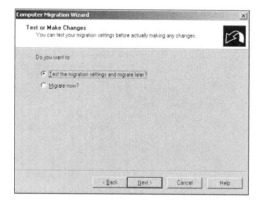

FIGURE 8.83

The Test or Make Changes page.

The Test or Make Changes page specifies whether Domain Migration Administrator writes the specified changes to the source and target domains. Click Next and the Data Source Page appears.

The Data Source page allows you to specify whether to use the modeling data and the options specified for the project. Click Next, and the Computer Selection page displays as shown in Figure 8.84.

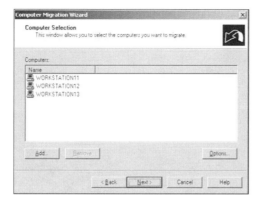

FIGURE 8.84

The Computer Selection page.

The Computer Selection page specifies which computers Domain Migration Administrator will migrate. To add computers, click Add and follow the instructions on the Select Computers window. Click Next, and the Organizational Unit Selection page displays as shown in Figure 8.85.

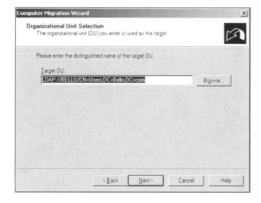

FIGURE 8.85

The Organizational Unit Selection page.

The Organizational Unit Selection page specifies the target container, such as an organizational unit, to which Domain Migration Administrator will migrate selected user accounts, groups, or computer accounts. Click Next, and the Translate Objects page displays as shown in Figure 8.86.

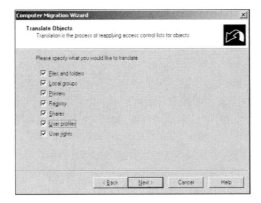

FIGURE 8.86

The Translate Objects page.

The Translate Objects page specifies the types of objects for which you want Domain Migration Administrator to translate security. Click Next, and the Security Translation page displays as shown in Figure 8.87.

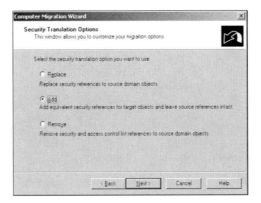

FIGURE 8.87

The Security Translation page.

The Security Translation page specifies how Domain Migration Administrator handles the security translation process. Click Next, and the User Account page displays as shown in Figure 8.88.

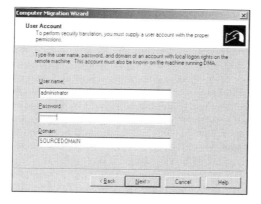

FIGURE 8.88

The User Account page.

The User Account page allows you to specify the user account name and password Domain Migration Administrator uses to perform the security translation process. Click Next, and the Computer Options page displays as shown in Figure 8.89.

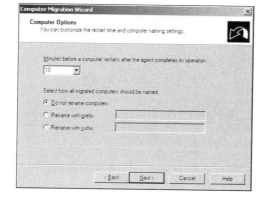

FIGURE 8.89

The Computer Options page.

The Computer Options page specifies how Domain Migration Administrator handles computers after it migrates the computer accounts to the target domain. You can customize the computer name settings and computer restart times with the following options:

- Minutes before computers restart after wizard completion   Specifies how many minutes after the task is completed that the computer on which the agent was run will restart.

- Do not rename computers   Tries to name the migrated computer account the same as the computer account in the source domain. However, if a naming conflict occurs, the options specified on the Naming Conflicts window control how the migrated computer account is named.
- Rename with prefix   Adds the specified prefix to the name of each migrated computer account in the target domain.
- Rename with suffix   Adds the specified suffix to the name of each migrated computer account in the target domain.

The Naming Conflicts page specifies how Domain Migration Administrator handles accounts in the target domain that have the same name as a copied account in the source domain. The fields are defined as follows:

- Ignore conflicting accounts and don't migrate   Leaves the account in the target domain unchanged. Checking this option overrides the update previously migrated objects option.
- Replace and update conflicting accounts   Changes properties of existing accounts in the target domain to match the properties of the account with the same name in the source domain.
- Remove existing user rights   Ensures the account in the target domain does not have more user rights than those granted to the account with the same name in the source domain.
- Remove existing members of groups being replaced   Ensures the members of the migrated groups in the target domain are the same as the members of the associated groups in the source domain.
- Rename conflicting accounts by adding the following   Adds the specified prefix or suffix to the name of the migrated account in the target domain to avoid the conflict with the other account with the same name in the target domain.

Additional Migration Utilities

There are several other migration utilities on the market. The following is a sample listing of migration tools. More are being introduced everyday. You should take your migration plan into consideration to find the right tool for your project.

Aelita Controlled Migration Suite

Aelita has available a Domain Migration Wizard, Enterprise Directory Reporter, Enterprise Delegation Manager, and Server Consolidator. These products can each be purchased separately. The graphical layout is well designed. You can generate reports about your enterprise, schedule when to perform the various phases of your project, and delegate tasks to other administrators. In addition, much like NetIQ Server Consolidator, you can track changes that were made to objects after the migration process was run. However, the scripting features might present problems to some users, as they are not particularly intuitive.

FastLane Migrator and Server Consolidator

Quest has a FastLane Migrator and Server Consolidator. The FastLane suite provides you with tools to address almost all of your migration needs. They provide support for reporting, task delegation, Novell NDS, and Exchange migrations. The user interface is nicely laid out; however, at times it is confusing in terms of what step to perform next given all the information that is presented to you. I do like the ability to point my users' accounts to new profile locations and I feel the process tracking in this product is excellent.

Desktop Migration

Microsoft provides you with some pretty nifty tools to automate deployment of your new desktop operating system. These include RIS, Sysprep, Setupmgr, and third-party tools such as DriveImagePro or Ghost. Microsoft however does not address how to migrate all of your user profile settings from a Windows 9x/NT 4 platform. One frequently overlooked aspect of migrating users to a new machine is the time spent by the user or technician copying data from one location to another (that is until you begin the daunting task). This includes writing down Web site favorites, changing the views in Outlook back to the way they were on the old system, or any other of a thousand and one user-configurable settings.

Tranxition Personality Tranxport Professional (PTPro) and Miramar Desktop DNA (DDNA) are two of the products on the market that can greatly reduce the cost of a desktop migration as well as increase customer satisfaction.

PTPro provides an excellent way to migrate users' data and most common preferences and settings across platforms and even different versions of applications. You can run it manually through the GUI interface or from a command line or batch file using configuration files. While being run from the old computer, you can select which application settings you want migrated and which data types to search.

You have options for turning on migration of various items in the control panel including keyboard, mouse, regional options, and display settings among others. You can select to have mapped drives, printer ports, and network shares recreated. You can also create file rules to include or exclude specific files, directories, or file types. The file rules can also filter based on size or date. These settings are usually saved to a network drive and retrieved from the destination machine.

NetWare Migration

It's a good idea to touch on NetWare migrations because most companies have NetWare servers in their current environment, so it's sure to be an issue you will need to address. Microsoft has a suite of tools for assisting you in your migration efforts away from a Novell platform. The first tool, Microsoft Directory Synchronization Tool, migrates your user and group objects from either a NetWare bindery or NDS tree.

As the name implies, this tool also keeps your two directories synchronized as you make changes in them. However, be aware that directory synchronization is only available from Active Directory to a NetWare bindery server and not NetWare bindery to Active Directory. Otherwise, the product works fairly well at keeping the two directories synchronized until you can have a pure Windows 2000 environment. If you plan to have these two environments coexist for a prolonged period of time, you might want to consider an Enterprise Directory Management solution, which will synchronize the heterogeneous environments.

After you have migrated the accounts to Active Directory, now you can start the file-migration process. Microsoft provides you with a tool called Microsoft File Migration Utility. This tool migrates your directory structure and permissions to the new Windows 2000 file server.

You also need to consider how you will support file and print resources for clients until the migration is complete. This can be accomplished through a variety of methods or any combination of methods that suit your environment. You can use Gateway Services for NetWare with which you will set up a Windows 2000 server to act as a portal to the NetWare server. This is a good solution if you are going to have the NetWare servers around only for a short period of time. If this is an indefinite solution, you might want to consider installing Microsoft's client on the workstations. This would be Client Services for NetWare. Be aware that Client Services for NetWare only supports the NWLink (IPX/SPX) protocol. Therefore, it might be advisable to install the Novell Client32 for Windows especially if you have NetWare 5.x servers.

Summary

This chapter provided an overview of how Windows NT 4 domain structures can be migrated to Windows 2000 and Active Directory. It also provided a description of the various Microsoft-supplied migration tools as well as an overview into several third-party migration tools.

CASE STUDY

Learning by Example: the "Molly Pitcher Pharmaceuticals, Inc." Company

To develop a migration plan for Molly Pitcher Pharmaceuticals, Inc., the existing Windows NT 4.0 Domain environment must be analyzed.

Existing Windows NT 4.0 Domain Environment

Molly Pitcher currently utilizes Windows NT 4.0 in a master domain model. There is a master domain at headquarters that houses all user accounts for headquarters employees. There are several resource domains, one for each department at headquarters. Also, each remote office contains a resource domain. Total number of domains is 19.

Domain controllers for all resource domains and the headquarters master domain are located in Valley Forge. BDCs for the master domain have been placed at each remote office to speed up user authentication.

Migration Plan

Because of the rather complex domain structure, it would be prudent to perform a domain restructure. All 18 resource domains can be restructured into OUs. Authority for the OUs can be delegated to the respective resource administrators. To ease the migration, an Upgrade and Restructure should be performed. In this case, the master domain housing all user accounts will be upgraded to Windows 2000. Once that domain is upgraded, the migration of security principals and objects from the resource domains can begin.

The migration of the resource domains would not need to be performed in any particular order. However, it would be more logical to fold the resource domains located at headquarters before the resource domains located at the remote offices.

Next, domain controllers in the master domain would need to be identified and documented. Any domain controllers that do not meet the hardware requirements of Windows 2000 would need to be replaced or upgraded.

To provide yourself with a backout plan, perform a full backup on all domain controllers. In the Master Domain, use Server Manager to perform a full synchronization of the domain. Once the synchronization is complete, pull one of the master domain BDCs offline and place it in a secure location. This BDC can be used to recover the master domain account database in case of a failure.

The first domain controller to be upgraded will be the master domain's PDC.

Immediately following the PDC, all sites should be created in Active Directory. This will allow the remaining domain controllers to be automatically added to their respective Active Directory Site when they are upgraded or installed.

The remaining domain controllers can be upgraded in any particular order.

Once the master domain is upgraded to Active Directory, the migration of security principals and objects from the resource domains can begin.

Migration Tools

Because an Upgrade and Restructure is being performed, user accounts and global groups from the master domain will be automatically migrated to Active Directory during the operating system upgrade on the domain controllers. However, objects from the resource domains, such as computer accounts, global groups, and other user accounts, will need to be copied/cloned into the new domain structure.

The easiest and cheapest way to migrate these objects is to use Microsoft's Active Directory Migration Tool (ADMT). This is a GUI-based tool that is relatively simple to use and provides all of the functionalities required for this migration. With ADMT, you can perform test migrations as well as run migration reports.

Trips and Traps: Troubleshooting AD

IN THIS CHAPTER

Okay, so now you've installed your Windows 2000 domain. Your users are running on Windows 2000 Professional, and you are happily using group policies and the occasional distributed bit of software to keep their machines locked down so tight they can barely change their desktop items, let alone mess with system .dlls.

Now, however, you have a host of problems associated with a new directory and management paradigm. Even if you've done your planning reasonably well, there is still going to be an inevitable break-in period during which you are learning things slower than you are breaking them. This is normal.

In order to get over the major hurdles of this time, this chapter addresses the following issues:

- **Domain mode issues**—The switch between mixed and native more is relatively trivial, but it's still important to consider what is involved to do so.
- **Directory and File Replication**—What is involved with inter- and intra-site replication for both your directories and your files.
- **Group policies problems**—How you can sort out the tangled web of group policies to determine what is going wrong.
- **Software installation**—What can go wrong and what are the best ways to avoid the problems in the first place?

This list does not imply that these areas are inclusive of every problem that can occur in Windows 2000. These topics do, however, allow you to consider some of the most complex changes that you are going to face as you move into your new environment.

Using Domain Modes

Chapter 7, "Supporting Active Directory Environments," mentioned that there are not that many practical differences between Windows 2000 in mixed mode and in native mode. This is in every way true. The switch between the two modes is really more a matter of when you will be able to complete the upgrades of your old BDCs than it is a technical issue.

In fact, upgrading to native mode may well be one of the simplest things you ever do in Windows 2000. All you really have to do is

1. Open the Active Directory Domains and Sites tool.
2. Right-click the domain.
3. Select Properties.
4. Select Native Mode (see Figure 9.1).
5. Click Okay.
6. Reboot the server.

FIGURE 9.1

The "momentous" decision.

That being said, there are a few things you should consider before performing the switch. Specifically, there are things that are just different in mixed and native modes. These behaviors are not that big a deal, but if you are not aware of them they will cause you heartache.

In Mixed Mode

When you bring up your first Windows 2000 domain controller (DC), you are in mixed mode. Mixed mode straddles the line between the more robust "native mode" in which you can use all of the features of Active Directory, and backwards compatibility with all of your existing infrastructure (see Figure 9.2).

While in mixed mode:

- You do not have access to universal groups.
- Windows 2000 Professional Workstations directly access other domains to query for group memberships in those domains.
- The PDC emulator is the only server in the domain with an `ldap.tcpwritable._msdcs._domainname` entry in the DNS records.
- You cannot use most migration utilities (as they require access to the `SIDHistory` attribute, which is disabled in mixed mode).
- The Schema and Enterprise Manager groups are global groups.
- NT 4.0 Services for Macintosh may fail (although there is a hotfix for this behavior).
- Domain local groups act like local groups on domain controllers in an NT 4.0 domain (that is, they are shared around with all of the domain controllers, but not with the member servers or other workstations).
- Downlevel BDCs can still synchronize their security data with the Windows 2000 domain.
- Advanced options in Remote Access are not available. These options include Verify Caller ID, Assign Static IP, and Static Routes.
- Services may still use the domain's NetBIOS name to gain access to its services.

9

TRIPS AND TRAPS: TROUBLESHOOTING AD

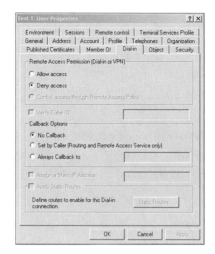

FIGURE 9.2
In mixed mode, you cannot use some configurations.

The practical upshot off all of this is that you are not really taking full advantage of the power of Windows 2000. Your domain has only one writeable copy of the database, your clients are reaching out across your WANs to get group memberships, and you cannot easily grant enterprise administration status to those individuals who need it.

In Native Mode

The "switch" to native mode should come as soon as possible in your Windows 2000 migration. Getting all of the NT 4.0 BDCs out of your environment should be one of your first priorities. Not only do you get to actually use Windows 2000, but you also get to use some of the tools that would otherwise go to waste (see Figure 9.3).

In native mode:

- Windows NT BDCs cannot synchronize their security settings with the domain.
- All domain controllers register as writeable.
- Windows 2000 Professional workstations query global catalogue servers to get group information from domains they are not members of.
- Scheme and Enterprise Administrators become universal groups.
- Domain Local Groups start behaving as described in the Microsoft Help files.
- You can access the various Remote Access Configuration options.

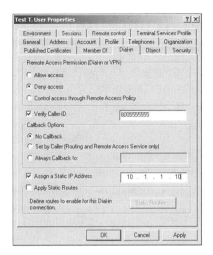

FIGURE 9.3

In native mode, you can use the configurations.

The conversion to native mode is especially important when you are using a hybridized migration model—one in which you are upgrading one domain and collapsing several other domains into the newly upgraded domain. In this scenario you should work as diligently as possible to ensure that you get your target domain into native mode as quickly as possible. This allows you to use the migration tools created by a variety of vendors, making your life a great deal easier. For further discussion of migration tools, refer to Chapter 8, "Migration Planning and Migration Tools."

What Doesn't Change

Okay, let's take this moment to dispel one final myth before moving on to addressing things that actually do go wrong. You cannot turn off NetBIOS just because you switch to native mode.

Just because your servers are not using NetBIOS to address each other (although you probably should be quick to jump to that conclusion), there are still services, applications, and various devices that are dependent on NetBIOS to function correctly. If you decide to take on the mandate of removing NetBIOS (and its evil henchman, WINS) from your environment, you have a long and difficult row to hoe. The more legacy you have (in terms of hardware, software, and services), the longer and more difficult the process will be.

The greatest barrier to removing NetBIOS comes from legacy applications that provide business critical functionality but that no one really understands anymore. Replacing these things takes time, patience, and customer savvy.

In short, if you want to really get rid of NetBIOS, it's a long and difficult project all its own.

9

TRIPS AND TRAPS: TROUBLESHOOTING AD

Directory and File Replication

There are two separate replication architectures in the Windows 2000 environment. These architectures mirror one another in some ways, but should not be confused with one another. Worse yet, they are also to some extent interdependent: some functions of Active Directory simply do not work properly unless File Replication is running smoothly.

This section focuses around two topics:

- **Active Directory Replication**—Considers how the directory entries are updated and what happens when something goes wrong
- **File Replication Service (FRS)**—Considers what data is replicated by default, which services rely on this replication, and how to tell when something has gone terribly, horribly wrong

Most of this chapter focuses on understanding at a basic level what is going on, what the symptoms are, and how to use free tools to troubleshoot problems when they arise.

These topics are not exactly the easiest to discuss—both AD Replication and FRS are complex topics that have stumped the minds of many a budding system administrator. This chapter discusses these topics at a very high level; going too deep into the mechanics of the replication schemes is beyond the scope of this book. And frankly, the information isn't all that useful unless you are dealing with some extremely confusing problems to begin with.

Active Directory Replication

You probably know from previous discussions that the Active Directory is a multimaster security database that governs access to resources in your enterprise. You also know that changes made to one of the databases in the Active Directory are automatically copied to all of the other databases.

Underlying this simple explanation is a host of complex technical details. Although these details are vitally important to the functioning of the database, they are also more than a bit esoteric.

This section addresses the following issues:

- What is really replicated?
- How does a server know whom to replicate with?
- What tools exist to help you when there are problems?
- What are the symptoms when good replicas go bad?
- What do you really need to do to configure AD Replication?

What Is Really Replicated

With the Active Directory architecture Microsoft tried to limit the amount of network traffic generated by the inevitable process of moving, adding, and changing accounts and services in the directory. In order to do this, Microsoft came up with a simple yet profound idea:

> After the initial replication to create the AD database on the domain controller, AD will only replicate the attributes of the objects that are changed by the administrator.

What this means is that if you change the last name of an individual, the directory does not replicate all of the information in the account object. Instead, it only replicates the actual attribute that changed (in this case, the last name).

Before you get overly excited about this, you need to realize the following:

- Not everything that you think of as an attribute is really an attribute. For example, all of the SIDs of the members of the group are lumped into a single attribute. Your best friend here is the Windows 2000 Resource Kit, which discusses how the schema is organized in painful detail.

- Because you are in a multimaster domain, changes that you make to the attributes of an object on one database might not show up for a little while on other databases.

- If you make changes to the same attribute in two databases (say, alter the group membership of group foo on one database and make a different change to the group membership of the group foo on another database), *only one* of the changes will be saved when the directory finally fully synchronizes. This can lead to some very strange results, especially if you have made several changes to the same object in different places.

- Each attribute in Active Directory has an update sequence number (USN), which is updated when the attribute is updated. This USN is compared with the known USNs of the server's replication partners, and if the USN is higher than the USN on the other server, it replicates. This is confusing to track, as the USN is unique to each server pair, and can easily be different from one site to another.

Practically, what this means for you is

- Wait for replication when possible. By default, if you make a change in a site, it will take five minutes for that change to propagate to the other domain controllers in the site. You can change this value if you like, but doing so can have unexpected consequences. Just be patient.

- When working with multiple sites, always work on the domain controller closest to the user. Choose a domain controller in the user's site, or the domain controller in the site closest to the user.

9

TRIPS AND TRAPS:
TROUBLESHOOTING
AD

- Make changes in one place and wait. Don't go hopping around making the same change in every database. Doing so can cause considerable problems, and can even cause one or more of your databases to corrupt.

The good news about all of this patience is that there are some changes, called urgent updates, that are immediately forwarded to replication partners within a site. These include

- Newly locked out accounts
- Changes to LSA secrets
- Changes to the RID manager

This means that if an account is locked out (or you lock it out), that information is shared as quickly as possible. Additionally, password changes are urgently replicated with the PDC FSMO and all domain controllers check with the PDC FSMO when they have a password mismatch to be sure that they have the latest copy of the password in question.

How Does a Server Know Who to Replicate With and When?

So now you know what AD wants to replicate (changes to attributes). But whom does it want to replicate with? Does each domain controller replicate with every other domain controller? Is there a "hub" domain controller that all of the others communicate with? Is all information replicated the same way? And how do sites fit into all of this?

Those are all excellent questions. Legions of trees have died providing the answers to them. I'll kill a few more providing some practical advice, and attempting to provide an explanation that isn't overly weird.

The simplest answer is that something called the Knowledge Consistency Checker (KCC) is responsible for answering all of these questions for you. In fact, 99% of the time the KCC takes care of all of these things in the background and you don't have to worry about them at all.

Generally, the KCC tries to set things up like this:

- Within a site (intra-site replication) the KCC tries to set up a ring topology, with each DC communicating with two other DCs. The KCC tries to create a redundant ring, where information flows in both directions as needed. If something happens to a DC in ring, the KCC reforms the ring without user intervention.
- Between sites, the KCC creates bridgehead servers in each site that connect to bridgehead servers in other sites. These servers replicate using the information established when you created the site links. If a bridgehead is removed, the KCC selects another one.

The KCC runs on each domain controller. Within a site, the KCCs of each domain controller function independently and create connection objects as required. Between sites, one KCC in each site (called the inter-site topology generator) is elected to build the replication topology.

How long does all of this take? The KCC runs every 15 minutes, and shouldn't take more than a few seconds to finish its topology calculations. However, in very large environments (with more than 10 domains and 125 sites) there can be problems with the time it takes to finish the calculations. There is a detailed description of this condition in Q article 244368.

What Tools Exist to Help You

There are three tools that you can use to assist you in your constant quest to manage and maintain your directory databases:

- **Active Directory Sites and Services**—The MMC snap-in where you can see the results of the inter-site topology generator's actions.

- **NTDSUtil.exe**—A built-in application that allows you to modify and repair your database.

- **ReplMon.exe**—An application on the Windows 2000 CD that allows you to monitor the replication status of servers in the same site.

These three tools give you most of the firepower that you need to deal with almost any replication issue. However, you might also need to use either backup software (to restore the database) or Dcpromo.exe (to demote and re-promote a damaged domain controller) in the event of a truly catastrophic failure.

Active Directory Sites and Services

The Active Directory Sites and Services MMC snap-in is available from Start, Programs, and then Administrative Tools.

This snap-in can be used to:

- Set up sites and site links
- Force a Knowledge Consistency Check on the topology (see Figure 9.4)
- Verify which servers a domain controller replicates with (see Figure 9.5)

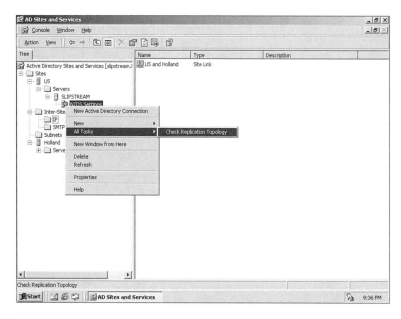

FIGURE 9.4

Forcing a topology check.

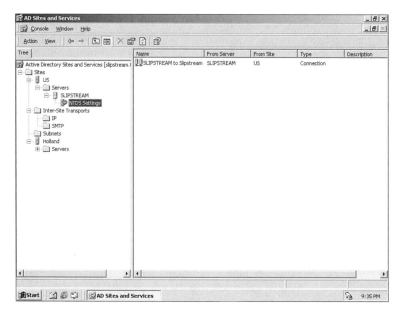

FIGURE 9.5

Looking at NTDS Settings in a DC.

NTDSUtil.exe

NTDSUtil.exe is one of those low-level, hard-to-use applications that Microsoft typically posts big warnings on saying things like "If you use this, have a current copy of your ERD ready." Although it is a remarkably powerful directory manipulation utility, it is also not that bad.

In order to use it, you have to start the domain controller you intend to use it on in Directory Services Restore Mode. You do this by:

1. Restarting the computer.
2. Pressing F8 when it prompts you to do so for advanced options.
3. Selecting the Directory Repair Mode option.
4. Letting the system finish booting.

When you finally have access to your user interface, you can start NTDSUtil by using Start, Run, and typing **NTDSUtil.exe** at the prompt.

The screen that appears looks suspiciously like a normal command prompt, down to showing you a drive path, as shown in Figure 9.6.

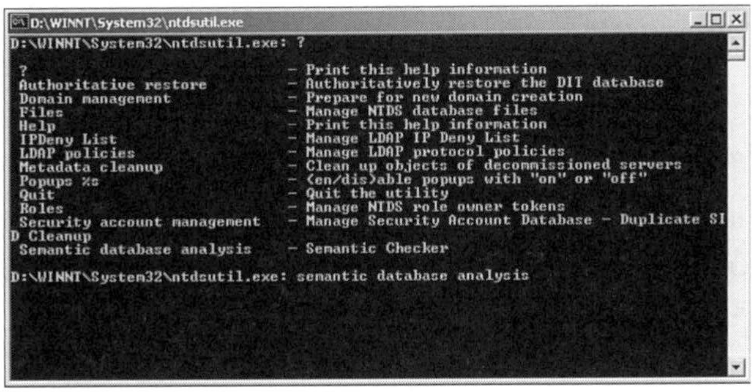

FIGURE 9.6

NTDSUtil: an executable or just another command shell?

There are a couple of important things to remember when you are using this particular piece of software:

- This tool directly manipulates the database, its files, and the schema. Do not use it lightly.
- Although there are short-cut abbreviations for just about all of the commands, go ahead and type them in long form. This will prevent you from accidentally using the wrong command.

- When in doubt, type **?** and press Enter. This will call up the context-sensitive menu that tells you what you can do from a particular part of the program.

- Quit always works.

- Always use the option to check only before using the option to check and fix. This is just good practice, and more so whenever using tools that can destroy the database.

Figure 9.7 shows the semantic checker in action. First you used the Go function to scan for errors and then you used the Go Fix function to fix the errors found during the scan. Because this database is actually in pretty good shape, there were no problems to fix.

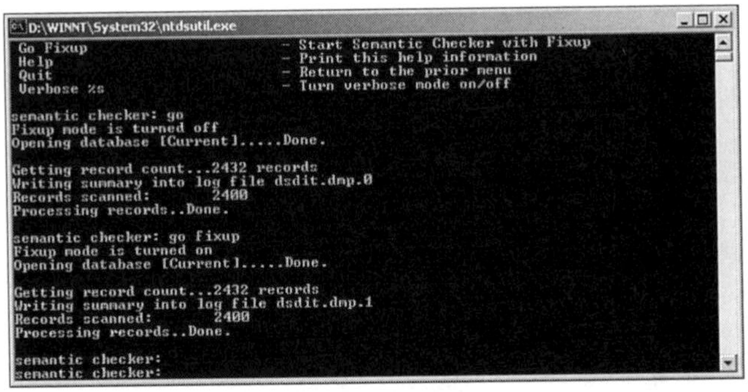

FIGURE 9.7

Checking for errors before asking a utility to fix them.

Once you reboot the server and let it come up in normal mode, the database should be fixed. Unfortunately, there is no way to be certain that it will stay that way, especially if the corruption is actually endemic to the entire system.

ReplMon.exe

In the Support folder on your Windows 2000 Distribution Disk you will find a set of tools that can help you in your daily administrative grind. Contrary to popular belief, these tools were not included just because Microsoft had nothing better to do with their time.

One of these tools is the so-called Replmon.exe, otherwise known by its GUI name of Active Directory Replication Monitor. After the installation of the Support Tools, you'll find it in the path shown in Figure 9.8.

Replmon.exe is the kind of tool that gives you as much as you are willing to put into it. For every server, it can give you a laundry list of information, as shown in Figure 9.9.

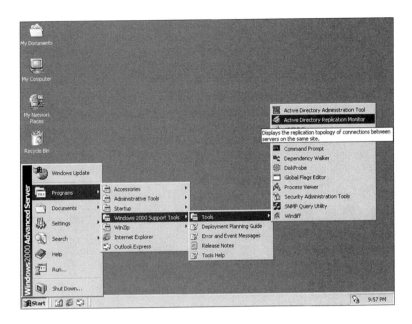

FIGURE 9.8

The path to the Replmon.exe.

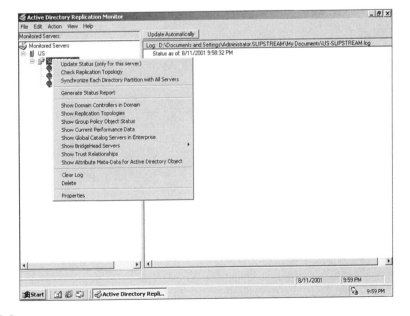

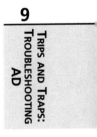

FIGURE 9.9

Replication Monitor functions by server.

One of the first things that you should do when you suspect that replication is not working (for whatever reason) is fire up the Replmon.exe and find out what's wrong. It will show you everything you ever wanted to know about the directory replication in your network, and will even touch a bit on File Replication.

This is not a tool for solving problems, but a tool for discovering what it is that is really wrong.

When Good Replicas Go Bad

There are some symptoms you can look for that tell you when a replica you are working with is not quite all it should be. These include

- Users are locked out when they try to access services in the domain.
- Directories contain accounts (computer, user, or group) that you deleted weeks or even months ago.
- When you change the group membership on one domain controller, it changes back to its original setting.
- Large numbers of replication errors show up in the event log on a single domain controller.
- Some accounts are marked by their SIDs rather than their common names, and those SIDs do not resolve no matter how much you refresh the display.
- New accounts do not appear in one or more of your sites.

You have a couple of choices in dealing with a bad replica:

- You can just demote the domain controller and then promote it again. This re-creates the database and forces the KCC to re-create the site replication topology. You can do this if the domain controller is one of several DCs in a site, and if no other services are running on it that require it to be a DC and are required in production when you do the demote/promote process.
- You can use NTDSUtil.exe to run a database-integrity check. This will fix any miscellaneous problems that arise during normal database operations, and will solve all but the most difficult problems.
- If you have accidentally deleted an account, you can perform what is called an authoritative restore. This restore increments the USNs by some incredible number (as much as 3,000,000) for every object in the AD. You need to be careful about this method, as it wipes out every change you've made since the last acceptable backup. You also need to be sure that your restored DB is less than 60 days old—any older than that, and you can cause serious database corruption that will cause you to rebuild your AD from scratch.

These are your best options. You can spend hours, even days, working on the things and not come up with any better results.

The File Replication Service (FRS)

Back in the bad old days of Windows NT 4, there was a file replication service that never worked quite right. LMRepl could handle a few scripts, but more than that and you were out of luck.

Windows 2000 has a fully functional File Replication Service (FRS). This service is active by default, and works pretty much without your intervention.

The File Replication Service uses the replication topology created by the KCC to replicate information intra-site and inter-site. This replication follows the replication schedules and timers established in the topology.

Despite following the same schedule, FRS and AD Replication do have some differences:

- FRS replicates entire files, not just the changes.
- FRS picks up a changed file as soon as it is closed. If the file is opened and closed several times, several copies of the file are picked up and replicated.
- FRS uses the timestamp to resolve conflicts. The copy with the newest timestamp is the winner in any cases of conflict.
- FRS uses a "staging area" of 660MB to prepare for copying files. If the data that needs to be moved is more than 660MB, there might be replication problems. AD does not use a staging area of this type.
- FRS does not compress data during replication.

What all of this really means is that, in the end, FRS is more vulnerable to network errors and is slower than AD Replication. It also means that when you have an interaction between FRS and AD (as in the case of GPOs), it is possible that delays in FRS replication will result in what appear to be AD errors.

What Is Replicated?

FRS, shown in Figure 9.10, replicates the following information:

- SYSVOL content
- DFS replicas

That's it. This service replicates nothing else.

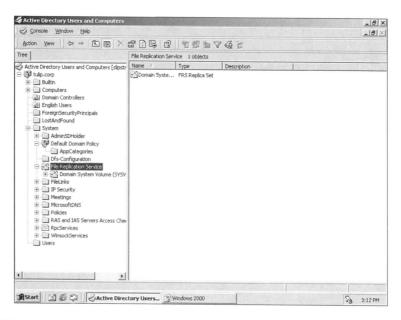

FIGURE 9.10
The FRS screen.

SYSVOL contains all of the basic text files that your network needs to operate (GPOs in particular), as well as login scripts and potential application packages. FRS is responsible for ensuring that the contents of all of the SYSVOL shares in the domain are kept in a state of convergence.

DFS operates slightly differently than ordinary FRS replication. FRS builds a full mesh topology with all DFS root and child replicas. Each member of the network can copy to every other member of the network. Thanks to the way that FRS works, this can cause considerable—even catastrophic—errors, especially on slow networks. You will want to change this behavior, using the Active Directory Users and Computers MMC, with the Advanced View activated. Look under the FRS node to see the DFS volumes and their roots.

What Does it Look Like When it Goes Wrong?

Other than kicking up the occasional error, when FRS fails, you will see the following kinds of problems:

- Users log in using retired scripts
- Retired or older versions of GPOs applied to workstations
- DFS content is inconsistent across sites
- Files in DFS shares appear to randomly revert to older forms

- New domain controllers cannot come online (because they cannot actually build their SYSVOL)

- The network swamps out at periodic intervals as DFS servers open RPCs with each other

At first, none of these will seem to be the result of FRS. Users will complain a bit, and maybe you will see an occasional error come across your desk. But these kinds of problems tend to grow over time, eventually leading to the kinds of instability seen at one of my clients who shall remain nameless. No matter what they did, they couldn't seem to get new scripts rolled out to the user community. Eventually, we isolated a single good domain controller, pulled all of the other domain controllers down to member servers, and rebuilt the domain.

What Can You Do?

A little proactive management will go a long way towards preventing most of these problems. Here is what you can do to help yourself:

- Do not use DFS for volatile documents, or documents that will be edited at multiple sites. There are a variety of document-management tools (including SharePoint Server) that can help meet these kinds of needs.

- Do not make changes to GPOs and scripts and expect them to immediately show up either within the site or outside of the site where the change was made. As with Active Directory, make the change in the site closest to the point where the change needs to be felt first.

- Monitor the various replication activities using the Replmon.exe included in the Support tools. Don't let the first indication that something is wrong be a phone call from one of your users.

- Do not attempt to replicate extremely large amounts of data (over 1GB) with the FRS. It is possible to do it, but each time you make a change to the FRS configuration, you will have to make custom changes to your servers.

- Do keep the servers up to the latest service pack. There are a number of FRS and DFS errors that are fixed in each service pack, and it would be a shame to suffer from a bug someone has already fixed.

- Be careful about following the advise in Q224512, which explains how to alter the replication topology of DFS to better fit with the needs of real networks. Although it will save a lot of network traffic if done correctly, making manual changes to an automatically generated topology leads to a great deal more work if you want to make changes later.

For all of the angst that people feel about DFS and FRS, the reality is that with a little planning these features are relatively self-maintaining. If you simply accept their limitations up front, rather than trying to do things that they are not suited for, you end up being in a much better position to assist your clients in the long run.

Group Policy

The single most exciting feature of Windows 2000 for most administrators is Group Policy Objects (GPOs). With just a little imagination, it is possible to see a network in which machines are taken out of the box and simply plugged into the network, and then automatically configured by layer upon layer of security settings until the box looks, acts, and feels exactly like it is supposed to based on the unique profile of the user who logs into it.

After all, that's what Microsoft promised in all of those hype-filled adds about the wonders of Windows 2000. GPOs seem to deliver on that promise, showing you how to build complex system configurations into the network itself.

All of that promise, though, comes at a heavy price. With 690+ possible settings per GPO, it's easy to get lost. Especially when you start adding layers of GPOs, applying several GPOs to a single OU, or filtering GPOs on a single OU using security groups.

The next few pages discuss the kinds of problems that you can run into with GPOs. It addresses the following topics:

- How to tell that things are going wrong—Some symptoms to look for before your network comes crashing down around your ears.
- The do's and don'ts of group policy—Some comments on GPO best practices, from people who should have known better to people who would like to know better before the disaster strikes.
- Group policy mergers and acquisitions—A few notes on that strangest of subjects, group policy loopback and the kinds of problems that it can cause.
- Tools that help you to understand—A discussion of the out-of-the-box tools that can assist you, as well as a few notes about the kinds of documentation you will want to keep around.
- Hacking group policies—What to do and what not to do.

By following a few simple rules, you should be able to achieve a reasonable, stable, and useful GPO set.

How to Tell That Things Are Going Wrong

One of the hardest parts of using GPOs is telling when you have made a configuration error. There are only a few error log messages associated with GPOs, and none of them point to a specific part of the GPO. Worse yet, it is usually not a single setting in the GPO that is causing a problem, but rather an interaction of settings that is neither easy to identify nor simple to fix.

Despite the lack of obvious red flags, there are a few things that you can keep your eyes open for. When you see the following things in your environment, you know that somewhere, something has gone astray:

- The client computers seize up for a period of time immediately following the application of the GPOs. This happens when the GPOs are applying a large number of settings all at once.

- Mobile users complain that their settings are different from location to location in the network, and these settings are both obvious and intrusive (like changes to the ways that offline folders work).

- The users get inconsistent policies despite logging in using the same account and being in the same site consistently. This can happen when a user is temporarily moved into a security group that is used to filter a GPO.

- Local group membership (like administrators or power users on workstations) is inconstantly populated and changes from day to day. This can happen when the restricted groups function is inconstantly or incorrectly populated in one or more of the GPOs.

- Users constantly gets the same software applications attempting to install themselves on the workstation.

- Logins are taking two to three times as long as they were in the original, pre-GPO change configuration. This happens when the security settings are either in conflict or are simply so large that they interfere with normal processing.

- The computer is not getting the GPO. This happens when the filtering is not set up correctly, especially in software installation.

As you can see, the list of possible symptoms is unfortunately rather broad, and for the most part are not the kinds of things that users are actually going to call in about. Worse, there are a lot of things that can cause these symptoms—GPOs are only one of several possible root causes for delays, incomplete security, and the like.

Dos and Don'ts of Group Policy

The following are tasks that you very much want to perform using GPOs:

- Limit the number of GPOs that apply to any single workstation or user to four or fewer. This vastly reduces the number of places that you need to go look to determine errors.

- Assign one person to work with the GPOs for an organization. This person should have a backup, but is the sole point of contact for any changes that people want to make to the GPO.

- Cluster functions (workstation configurations, software assignments, and software configurations) into as few GPOs as possible.

- Link each GPO to only one OU, no matter how tempting it is to link it to multiple OUs.
- Put settings in the highest-level OU that they possibly can be in. For example, if you want the everyone group to be a member of the power users group on all workstations in your environment, set the restricted group setting at the highest workstation OU, rather than on each OU below it.
- Decide whether a GPO will be used for computer or user configurations, and stick with that decision. This not only allows you to reduce the time associated with processing the GPO, but also gives you a framework for whatever changes you want to make.

You should correspondingly try to:

- Avoid the use of GPO security (also called filtering) to assign GPOs to users. Although this is tempting, it is also very difficult to manage, and can lead to unexpected consequences in complex networks.
- Limit the use of login and logoff scripts to a single GPO. Otherwise, you will end up having to do some very complex integration testing with your scripts, leading to either delayed deployments or unexpected errors.
- Avoid using GPO loopback whenever possible. This helps you reduce the complexity of your troubleshooting, and also helps avoid the problems associated with inconsistent application of policies across a network.
- Limit the application of Registry settings. Each Registry setting takes a certain, relatively short amount of time to process. Hundreds of Registry settings can take several seconds to process, and thousands can extend your user logon times by several minutes.

By checking to see whether these rules are followed, you can often identify a root cause of serious GPO problems relatively quickly.

Group Policy Mergers and Acquisitions

Other than flat out network errors, there are two things that can cause a GPOs not to be applied when you think that they should be—the OU can have inheritance blocked, or the workstation GPO can have loopback enabled. If either of these conditions is true, you might end up with workstations that have radically different configurations than you think they should.

Blocking inheritance is described in some detail in Chapter 7. In essence, it allows an administrator to specify that all of the objects in a given OU will not receive the GPOs from any of the OUs above the given OU. This feature is particularly useful for so-called unmanaged resources, or for OUs that need very particular security configurations. It can also be useful for helping to establish security boundaries related to administrative boundaries within a specific domain.

GPO loopback (see Figure 9.11) is often confused with block inheritance, and is sometimes activated by mistake. Although block inheritance is an OU-based setting, GPO loopback is a GPO-specific setting.

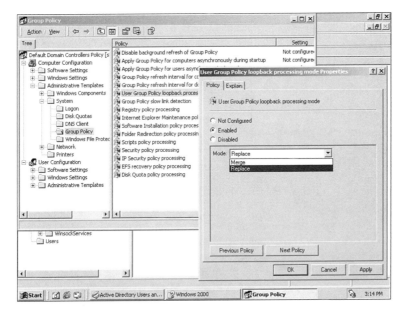

FIGURE 9.11
GPO loopback is located in the Computer Settings section of the GPO in question.

Loopback is not the same as block inheritance, although it can appear to behave in a similar fashion. In particular, whereas block inheritance has one setting (on or off), loopback has two:

- **Merge**—In this case, the computer reorders the GPO settings so that its GPOs are applied after the user's GPO are applied. This delays the logon time, but ensures that the settings for the computer are applied to the workstation rather than the users—unless the users settings cannot be changed due to settings enforcement regardless of application order.
- **Replace**—Prevents the computer from gathering the user's GPO information when he or she logs onto the workstation. Replace is used when you do not want the user's GPO applied to the workstation at all.

One of the first things to check when you see that GPOs are being inconsistently applied is to verify whether GPO loopback (rather than block inheritance) has been applied to a particular workstation GPO.s

Tools That Help

Okay, so let's say that you've already decided to ignore all of the advise given to you in the rest of the book and you've built a tangled web of GPOs that do all kinds of things you only barely understand. How can you tell what the resultant set of policies being applied to your workstation/user combinations really is, and how do you tell where each setting comes from?

Your first and most important tool is the change logs that you should keep for your network. These can be random scraps of paper, a complex database, or even part of a fully fledged asset management tool. Whatever the case, you should check the change log as soon as something starts to go wrong. With luck, it will at least tell you what has changed.

Barring proper administrative procedures, there are also a bevy of tools to help you out. Some, such as Full Armor, are available for purchase. Some, specifically GPOTool.exe and GPResult.exe, are available for free from Microsoft. As always, you get what you pay for.

GPOTool.exe, shown in Figure 9.12, is a one of those tools that really should have come installed with the basic operating system. It allows you to check the status of all of the GPOs on the network and in the domain from one easy command line.

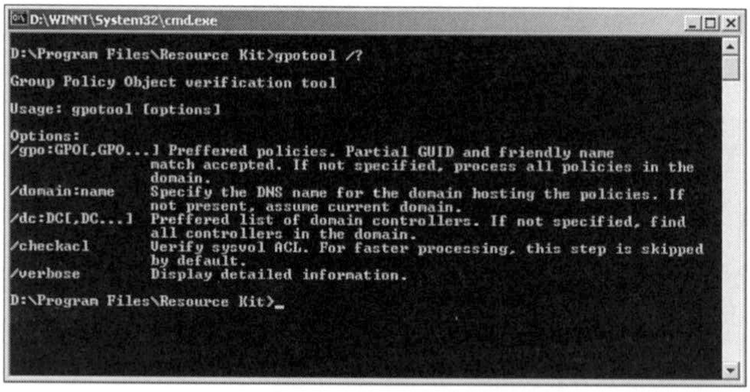

FIGURE 9.12

The GPOTool.exe is a command-line program with a fair number of switches.

When you run the tool, it checks each of the GPOs in your network and reports on any problems, as shown in Figure 9.13.

FIGURE 9.13
The GPOTool.exe results.

You use GPOTool.exe when you see symptoms that indicate a problem with replication: changes disappearing, old scripts or GPOs being applied, that sort of thing. It allows you to pinpoint problem areas for investigation quickly, bypassing lengthy analysis.

GPresult.exe is a much more complicated to read than it is to use. Like GPOTool.exe, it is a command-line program that can be downloaded for free from Microsoft, or installed directly from your Resource Kit.

Also like GPOTool.exe, Gpresult.exe is a powerful tool that can generate a great deal of information. Specifically, it can (when used with the /s switch) tell you the exact setting provided by each GPO to the workstation. Unfortunately, this information is output in a rather user-unfriendly fashion, as shown in Figure 9.14.

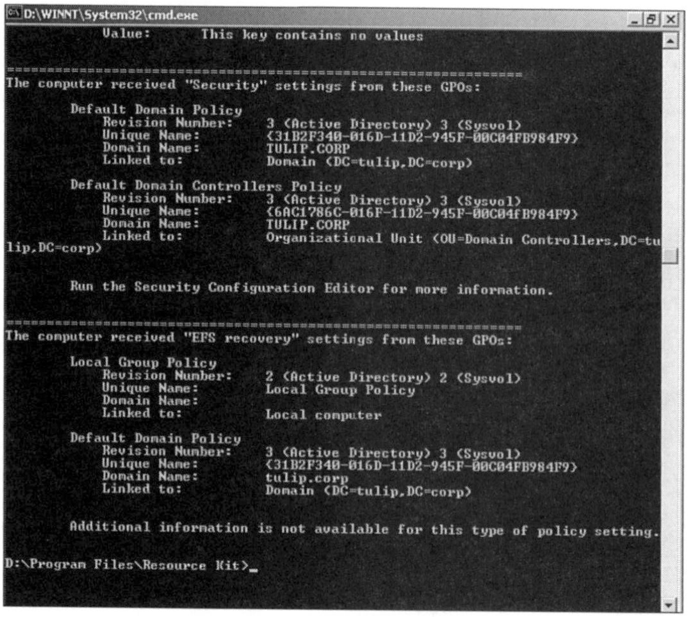

FIGURE 9.14

The results of a Gpresult.exe run.

Gpresult.exe can be used on any workstation or server that is experiencing what appears to be odd GPO problems. For best results, you should take a set of results from a "healthy" workstation with a configuration that you want to use, and compare the two.

Hacking Group Policies

Creating .adm templates is a relatively simple process, as is adding whatever Registry keys to an existing GPO you care to. The question is—why? Why would you go around randomly hacking the Registry? Is there really any value in doing something that generally comes with large disclaimers on it?

Well, unfortunately, the answer to that last question is yes. There are reasons for you to think about applying Registry settings globally. These include, but are not limited to:

- Your company has developed an in-house application that needs specific Registry settings for individual users.
- You have a Registry fix for a problem that is plaguing your environment and you want to apply it globally to all existing and new computers or users.
- There is a Registry setting that you need to apply globally for legal or political reasons.

That being said, be very careful about what you choose to do here. The GPO editor is, in effect, RegEdit for your network.

As with any Registry edit, you should be careful to limit your activities to those keys that you intend to effect. Generally, this means is that you will want to add specific Registry keys, as shown in Figure 9.15, rather than creating your own .adm templates.

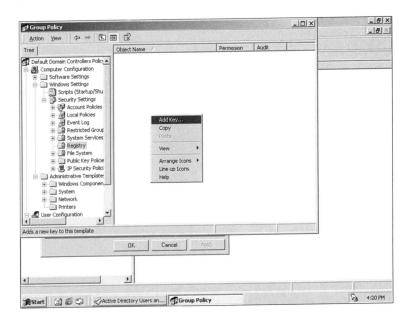

FIGURE 9.15
Here you add a Registry key to a GPO.

If your software developers have created an application that uses Registry keys for configuration options, you suddenly find yourself in a situation where developing an .adm file becomes necessary. After all, you need to support proper programming on their part.

Before you get started, you should make sure that the developers have actually given you a complete listing of the configuration parameters, the Registry keys involved, and the values you can set. It would be unfortunate to get though this process and end up with something that didn't work.

As with everything else in infrastructure, your best option here is to borrow the set up from another, working example of what you want to create. In this case, try grabbing something from an existing .adm template, as shown in Figure 9.16.

You can grab an entire GPO hierarchy (containers and keys) and copy them into another .txt file. You can then edit the values as shown in Figure 9.17.

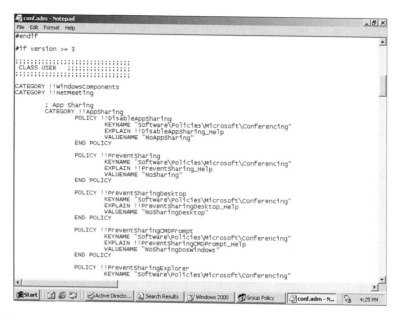

FIGURE 9.16

You can open an .adm file in Notepad.

FIGURE 9.17

Here, the administrator has changed a few things in foo.

Then you save the file into the WINNT\inf directory and add the .adm file to the GPO of your choice, as shown in Figure 9.18.

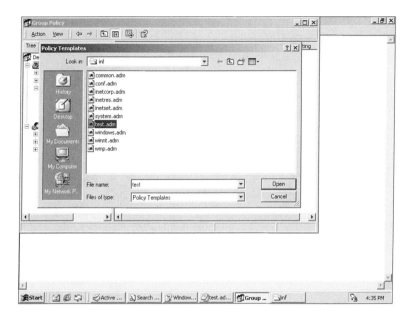

FIGURE 9.18

Adding to a GPO.

Creating a GPO .adm file (see Figure 9.19) actually takes a lot of time and effort; it's not something you should do lightly. If you have to get involved, however, the help files included with the software are actually rather complete.

9

TRIPS AND TRAPS: TROUBLESHOOTING AD

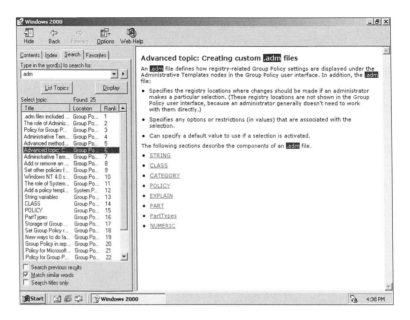

FIGURE 9.19
Adding a GPO.

To create a GPO .adm file, always refer to the help file. After you read it thoroughly, you will better understand what is involved.

Software Installation

Any GPO can deploy software packages to either specific workstations or specific users. If anything happens to prevent the installation, the system doesn't log anything unless you take some steps to make it do so.

This section discusses the following topics:

- Where to specify packages for installation
- Who can install what on a workstation
- How to tell what went wrong in an installation

As with the other sections, this section focuses on ways to prevent problems from happening in the first place, and then focuses on how to determine when a problem is occurring so you can better determine the causes.

Where to Specify the Install

If you use the following rules of thumb, you can avoid a number of problems up front:

- Install software that everyone will receive in the image, rather than using a package. This includes common productivity applications (Microsoft Office, Adobe Acrobat, and so on) and environment-specific tools (like the general PeopleSoft client).

- Deploy patches and additions to software common to the entire environment directly to computers. This will cause the computer to start loading the patch as soon as it applies its policy, avoiding user intervention.

- Deploy software that is required only by a group of people directly to the users who need it. For example, if you have a GPO that is filtered for the Finance group, you can use it to deploy software directly to that group.

- Do not create GPOs just to facilitate software installation. There are a lot of other software distribution mechanisms that allow for much finer grained control of distribution than GPOs.

In any case where you need finely grained control (workstation-by-workstation or user-by-user) deployment of software, you need to use a tool other than GPOs. System Management Server provides one option, whereas other vendors provide a wider range of choices.

Who Has Installation Rights

Generally a normal user cannot install software on a workstation. This can lead to problems with your user community, especially as they try to install various plug-ins for Internet Explorer.

However, a normal user can install a package that uses the Windows Installer Service. This is because the Windows Installer Service runs in a privileged mode, acting as a local administrator.

Additionally, any user who is a member of the power users group can install software. However, the user typically cannot install software that adds services to the workstation.

How to Tell What Went Wrong

The Windows Installer Service (WIS) can also provide you with a detailed error log, if you ask it to. Generally, the easiest way to configure the WIS is to use a group policy that affects the machines in question. You'll find it under the Computer Configuration, Administrative Templates, Windows Components, Windows Installer section. Select Logging, and choose your options, as shown in Figure 9.20.

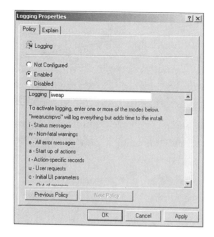

FIGURE 9.20

Turning on logging for the Windows Installer Service.

Use this functionality either when you have reports from the user community about something going wrong, or when you are testing new packages in your labs before sending them into the wild world of production.

The logging option is a string of letters, telling the Windows Installer Service to log the following:

I—Status messages

W—Non-fatal warnings

E—All error messages

A—Start-up of actions

R—Action-specific records

U—User requests

C—Initial UI parameters

M—Out-of-memory or fatal exit information

O—Out-of-disk-space messages

P—Terminal properties

V—Verbose output

+—Append text to an existing file

!—Flush each line to the log

The log file (called MSI*.log, where * is a string of random numbers) for each installation attempt is stored in the Temp folder on each workstation. If you are using logging in a lab, you shouldn't have much trouble getting the information. However, in production you should use either a script or SMS to gather the log files after they are generated, so that you have your data in one central location. Also realize that the more options you activate, the longer the installation process is going to take.

> **CAUTION**
>
> Given that this feature can have a rather adverse effect on the performance of application installation, you should be careful to turn it off after gathering your data for analysis. There is very little point in punishing the user community for trying to do their jobs.

The kinds of errors that you can run into using scripts are as varied as the scripts themselves. No two seem to fail in quite the same way. However, by examining the logs of several computers, it is usually possible to build a pattern of failures that can point you back along the path of the installation script to the point of error.

Summary

This chapter covered many of the methods and tools used to troubleshoot Active Directory.

It covered issues that are related to domain modes—native and mixed modes—as well as how to troubleshoot them.

The chapter also covered replication issues, including intra- and inter-site replication issues with both directories and files.

Finally, the chapter discussed GPO issues, along with some of the tools Microsoft provides in the Windows 2000 Resource Kit.

Introducing .NET and the Next Generation of Windows

IN THIS CHAPTER

If you read the trade magazines or visit the Microsoft Web site, you have likely heard about .NET and how Microsoft is pushing .NET as its new vision for the next generation of computing.

This chapter provides a brief overview of .NET and the various components that it contains. It also examines the new versions of Windows server, called Windows .NET Server, and its affect on Active Directory.

The .NET Initiative

In June 2000, Microsoft's Chairman Bill Gates announced a new initiative called .NET. Pronounced "dot net," .NET marks Microsoft's embrace of the Extensible Markup Language (XML) into all of its products, including operating systems, programming languages and tools, as well as Web services.

The .NET initiative provides a framework for information, devices, and services to be brought together into a single, unified environment. .NET, by using XML, facilitates the creation of XML-based applications that can share information among themselves as well as be presented on a variety of devices, including standard PCs, handheld devices such as PDAs or Web-enabled cell phones, or any other type of smart device such as tablet PCs or even game consoles.

As a result, an organization can use the various components found in the .NET framework to build comprehensive XML services to meet their needs.

So what does this mean?

First, you need to take a look at XML and what it can do. XML enables the creation of flexible information formats that, along with the data, can be shared via the World Wide Web, intranets, or any other type of network. XML describes the format of the data and what the data is. As a result, any platform can then display the data in a format that is appropriate for that platform.

Take for example, the methods a user can use to access their inbox on an Exchange Server 2000. Exchange Server 2000 supports XML and will provide an XML data stream to XML-enabled clients. These clients can then present the XML data stream how the user prefers. The user can access the inbox via Outlook, or can use a Web browser and use Outlook Web Access. In previous versions of Exchange (that did not support XML), if the user wanted to sort their inbox by sender, subject, or received date, the Web browser would need to request the data from the server. Then the Exchange server would sort the data and send it to the client. With XML, after the Web browser receives the XML data stream, it can sort or resort the inbox without needing to request the server to send the data again. This speeds up the user experience, while also eliminating excessive network traffic. Also with XML, the user could use other XML-enabled applications and devices to access their inbox. These applications and devices would reformat the data as needed.

Microsoft has designated five separate areas that create the .NET initiative.

.NET Experiences

.NET experiences are the results of utilizing XML-based Web services and their underlying infrastructure. An example of a .NET experience is the MSN Web site. You can view the beta version of the XML-enabled MSN Web site at `beta.msn.com` (see Figure 10.1).

FIGURE 10.1
The XML-based version of MSN found at `beta.msn.com`.

Another example of a .NET experience is the new "cartoon" interface found in Windows XP (see Figure 10.2).

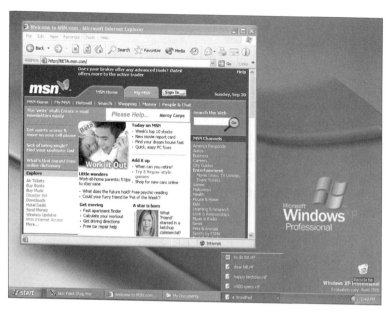

FIGURE 10.2
The Windows XP .NET experience.

Clients

.NET clients are considered "smart" devices. A smart device can access XML Web services. These devices can be desktop PCs, portable PCs, high-powered workstations, PDAs, Tablet PCs, Web-enabled cell phones, and game consoles. Many Microsoft operating systems are considered .NET clients, such as Windows CE, Windows Embedded, Windows 2000, and Windows XP.

Services

.NET services can be created by developers, third-party vendors, or Microsoft. Microsoft is preparing to release the first of the .NET services, called ".NET My Services". .NET My Services is being built upon Microsoft's passport user authentication system. It allows data to be stored and utilized on a user-centric level. .NET My Services includes characteristics such as the user's address, phone number, address book, inbox, calendar, electronic wallet, and so on. These different characteristics can be used, with the user's permission, by other organizations to facilitate and complete transactions. For example, users can purchase an airplane ticket using the credit card information found in their .NET My Services wallet. The airline could then automatically add the user's itinerary to their .NET My Services calendar.

Servers

.NET servers make up the .NET infrastructure that is utilized to deploy and manage XML Web services. The heart of the .NET servers is Windows .NET Server, Windows .NET Advanced Server, and Windows .NET Datacenter Server. The following servers build upon the functionality of Windows .NET and add various XML-based capabilities.

- **Microsoft Application Center 2000**—Deploys and manages highly available and scalable Web applications.
- **Microsoft BizTalk Server 2000**—Builds XML-based business processes across applications and organizations.
- **Microsoft Commerce Server 2000**—Builds scalable e-commerce solutions.
- **Microsoft Content Management Server 2001**—Manages content for dynamic e-business Web sites.
- **Microsoft Exchange Server 2000**—Enables messaging and collaboration anytime, anywhere.
- **Microsoft Host Integration Server 2000**—Bridges Windows networks to data and applications on legacy systems.
- **Microsoft Internet Security and Acceleration Server 2000**—Used for secure, fast Internet connectivity.
- **Microsoft Mobile Information 2001 Server**—Enables application support by mobile devices like cell phones.
- **Microsoft SharePoint Portal Server 2001**—Finds, shares, and publishes business information.
- **Microsoft SQL Server 2000**—Stores, retrieves, and analyzes structured XML data.

Tools

.NET tools are used by developers to build and deploy XML Web services. They include all of the functionality required to implement the .NET initiative.

The .NET tools that Microsoft provides are Visual Studio .NET, and the Microsoft .NET framework.

Visual Studio .NET is a multilanguage development tool that enables developers to build XML Web services. It includes the following languages: Visual Basic.NET, Visual C++.NET, and Visual C#.NET. Visual Studio .NET includes all of the components needed to build .NET applications.

The .NET framework is a platform that provides a standards-based, multilanguage application environment. It manages memory, addressing, reliability, scalability, and security aspects of an application. The .NET framework includes several components, including the Common language runtime and ASP.NET.

10

INTRODUCING .NET
AND THE NEXT
GENERATION OF
WINDOWS

Windows: The Next Generation

Windows is at the heart of almost everything that Microsoft does. As a result, the next generation of the Windows family of operating systems is fully immersed in the .NET initiative.

Windows XP

Windows XP marks the accomplishment of Microsoft's long-sought goal of converging the Windows 9x and Windows NT families of operating systems. It combines the security and reliability of Windows NT and 2000 with the ease of use features of Windows 98, such as plug and play.

Windows XP comes in two flavors: Professional and Home Edition.

Windows XP Professional is designed for the business user. It includes a new user interface, sometimes referred to as the "cartoon" interface (see Figure 10.3). This interface has a very smooth and colorful look to it. One of the first things users will notice is the bare desktop. By default, the only icon on the desktop is the Recycle Bin. All of the icons usually found on the Desktop, such as My Computer, My Network Places, Internet Explorer, and so on, are now found on the enhanced Start menu. The enhanced Start menu (see Figure 10.4) displays your five favorite applications, as well as your default e-mail and Web browser.

FIGURE 10.3

The cartoon interface found in Windows XP.

FIGURE 10.4
The enhanced Start menu found in Windows XP.

It also includes a new feature known as Fast User Switching (see Figure 10.5). This feature, meant for home use, allows users to use separate sessions within the computer. This eliminates the need to log off and save a user's application whenever another user wants to use the same computer. Windows XP uses Terminal Services to create and manage the separate user sessions.

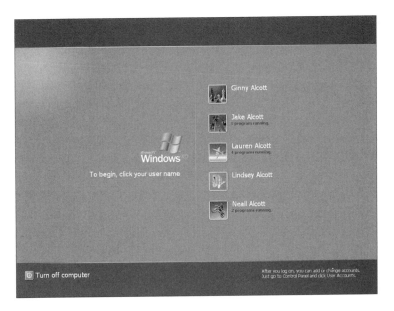

FIGURE 10.5
Fast User Switching in Windows XP.

Windows XP will also perform file grouping. File grouping groups multiple instances of an application under a single task bar button. In earlier versions of Windows, a separate task bar button is created for every instance of the application. This helps reduce the clutter on the taskbar.

For users who require assistance from technical support or help desk staff, Windows XP includes a feature called *remote assistance*. Remote assistance allows a user to request for help from the help desk, allow the help desk to connect remotely to the user's desktop, and help the user.

Windows XP also includes new versions of many utilities, such as Windows Media Player 8, Windows Movie Maker, Internet Explorer 6, and Outlook Express 6.

The Home Edition of Windows XP includes a subset of the features found in Windows XP Professional. It is meant for home users who require a fast, stable OS without all of the firepower found in its big brother.

Some of the features not included in Windows XP Home Edition include the Encrypting File System (EFS), Remote Desktop, Offline Files and Folders, Multi-processor support, Access Control, Group Policy, Roaming User Profiles, Automatic Software Installation, Remote Installation Services (RIS) support, and the Multi-language add-on.

Windows .NET Server

The Windows .NET Server family will be the next progression in the Windows server family of operating systems, the latest of which is Windows 2000 Server. The members of the .NET Server family, Server, Advanced Server, and Datacenter Server, are expected to be released in early 2002.

Active Directory Changes

Windows .NET Server includes many changes to Active Directory. Although most of these changes are relatively minor and fix or enhance issues with the version of Active Directory found in Windows 2000, it also includes a few new features that make Active Directory more robust and flexible. Also, the maximum number of directory objects is increased to more than a billion.

Please keep in mind that most of the changes found in .NET AD are changes in the directory schema. As a result, the schema found in .NET AD is not compatible with the schema found in Windows 2000 AD. You must first upgrade the PDC emulator to Windows Server .NET, which will then allow the schema changes to be replicated to the Windows 2000 DCs.

One fix found in .NET AD is the way AD will replicate the member attribute found in the Group object. Windows 2000's AD replicates the member attribute as a single object during replication. The problem with this method of replicating this particular object is the way many medium-to-large networks perform user administration. If multiple administrators make multiple changes during a single replication cycle, only one of the modifications will be successfully replicated to all domain controllers. The other changes will be lost. For example, two users, Matt and Adara, need to be added to a group named Systems Support. One administrator adds Matt to the Systems Support group and at the same time another administrator adds Adara. Only one of these additions ends up being replicated because the entire membership list is replicated, not each entry in the list. In .NET AD, Microsoft solved this issue by having each entry in the membership list replicated, instead of the entire membership list object. As a result, all changes to the membership list will be replicated to all DCs.

There are other changes that were made to the replication engine, including the way intersite connection calculations are computed. To take advantage of these replication changes, you need to upgrade all of your DCs to Windows .NET Server. After the upgrade is complete, you need to increase the functionality level of your forest. In Windows 2000 AD, the functionality level is 0. In Windows .NET AD, you will need to increase the functionality level to 1 to utilize the new replication engine.

A major new feature found in .NET AD is called the *forest trust*.

In Windows 2000 AD, you create separate forests when you need to implement separate schemas or when your organization needs to have separate IT infrastructures. If users in one forest need to access resources in another forest, you can create a shortcut trust between the user's respective domains. These types of trusts work well on a small scale, but they are not transitive, so if the users needed access to other domains, more shortcut trusts would need to be created. In .NET AD, you can create a forest trust that will create a two-way relationship between the forests. This allows security principals, such as users, groups, and computers, in one forest to be placed on Access Control Lists (ACLs) in the other forest.

Forest trusts are not transitive, so they might not be the perfect solution in all cases. For example, if Forest A has a two-way forest trust with Forest B and Forest C has a two-way forest trust with Forest B, Forest A and Forest C do not trust one another. A forest trust needs to be created between Forest A and C. Despite this however, forest trusts are a step in the right direction.

.NET AD also includes a new Active Directory Migration tool. In Windows 2000, this tool can be used to migrate user accounts and groups to specific Organizational Units within Active Directory. However, it cannot migrate user passwords or their profiles. The .NET Active Directory Migration tool will migrate user passwords and profiles.

Domain controllers in .NET will cache global catalog queries. This will help make queries faster for users as well as enabling users to log on without requiring a valid physical connection to the GC.

.NET AD will also support dynamic LDAP updates, which are defined in RFC 2589. LDAP in its original form provides access to static directory information. With dynamic LDAP updates, information can be added to the directory that changes periodically and can eventually timeout and be removed from the directory automatically. This allows certain information, such as whether a user is currently logged on to the network, to be added to the directory. When the user logs off, the information is updated or just simply times out to reflect the user's new status.

Another new feature that is scheduled to be included in .NET's AD is *schema delete*. Schema delete allows an administrator to delete objects and attributes from the directory schema. This new feature helps eliminate clutter and completely uninstalls directory-enabled applications. For example, when Exchange Server 2000 is installed, it makes more than 1,000 changes to the Active Directory schema. However, after it is uninstalled, the changes cannot be removed from the directory. Multiply this by adding more directory-enabled applications and the problem becomes very evident. As a result, the undeleted schema objects and attributes continue to be replicated needlessly. Windows 2000 includes a retire schema feature that marks objects so that they aren't replicated, but these objects can never be removed.

Other .NET Server Enhancements

Besides the changes to Active Directory, .NET Server includes many other new features.

Windows .NET Server, like Windows XP, will include a 64-bit version of the operating system. These 64-bit OSes can run on hardware platforms that utilize the new Intel Itanium processor. This will allow operating systems to support multiple gigabytes or even possibly terabytes of memory.

Also included in .NET Server will be more robust remote management capabilities. By pushing "headless" server technologies, Microsoft is acknowledging that most organizations do not require their servers to have a mouse, keyboard, or monitor. These components raise TCO as well as require physical space for the components and their associated cables. .NET Server will provide three remote management methods.

Terminal Services was introduced in Windows 2000 as a remote management method. In .NET Server, this capability is called Remote Desktop. It utilizes the Remote Desktop Protocol (RDP) to transmit mouse movements and keyboard input from the Remote Desktop client to the headless server and the server transmits video updates to the client. This allows you to access the server and its desktop from the workstation. At this point, you can administer the server as though you are physically sitting at the server. Remote Desktop in .NET Server includes a number of enhancements over Terminal Services such as support for 24-bit video and high resolution, drive, printer, serial port, and audio redirection. Remote Desktop utilizes an MMC-based interface, which allows you to create a list of headless servers on the left side, whereas the details pane displays the selected server's desktop.

Another method to connect with a headless server is by using the Emergency Management Services (EMS). EMS enables you to make a connection via a null-modem cable from another computer. This allows you to access the server in the event that its network configuration or network adapter fails. EMS then provides you with a command-line interface similar to the recovery console.

You can also utilize the Telnet service, much like you can in Windows 2000. The Telnet service enables you to access a command prompt on a headless server.

One more new feature found in .NET Server is the addition of an Effective Permissions tab when looking at the Advanced Security dialog box. This enables you to select a particular file or folder on an NTFS partition and determine a user's or group's permissions. This helps eliminate the complex and sometimes confusing methods of determining the effective rights for the object.

.NET Server contains many more features, and because it is still in beta, the list is subject to change. Keep an eye out for it. It looks like it will be an upgrade worth making.

Summary

This chapter provided a quick overview of the technologies that Microsoft will be releasing in the near future. Microsoft has dedicated a lot of resources to .NET and it will be encompassing many of their future endeavors.

INDEX

A